1

GW01451733

Published by

George Monta

George & Somchai
129 Marine Parade
Brighton
BN2 1DE
geosom@hotmail.com
www.montaguesilver.com

www.geocities.com/georgememoir/gem

First Edition
Printed in Bangkok, Thailand
Jan 2003
By

alphagraphics®

DESIGN ■ COPY ■ PRINT
Silom Branch

Tel. (662) 266-5335-8 Fax. (662) 266-5330
www.alphagraphics.com

ISBN 0-9544231-0-0

With Acknowledgements to-

The Slough Observer The Slough Windsor
& Eton Express
& The Maidenhead Advertiser

For some of the Photographs used

Prologue

I don't believe in astrology but it is a lot of fun. As my star sign is Gemini I thought it would be fitting to use the two figures in the tile. For much of my busy life I was ('in the closet'). Hiding my sexuality, living a double life. A sort of Jekkel & Hyde. 'A GEMINI' is me as most friends', Scouting colleagues, Boys from Bucks, five neighboring counties and London (all of whom will now be middle aged or late middle aged) knew me. Some I hope will read it.

'THE OTHER GEMINI' is about my gay life and all my gay friends will identify with this part. I also hope members of the general public particularly those who may have prejudices and homophobic views will read it. You don't have to read it all. It is not a novel. Chapters on Sailing or 'My Wheels' and one or two others will be boring to some I know, so you can skip them. I shall be giving it away to all that I can find. If you have to pay for a copy then it will not be very much I have no interest in even recouping what it has cost me.

Kind thoughts and best wishes to all who used to know me sorry it's been so long, (but I have not felt able to publish while a person mentioned was still alive) and to all those who know me now. I shall welcome any comments favorable or otherwise.

GEORGE
Meaning Prosperous

You will succeed
Is foretold in your name.
For there's nothing can stop you
Once you've set your aim.
You know the way to
Make a chore seem like fun.
You get things to happen
You see things get done.
You'll prosper from
Each idea you generate.
And reap rich rewards
From all that you create.

This was on a birthday card

You've a baritone voice as we've found out,
But we love you best as a big boy scout,
The voice that sings so strong and fine,
Also sings out a bob a time,

Now our George is a very good scout,
And during a social o'boy can he shout,
His manly physique and his tone so strong,
Our hearts are enraptured with voice and song,

CHAPTERS   **PAGE**

I dedicate this book to
The memory of my parents
&
With my love and thanks to my partner
Somchai. without whose care and devotion this
Book would never have been finished printed or illustrated

Acknowledgements to the Slough Observer, the Slough Windsor & Eton &
the Maidenhead Advertiser for some of the photographs used

For Adults only

ILLUSTRATIONS PAGE

Mum & Dad

CHAPTER 1

Pre school Days

My Mother 1899-1981

I know very little about my mothers life prior to her being "in service" (as it was called in those days') at a house in Boscombe near Bournemouth. My maternal grandparents were separated and she had only one brother, (Uncle Sid) and no sisters. I never heard about any other relations except for her cousin Auntie Hetty who lived in Reading. We rarely saw her parents; she seldom spoke of them or her childhood and we lost touch completely with Uncle Sid, he was some years younger. When my mother died I was never able to tell him of his sister's death. When her mother died, (my maternal Grandmother) soon after the end of the war and her father (my maternal Grandfather) a year or two later, my mother and I were the only ones at the funerals. I remember thinking how lonely their last years must have been. I regret not talking to her about her early life, her school days, her teens, had she had any other boy friends before dad? Perhaps we did ask her but I can't remember her telling us anything, as she never talked about it. I'm fairly sure that she did not have a happy childhood. From the time she married my Father, he and all his family and friends became the only ones she kept in constant touch with, she was the letter writer. She had three sisters-in-law and eventually twelve nephews and nieces most of whom had offspring; she kept in touch with them all. She certainly did all she could to give us a very happy childhood.

My Father 1892-1982

His father, (my Paternal Grandfather), had run a drapers shop in Hampshire and I see from the family bible, that he died in 1920 at the age of 58 and was buried in Reading cemetery. At that time he, and I suppose my grandmother must have been living with his sister Aunt Bess at 46 Belmont Road, the address on the wedding certificate. Number 42 is given as mother's address, so they had been living next door but one to each other. Father had trained as a gardener, then became a policeman, he Joined the Grenadier Guards at the outbreak of the 1914 war, was wounded, then captured spending some time as a prisoner of war in Germany. When the war ended he re-joined the Police Force, he was stationed at Bournemouth. Mother must have followed him and was working as a domestic servant in Boscombe. She was not able to leave the house except on her night off, so PC Montague would often court her in true "Romeo stile," whilst still on duty from beneath the balcony of the house. He was told he was not a good policeman; he was too friendly with the general public.

(Note) The family bible was presented to my Great Great Paternal Grandmother Sarah in 1869, and on the first few pages is a complete family tree record. Her husband Joseph I see lived to the age of 93.

I was born on Tuesday the 5th June 1923

At Clapton Mothers Hospital London The only thing mother ever told me about my first three years was that I loved to go up and down in the "water cliff lift" at Boscombe, which cost a half penny a time and that I once sat in fathers police helmet. Since mother was working, I must have spent most of my first three years living with my maternal grandmother in Reading. It never occurred to me until many years later that if mother and father were both working in Boscombe, and their home was in Reading, why was I born at Clapton in London? I would like to be able to say that I shall be telling you more, but I never did find out the whole answer. Dad left the police force when I was three and my bother Edward was just a few weeks old. We moved from Reading to Hitcham in South Buckinghamshire in the summer of 1926. "Hitcham House" was the home of the "Squire of the village", a wealthy brewer Col. Handbury. He owned this large country house and estate, which included a farm and a typical Victorian walled kitchen garden. In the centre of this garden was the estate laundry with a "tied" cottage attached, in which I was to spend the next fifteen years of my life. At this time about twenty six servants were employed on the estate, six on the farm and the dairy, about ten in the house consisting of a butler, two footmen, a cook and kitchen maids, up stairs and downstairs maids, six gardeners, two chauffeurs and an estate carpenter. Mother was taken on as Laundress and father as a Gardener for four days and to help mother in the Laundry for two days.

The House, Garden, Farm & The Park

The house was a very old "two up two down". There was no bathroom; the toilet consisted of a bucket in a small privy out side ten yards from the back door. If it was raining you just had to run for it. In those days we had long hard winters with lots of snow and thick ice on all the ponds. The living room was a little larger than the kitchen, with a single gaslight hanging from the centre of the ceiling. It had four doors, one in each wall, one into the kitchen, one into laundry, one lead into a small pantry and the stairs, the

MY DRAWING OF THE KITCHIN RANGE

other was the front door, which was only opened in the summer. With only a small coal or log burning fire, it was very cold and draughty in the winter.

The kitchen was the warmest room in the house. The centrepiece was a typical 'black-leaded cast iron range. A small coal burning fire with a removable top plate, on which sat a large black kettle. At the side was one small oven. In front protecting the whole unit was a brass topped wire guard about 30" high. Over the top was the "mantel piece" (shelf) that had a short red velvet pelmet with tassels. (See sketch) This room had two gaslights, one on either side of the fireplace. On this mantelpiece was kept dad's tobacco, (he always smoked a very strong shag called 'black Beauty'), his pipes, matches and pipe lighters were made by us kids with pieces of tightly rolled newspaper. Writing this reminds me of the only time I ever disagreed with my father. When I was grown up I remonstrated with him over smoking. He said. 'Son, if you were injured in the front line the first thing you would ask for would be a cigarette' I had to disagree with him on that occasion.

The kitchen fire rarely went out, it was stoked up at night, the damper shut down, then with a tickle in the morning it would flare up to boil the kettle for the first cup of tea of the day. There were no storage cupboards or worktops, just a very well scrubbed pine table. Every thing was kept in the larder under the stairs on the other side of 'sitting room'

My TAPESTRY OF OLD GARDEN COTTAGE

My paternal grandmother had come to live with us and so to start with I would have slept in the small bedroom with her with my brother in the cot in my parent's room. As the family grew, with first my sister Betty and then brother John, I graduated to a bed in the ironing room of the laundry, in a corner screened by curtains. The laundry had gas lighting so I had my own light, where-as I had always had to have a candle in a candlestick when I when to bed upstairs. The house had been built on the site of what had once been a very large country house and incorporated four large wooden columns, with brick work in between, so that part of each column was visible outside and part inside. I remember it being said, that the name of the house had been Blythewood, which is mentioned in the Doomsday book, (a seventeenth century catalogue of properties of note). Many walls of the old house had been retained as fruit walls, some of which still had the old 'glass-less' windows. I think most of the bricks from the original house had been used to build the fruit walls, and the perimeter walls of this very large Victorian kitchen garden.

Leading from the house was what had once been a grand entrance drive, on each side of which were beautifully kept flower borders edged with a small box hedge and at the back were neatly trimmed six feet high yew hedges. At the end of this drive were large ornate wrought iron gates. Half-way along was a large round Goldfish pond about two feet deep, with a life- sized statue of a lady looking into it. On the edge of the pond was a box, which always contained large biscuits. Once a day we would break some of these with a stone, the tapping on the side of the pond would be the signal for the fish to come up and eat. This pond was to have an indirect bearing on what I was to do with part of my life.

The whole of this garden was cultivated. Flowers bordered all the many paths behind which grew every conceivable vegetable. On the walls were fruit trees of every kind that would grow outdoors and in the green houses, all those that needed heat like grapes and figs. On the other side of these walls were two large orchards, one for cherries and the other for apples. There was a paddock that was the home of a white donkey named Snowball, my brother and I would often try to ride on him but I don't recall us being successful. Snowball would 'he haw' so loud you could hear him from a mile away, he was always in his paddock except on the rare occasions when he was put into a small two wheeled cart in which Mrs Hanbury would ride, together with any children staying at the 'big house'. When any of the Hanbury family or their guests were walking around the grounds, we children were told not to be seen or heard.

The size of the park that surrounded this garden on three sides was about 300 acres, containing some very fine trees. There was Walnut, Sweet Chestnut, (the nuts of which we collected when they fell). Some very fine examples of English timber, Elm, Ash, Sycamore, Lime, Horse Chestnut and many large Oak trees, the finest of which I shall have more to tell you about. My bother Edward and I spent a great deal of our time playing and climbing trees, we also had jobs to do. Rubbish from the house and that which would not compost we had to take in a wheelbarrow out to what was always referred to as 'the pit', a large attractive hollow. This tip had been used I would think for a great many years, for when we were older we would dig there and find all sorts of antique bottles and other interesting items. At the other end of this hollow was a sheltered cowshed, the rubbish had to be tipped at one end that the cows couldn't get to, then the wheelbarrow was taken into the cowshed and filled with 'cow dung' for the garden.

When we were old enough we had to dig a hole (in a different place each time), then fetch and empty the toilet, the 'dubs bucket' as it was called. Like many other jobs such as weeding the gravel paths, sweeping away the snow we didn't like very much. Our parents were much too poor to give us pocket money, so we sometimes dug up weeds on the seemingly endless gravel paths to earn some. This job was done on our knees using an old knife; it made our knees and fingers sore. We had very little money, but unlike many of our contemporaries we were not really poor. In fact we lived on the fat of the land as far as food was concerned. Grandmother and then as we got older we boys used to do the shopping. There were very few items on the list. Flour, Tea, Sugar, Salt & Pepper, Vinegar, Scots Porridge Oats, and rice for rice pudding. That's about all I can think of, every thing else was grown, made, got from the farm or shot. We used a lot of vinegar; mother would send me down to the shops for an extra bottle, for she was always preserving some produce or other that dad brought in from the garden. I would then drink little swigs of it on the way home. Mother told me off, saying it would dry up my blood. The one thing we did not have was fish, even though it was very plentiful and cheap we still could not afford it 'they say' that fish is good for the brain. Perhaps that accounts for it!

All the produce you could name grew surrounding the house. But father had his own garden, where if it was daylight he spent most of his spare time. Every day he brought in fresh vegetables. He always grew enough potatoes to last for the whole year. In the summer he dug them fresh every day. I've never tasted better than that first root of very small new ones, dug in the early summer, lightly boiled with a sprig of home- grown mint. In the autumn all the potatoes were dug up, we had to help clean them. Then they were put into the corner of the 'coal shed' in a pile covered with straw and sacking. In the winter evening's father was always in his chair, reading library books. He read two or three a week.

He also studied 'Suttons' catalogues, deciding what seed potatoes to order for the next year. King Edward and Epicure were two of his favourites. In the spring we would help him plant them out. A long line on a special iron reel would be carefully laid out. Then with what was called a 'dibber', made from the broken handle of an old fork or spade. This was cut with a point to the exact length that was required for the distance between each seedling. We would make a hole, then lay the 'dibber' down with the handle touching the hole we had made, then lift up the dibber and make another hole all about five-inches deep in the well dug and manured soil. Dad would drop in the potato seedling making sure they were the right way up. When the green tops had grown to about four-inches high he would 'hump up' the rows, so that the seed was now seven or eight-inches deep. This would all be done when dad thought there would be no more frosts. Occasionally there would be a late one forecast, we then had go and cover them all up with old newspapers. If there was an unexpected frost, (the forecasts were not as good in those days) the tops would be burnt black, the crop would be delayed and dad would be very irritable. In a good year each root would yield ten, or sometimes fifteen fold potatoes, most of them larger than the original seed.

We could never afford to buy meat. Father had a shotgun and several times a week he would disappear then we would hear shots. The park was teeming with rabbit, hare, partridge and pheasant. Dad would return with dinner for the next few days. When I got a little older I used to make wire 'snares' like a hangman's noose, which I would place in a 'rabbit run' in the long grass, just where they ran under the fence. More often than not, when I went out again just before dark, there would be a fat rabbit, if it was not dead I would give it a sharp blow with an open hand breaking it's neck, we did not think it was cruel in those days. This was the only way dad could feed his family; even the cost of cartridges was a problem. There were so many rabbits they were classed as a pest; and they did a great deal of damage and had to be kept down. Fortunately for us, it was many years later that Myxomatosis, 'a virus disease' almost wiped out the total rabbit population, since when, very little wild rabbit is eaten. I learnt to skin and paunch rabbits and hares at a very early age.

Once when dad was ill. I was only about twelve years old at the time; mum said 'Oh dear!' 'There's nothing for dinner'. Without telling any one I took the gun and having always watched my father I knew just what to do. You had to approach the warren very slowly and 'up wind' so that the rabbits did not smell you. I remember the recoil kick as the gun went off, it nearly knocked me over, but dad had told me that you must keep the butt pressed tight into the shoulder I came back and proudly presented mother with one large rabbit. On special occasions we would have a chicken, or a cockerel from the farm. On very special occasions such as Christmas we would be given a goose. Father and we boys all wore boots, these were never polished, but well rubbed over every day with lots of special grease called Dubbin, which we had to buy. The fat we got from the goose saved us buying Dubbin for many weeks. It was years before I tasted Turkey, they were for the big house only.

There were four Public Houses, 'Pubs' all about a mile away. The Crispin, the Pheasant, the Maypole, and the Oak and Saw. On special occasions, such as when we had visitors, or holidays and during the summer we would all go to one of these, where we could all sit outside. Dad would have a pint of mild and bitter, mother and grandmother would have a Guinness or a glass of Stout. We children would be given lemonade and a halfpenny current bun, (it was more like a large biscuit really) about three inches square and half an inch thick, very hard and with a few currents. I was fourteen years of age when dad let me have my first half pint of beer. On Saturday evenings in the winter, from the age of about eight, I was sent around to the Pheasant, (the nearest pub). All the pubs in those days had a 'Jug and Bottle' where any one including very young children could go and knock on the 'stable like half door', the top half of which only would be opened. I would take with me three large plain glass bottles to collect the 'weekly treat' and If we had been good, a 'halfpenny' bun each for us children.

On a Sunday afternoon when the weather was fine after Sunday school, mother would take us on a walk around the 'block'. That was right round about half of the Hanbury estate, a distance of about three miles. First brother Edward, then sister Betty, then brother John (there was about three years difference in our age's), would be in the old Pram that had two large wheels and two small wheels. When John was a baby all three of them would get a ride, I being the eldest never did, I had to help mother push. Along the road at the southern end of the estate were three shops, one was the paper shop called Wakeford's owned by Mr. Wakeford, for whom I was later to work as a paperboy, this shop sold sweets. Mother would buy us a small packet of chocolate drops each. The other shop was a general store, selling a great many things, one of which was bicycles, some new, some second hand, I looked at these longingly, deciding I was going to earn enough money and buy one some day. This shop also charged accumulators, (glass, acid filled batteries); the power supply for our wireless, (as it was called then). Once a week we exchanged the flat one for a fully charged one.

Mother had more energy and worked harder than any other person I've ever known. From six in the morning till late at night she would be on the go working in the laundry. Five and a half days a week she did the washing and ironing for a minimum of fifteen people from the" big house' where most weekends they would have guests. In the evenings she would be cooking, preserving fruit, making jams, pickling onions and other produce that dad brought in from his garden. All the cooking was done on the kitchen range. A small coal burning fire heated the oven, yet her cooking was of the very best. Rabbit stew, jugged Hare, roast Pheasant or Partridge, vegetables picked fresh that morning, Brussel Sprouts picked with the frost on them. There was always a desert (sweet we called it) Apple, Raspberry, Gooseberry, Cherry, fruit pies, Rice Pudding. Our favourite, was a suet pudding, cooked in a basin, with treacle in the bottom, wrapped in a cloth, in a saucepan of boiling water for a long time, then turned out onto a dish so that the treacle all ran down the sides, we called it 'Noble Pudding'. What a shame it is that these things you can't have when you get older, if you want to keep a reasonable waistline.

Not having such a thing as a refrigerator, every thing was cooked fresh each day. The milk from the farm could not be collected until after breakfast, so every evening what was left had to be scalded, that is heated to just below boiling point. There is a saying that 'a kettle never boils if you watch it'. But we had to watch that milk most carefully, if we took our eyes off it for a few seconds it boiled over. Then that person would get none on their porridge in the morning, this was even more of a blow, for when cold, scalded milk has thick cream on the top. Meal times were breakfast, which was always porridge; cornflakes didn't come in until after the war. Scrambled eggs on toast, and thinly sliced fried potato, the toast had to be done, laboriously with a toasting fork in front of the open fire. Lunch was a word we never used; the main meal of the day was dinner at midday. It was many years before I felt comfortable using the word lunch, even when taking customers out for a midday meal. It was like using the word 'one', when referring to 'one's self, I still do not feel comfortable saying that even now. The last meal of the day for us children while still at school was Tea, bread and jam, cake and tea, we did have coffee (of a sorts) sometimes, it was named Camp and contained chicory, I believe it can still be bought.

THE LAUNDRY

The washing room was a most unlovely place with windows on one side only, through which the sun never shone. A cold stone floor so that in the winter it was almost freezing unless the coppers were alight, when it would still be nearly as cold but full of smelly steam. At one end were two, (what we called,) 'coppers' large brick built structures, each with a copper bowl about two feet in diameter. These bowls each held about twenty gallons of water. On the top was a wooden lid and then underneath was a wood burning fire with an iron door. Dad used to work in the washing room on Mondays and Tuesdays. Early in the morning before breakfast he would light the fires, fill both coppers by hand with buckets of water, then when they were boiling in would go the washing most of which would be white linen, a few hands full of soda would be added. Then this would all be boiled for several hours. Every now and then dad would climb a small stepladder and turn the bubbling mass with a three-foot long stick. I can even now remember the smell of that room.

The next operation was to lift out the two great steaming hot every heavy bundles of washing, these then had to be transferred into several large wooden tubs, where every thing would be rinsed again and again in cold water. With no such thing as spin dryers every thing had to be put though the 'mangle'. A large machine with two wooden rollers, one spring loaded with a handle that turned both rollers through which the clothes would be squeezed. Those items with buttons on had to be wrung out by hand or the buttons would be broken. All items badly soiled like the servant's aprons, shirts collars and cuffs were scrubbed by hand. I can see mum and dad now bending over the tubs scrubbing away for hours with large brushes using Sunlight soap. Tuesdays and Wednesdays were 'drying days'. If the weather was bad then a fire had to be lit in the 'drying room'. This had two large heavy racks on pulleys hanging from the ceiling. A system of pulleys and cords lead down to a windlass on the wall to raise these racks once loaded. In the centre of the room was a cast iron 'Tortoise' wood or coke burning stove, if wood was being used this had to be constantly fed with logs.

Unlike the wash house, (as it was always called) the ironing room was a lovely room with a wooden floor about 30 foot square with large windows all along two sides that caught the sun most of the day. In the centre was a supporting pole that we children used to play around and climb. All down one side of this room was a twenty five foot long ironing table covered with old blankets and linen, at which mother would stand for hours on end, some times late into the evening doing the ironing. Most of the irons were what we called 'flat irons', about the same size as today's electric ones, but in solid cast iron with a steel handle weighing 10 pounds. (I know that because it said so in letters cast on). A few were smaller at five pounds. Then there were a few very small, with round bottoms used for ironing starched collars and cuffs. These irons were heated on a special square stove with slopping flat sides, with a ridge to hold the Irons; the round ones were heated on the top. The stove was in the corner of the ironing room furthest from the ironing table. Each heated iron would stay hot for about five minutes. So we worked out that mother would walk several miles each ironing day. She used to spit on the irons to test if they were hot enough. The reason for the long ironing table, was for the white linen table clothes used at the big house, where they had frequent house parties, dinners and banquets.

Personal washing was done first thing in the morning and last thing at night using a large china jug and bowl, with warm water on ironing days only. Mother would call out 'don't forget your neck knees and behind your ears'. If we didn't do it well enough she did it for us and it hurt. We also had to wash our hands every time before sitting down at the table. Friday night was bath night. We had an old 'hip bath' into which we put about six inches of water, that had been heated on top of the ironing stove in a couple of large heavy cast iron pots. The ironing room was still warm. The bath was put close to the fire and the clothes racks full of airing clothes were put around to form a screen from the draughts. Despite having no bathroom we quite enjoyed bath night.

When mother did sit down, it would be behind the sewing machine on which she made many of the clothes we wore, including my sisters dresses. If not using the old hand operated Singer machine, then she would be knitting, making scarfs, socks, gloves and jumpers most often with wool that she had un-picked from something that was too small, or that she had picked up at a rummage sale. On the very rare occasions that she bought a new scane of wool, one of us would have to hold it out on our out stretched arms so that she could wind it into a ball. It made our arms ache. Hardly a night would go by without her darning the heels of a pair of socks, making or mending something or sewing on a few missing buttons. All our clothes that we wore to school, had to have our names on. This would be done where possible with 'Indian ink' straight onto the garment. Or it was written onto a piece of linen that was then sown on.

All the washing was done without any labour saving devices, in the home or the laundry. Clothes were hand scrubbed and this included items like evening dress shirts that had to be starched. Our family doctor was a Dr Summers. He was an unforgettable character; he attended the whole family right from the moment we moved to Hitcham until after the death of both my parents. One day he saw the result of mothers ironing on one of the Colonels 'dress shirts. From then on when ever he had to attend a special function as an ex. Army medical Colonel, she would be asked to wash and iron the shirt he would be wearing.

Every thing was dried outside whenever the weather permitted. Many times there would be a shout, 'it's raining! We would then all rush out to help bring in the washing. As the many items were ironed they would be 'aired' around the fire on large wooden racks. If it rained for several days then all the washing had to be dried in the drying room. When finally dry and ironed, it all had to be folded and put into wicker baskets, which when full were far too heavy for one person to lift. This process would continue until every item was packed into what became five or six baskets full. This would sometimes take until late on a Friday evening to complete. Then early on Saturday morning a two wheeled cart drawn by a horse named Tinker would be backed up to the laundry door. This cart would contain five or six more large wicker baskets full of dirty washing. The baskets with the dirty washing would be unloaded and the clean washing loaded. The dirty washing would straight away be sorted with the very dirty items being put 'in soak', with soda all ready for another weeks washing on Monday.

CHAPTER 2

School years 5 to 14.

The nearest school was about a mile away at Burnham, the largest village in the county of Buckinghamshire. But mother knew of a family with a boy a few years older than I, who lived a quarter of a mile nearer that school than we did, but did not go there. He passed the end of our drive on his way to Taplow Church of England School over a mile away in the opposite direction. His mother said it was better and much smaller. So soon after my fifth birthday, Bill Woodley (was his name), would call for me and escort me. He came out of school half an hour after me so I had to wait for him. My very first memory was when during this half hour I was playing with a lad named Peter Dewdney. He was waiting for his mother to collect him, when I must have been a bit rough and hurt him, he was crying saying "He was going to tell his mum", who was about to arrive to collect him. She came into the classroom while he was still crying. I remember being frightened and hiding beneath one of the desks. On returning home from the war I discovered that Peter had been killed while serving as an air gunner in the R.A.F.

For the first year I was in the 'Infants', (now called primary), the teachers name was Miss Challen. Except for the headmaster all the teachers were females, although I'm sure some of them were married we had to call them 'Miss'. I enjoyed my time in the infants, Miss Challen was young, pretty I thought and I liked her. Then the next year I moved up to Standard one, the teacher there was a Miss Tanner, quite old, very strict, when she bent down to talk close to you you'd get spit on your face. I didn't do well at all and when the following year the whole class went up to standard two, myself and one other boy had to stay behind. I was a slow learner, I think I must have had and to a certain extent still do have, a sort of mild of word blindness. (Very sight Dyslexia) For although I have never had too much of a prob-lem with reading I was and still am a very poor speller. (Thank goodness for the 'spell checker on this PC) I nearly always know if a word is spelt wrong, but I can't spell it right. Words like Yacht (even when I had one) Lieutenant, Colonel, Consciousness, Distraught, Necessary and many others. I always have to look them up or use the spell checker.

At woodwork, sport and gardening I excelled. I suffered from shyness; I also had a bad stammer just like King George VI. I told you I'id tell you more about the round fishpond. Apparently I fell into this pond when I was about three years old and very nearly drowned. My grandmother saved me. I was told that was very likely the cause of my stammer. When I was about seven years old while walking home from school, I met Mrs Hanbury (the wife of my father's employer). Answering her questions, I stuttered a great deal even more that usual, we children were always in awe of her. I addressed her as Miss, but she told me I must call her Madam. Follow-ing this encounter she had a word with my mother, telling her to put me in the church choir, as singing would cure me of my stuttering. She was right and years later when as an adult; still in the choir, often sing the solos, she told me that I ought to have my voice trained. I did and singing was to take up a great part of my life. So I owed Mrs Handbury a great deal.

About this time my family went though a very bad time. My brother Edward caught pneumonia. This developed into double pneumonia. My sister Betty who was only a baby at the time, also caught it. The doctor suggested that I be sent away if possible. I was collected by my Aunt Gertrude, (my fathers sister) and Uncle Harry and taken to London. It was the first time I had ever been in a car. They had an old T Ford; it was also the first time I had ever been more than a few miles away from home. They lived at Hammersmith London, in 'Black Lion Lane'. At the end of this road in those days was a footpath leading down to the river. I spent many hours there watching the river traffic and was particularly fascinated by the 'pump house', in which was a huge cast iron, steam operated 'beam engine' clearly visible through the large windows, pumping some of London's water. Little did I guess then, that I should always remember the sheer size of those casting's, when years later I became a Pattern Maker spending nearly sixty years of my life directly connected to found-ries and castings. None were ever as large as that old beam engine. Many years later I went back to find that Black Lion Lane had been cut in two by a dual carriageway and the Pump House had been pulled down. I enquired in the Black Lion pub what had happened to the pump? They told me it had lain on the riverbank for years, but had recently been moved to a local museum. I promised my self I would renew acquaintances with it one day.

My brother was ill for a long time, twice he nearly died, but they did not give up. Mother and grandmother between them fought until he turned the corner and got well. After spending some time in London, I think it was about a month, another Aunt begged my Mother to let me go and stay with her. Auntie Hetty and Uncle Tom had never been able to have children of their own and so I was sent down to Reading to stay with them. Uncle Tom was the manager of the Undertakers dept. of one of the largest stores at that time called Heelas's. He went to work every day in 'Morning Dress'. They had a Ford Popular saloon (The first car in England to be sold for 100 Pounds). I was very sorry that my Brother was so ill, but I very much enjoyed the long holidays. It was at Reading that I first developed my love of popular classical music. They had a 'wind up' Gramophone and twelve inch records of Strauss. Beethoven, Chopin, Bach and my favourite Handle. Whenever I hear this music, I think of Auntie Hetty and Uncle Tom. I must have behaved myself and been no trouble for when my brother was better and it was time for me to go home, Auntie Hetty Cried.

We lived very near to the village church; the Vicar was the Rev. Canon Evans a wise kindly man and a great character, my father thought very highly of him. He had a great influence on my early years. He told father that Montague was a very noble name. As Mrs. Hanbury had suggested, I joined the church choir, but as they were short of boys I joined much earlier than I should have done, I could hardly read. The shortest cassock was much too long, but this meant that I was in the choir club, which the vicar ran and I got paid!

It must have been about this time that I was taken to the pictures for the first time. Surprise surprise! It was by my father who very rarely went anywhere. He took me to Maidenhead to see 'Ben Hurr', a silent film showing at a small cinema in one of the back streets of Maidenhead. The Commodore cinema was built a few years later on the Bath Road about a mile away. To us this was like a palace. Two thousand seats with a balcony and an electric organ that came up from the depths in front of the stage, it was very colourful. The Organist played poplar music on three keyboards, foot pedals and dozens of stops, similar to our church organ but much bigger.

There were several famous artists who travelled around the country playing at all the best cinemas as well as on the wireless. I was thrilled to see and hear Sandy McPherson, also Sydney Torch, both of whom I saw and heard again many years later at the Winter Gardens Blackpool. The 'red letter' day of the week at the Commodore was the Saturday morning 'tuppenny rush', two old pennies to get in. Many times we had not got enough money, so we would have a 'whip round' with a halfpenny here and a farthing there. Then one of us would pay to go in, going straight down to an emergency exit door that he would open to let the rest of us in. In those days we would see one full-length film, plus another short one, the news no advertisements and we were entertained by the organist.

About the age of ten I started to help the local milkman on a Saturday morning and holidays, his name was Rex Talbot. The milk cart had two very large wheels with a sloping platform open at the back just like a roman chariot, but drawn by one horse not two or four. There were no milk bottles. Two or three large milk churns held all the milk. There were three metal measures, one for a half a pint, one for a pint and one for a quart. A smaller container would be carried to the door, or people would come to the cart with large jugs, into which the milk would be measured. One advantage over the present day milk float was, that the horse would 'walk on' all on his own to the next house. Tubs of cream were also carried; several tubs were delivered to Cliveden, the home of Lady Astor. She was by then the first ever lady MP. When Rex was not looking, I sometimes lifted off the lids of these tubs the underneath of which would be covered with thick cream. I would lick the lid clean, then carefully put it back. We would enter the estate though the trade-mans entrance. The estate contained many Golden Pheasants and Peacocks, to keep them in there was an electric gate, which opened when the cart passed over a plate in the drive, then closed again by another plate on the other side.

Rex finished his milk round about midday on five days a week, except Fridays. That was the day he had to collect all the money, so he finished very late on that day. At the same time as delivering the milk he would collect boots and shoes for mending, for he was also a skilled cobbler. So after school several evenings a week I would help him in his cobblers shed putting on protectors, cleaning and polishing shoes, also helping to work his treadle machine. Rex had an influence on me as a work-a-hollic; His day started at 4.30 in the morning, and didn't finish until late in the evening. Six days a week. Whilst in the army, during the war, Rex was a prisoner of the Japanese and spent a horrific time on the Burma railway and the Bridge over the river Kiwi, (which I was to visit whilst on holiday in Thailand, years later). After the war Rex showed me a Samurai sword he had taken from a Japanese officer, that he had seen being used to cut off the heads of some of his comrades. Some years later he asked me to take it away. He told me 'He could no longer stand the sight of it'. I still have this sword on the wall of my dining room.

For both jobs that I did for Rex he would pay me, the money I saved until I had enough to buy a bicycle. Then I was able to get a job as a paperboy delivering evening papers. They were, in those days the Star, Standard and Evening News. With the three jobs together with my 'choir money' I earned about four shillings, (twenty pence) a week. Mum & dads total wages in those days was about two pounds ten shillings, (two pounds fifty pence). But they paid nothing for rent, rates, coal or gas, all of which went with the job and the 'tied' cottage. But if dad or mum had lost their job, they would have had to leave the cottage at one week's notice.

The evening papers came down from London on an express train to Taplow Station about six o/clock in the evening. The train didn't stop but thundered through at about a 100 miles an hour. (It was what was called a 'slip train') the last one or two carriages' were 'slipped', (disconnected) about half a mile from the station, then a 'brake man' controlled them bringing them to a halt at the platform. There was one night that I shall never forget, it was Thursday the third of December 1936. I was thirteen years old at the time waiting as usual on platform 2 for my papers. The slip train came and went but no papers, I waited for two hours. It was very cold. (It's always even colder on a draughty railway platform). Then out of the guards van of a 'stopping train', I saw my papers being off loaded, there in big headlines, THE KING ABDICATES. By the time I had finished my paper round that night, it was very late. My parents were not too worried, they had heard the news on our 'accumulator' powered wireless (Radio) and guessed what had happened.

I was very proud of the bicycle that I had purchased with my own money. I put a little 'mile o meter' on the front wheel. Some times I did twenty miles in one day. My paper round involved cycling at night, we only had to have a light on the front in those days with a reflector at the rear. This lamp was a 'self making' gas light, containing a chamber at the bottom holding 'carbide crystals'. Above that was a small tank filled with water. A valve was adjusted so that the water dripped slowly onto the crystals that then gave off a gas. I had to remember always to have matches with me. This light was not much use to see by, but meant that I could be seen from the front at least, there were very few cars about in those days.

One thing I used to do, that I don't think I ever did tell mother. Some one must have bought me a milk shake a pineapple flavoured one. I though it the most wonderful drink I had ever had. In those days unlike today (yes I still have one now and then), they would pour into the mixer a glass and a half of milk and some ice cream, fill up your glass, then leave the container on the counter so that you could have another half a glass full, once you had nosily sucked up the last drop with the straw from the first glass. The cost was three old pennies, (just over 'one pence). To day if there is a little that they can't get into the glass they tip it into the sink. This always annoys me intensely. Once I had my own money and bicycle, I would cycle the three miles into Maidenhead just to buy a milk shake.

When I was young we always had very cold winters with severe frosts for months on end and often up to as much as a foot of snow. Despite a good pair of woollen gloves, (hand made by mum), when riding my bike my hands were always so cold that I would have no feeling in them. Dad would make me stand and vigorously throw them under each armpit to get back the circulation; the pain would almost make me cry. There were several ponds in the park, we would go fishing for gudgen and perch; quite small fish about three inches long, once we had caught them we would throw them back in the water. All these ponds formed by natural springs, were full of wild life, with many Moorhens we called them, (Cootes is the correct name) and we would collect their eggs. There were also dragonflies and frogs. Every year some frogspawn would be put into a jam jar, then we would watch them grow into small frogs. These ponds froze over every winter for many months. To start with we would test the ice at the edge by jumping up and down until we were sure that it would bear our weight. But almost every year we would hear that yet another boy or girl had drowned while skating on thin ice. We did not have any skates, but this did not stop us from having a lot of fun, we would make a sledge out of scrap wood and then take it out to 'Berry Hill', just on the opposite side of the river from Maidenhead. We had just as much fun with our home made sledge as some of the 'posh' kids there with their toboggans.

Boxing was one of the most popular sports at this time, some of the most famous names then were, Len Harvey, Benny Lynch and Tommy Farr. Tommy was at this time training for his fight with Joe Louis, the American world heavy weight champion. On the Bath Road only just over a mile from our house was a public house and hotel, which had a large gym at the back, where most of the top boxers of the day would train. There was a facility for the public to watch; whenever boxers were training I would be there, sometimes when I was supposed to be at school. Like most people in those days I followed boxing very closely. I maintained my interest for many years, doing quite at bit of boxing, including being a sparing partner to a future world flyweight champion. But now, having seen several deaths and many that have become 'punch drunk' and brain damaged I am against boxing.

I'm sure we were never given homework at school. The last exam we took would have been to see if we were clever enough to go to Grammar School. Only two of my schoolmates did go to Grammar School, although several more passed the exam. They were mostly from very poor families and were needed as extra breadwinners. These were the days of the depression and the general strike. I can remember asking mum to put some extra food and fruit in my lunch box, so that I could give some to a couple of friends who were particularly poor, always hungry and came to school in clothes full of holes and no socks. There were jobs for fourteen years old boys but not for men, a record number of them were either unemployed, on short time, or had had their wages cut. There was no unemployment pay or social security. So for most of my friends it was very necessary for them to leave school, get a job and help out with the family finances. Most of us were pleased to leave school, being then able to wear long trousers all the time. I bought my own pair of long trousers with my own money before I left school. But I was only allowed to wear them on Sundays. I could never have passed the Grammar school exam and would have come very near to, if not bottom of the class. I left the little village school at the age of fourteen, barely literate or numerate.

From the beginning of August to half way though September the whole of the Hanbury Family, household servants, grooms and chauffeurs, would migrate to a shooting lodge called 'Lenderick Lodge' in Scotland for the annual Grouse and Stag shoot. This was in the Trossachs, quite near the well known Loch Lomond and the 'Brig O' Turk' bridge. Mrs Hanbury whom it seemed had taken an interest in me offered me (though my parents) a job as a 'pony boy'. I of course jumped at the idea. Mrs Wilder, the cook was to be my Chaperone. On the day we left we all went very early to Taplow railway station. A special carriage was waiting, half of which was 1st. Class and the other half third Class. We all sat in the part according to our 'station in life'. After a very long day we arrived. I was thrilled at the sight of the Lochs and the mountains Ben Lomond, Ben Ledi and Ben Venue, I climbed them all. We fished and caught a large pike in Lock Vennacher. Getting up very early, we would go right up into the mountains, where the Colonel and his guests would first stalk and then shoot the deer, they would always try to get the 'royals' those with twelve or more points to their antlers.

My job was to lead a pony following the hunt at a good distance and then, when a kill had been made and the stag had been loaded on to my pony, I would follow them home. There were three ponies altogether, rarely were there less than two stags shot and sometimes three. I learnt a great deal about preparing 'game', (plucking and paunching the birds) how to skin the deer and prepare the fish caught in the lochs. After the twelfth of august, it was Grouse, Blackcock Snipe, also Rabbit and Hare, which I already knew how to skin and paunch. I remember feeling sad when the skins and the heads of the deer, minus the antlers (if they were 'royals') were put into a large pit and surprised when the Grouse were 'hung' until lousy with maggots, before they were plucked and cooked.

Looking back I can see that I was very lucky to have been able to have such a 'holiday', which even though I worked I looked upon it as. There were three other Scottish lads who lived in cottages at the hunting lodge, sons of the men who were, while we were there, the beaters who drove the birds towards the guns. These boys were about the same age as myself, so I spent a great deal of my time with them at work and at play. On returning home dad said to me, 'what are you talking like that for?' I had apparently picked up in that short time, a slight Scottish accent. Many years later, I took my whole family in a Dormobile camper van to revisit the area, but was very disappointed. The house seemed so small and all the Bens (mountains) had been planted with conifers.

CHAPTER 3

I get my first proper Job in 1937 at the age of 14 :

At the local Youth Employment office I was asked what I wanted to do, I told them I was good at woodwork and I wanted to be a Cabinetmaker. They sent me to see a Mr Brett who was running his business from a private house, using his large garage. His wife showed me to an outhouse where Mr Brett was deep cutting a piece of wood on a circular saw, without looking up he said, 'what do you want?' I told him I wanted a job. 'What makes you think you could be a patternmaker'? He said, I probably just looked at him with my mouth open, I had never heard of that craft. (To me patterns were what mother used to make my sisters dresses). He took me into the workshop, then his phone rang and he disappeared to answer it. There was another man working at a bench, his name was Ted Rowell. Ted started to talk to me telling me and showing me what pattern making was all about. I was told I could start on a month's trail. I went home and said, 'Mum! I'm going to be a pattern maker'. That turned out to be a very lucky day for me. Cabinet making and joinery became largely mechanised, but pattern making was a highly skilled and well-paid job. A good patternmaker was never out of a job. That is a fact that is still true to this day.

I was engaged on a five-year apprenticeship, to be followed by two years as an improver. During the following weeks I discovered that the craft I had chosen was very highly skilled, like engineering in wood, 'tooling for the foundry trade', but it also included being a woodwork specialist and Model Maker. The wages for a fully qualified 'journeyman' (skilled craftsman) patternmaker at that time was two shillings and sixpence and hour, (twenty-six pence), most other skilled workers only got two shillings, unskilled workers got one shilling an hour. Many years later I told this to colleagues in the R. A. F., they did not believe me.

I soon discovered that my employer was more interested in getting me to do all sorts of odd jobs, than he was in teaching me my craft. I had to clean his car, work in his garden and clean out a large cage of Budgerigars. He was a 'chain' smoker, the first I had ever known and he used only one match a day constantly lighting each new cigarette from the 'stub-end' of the previous one. At least twice a day, sometimes three times, he would send me to the shop at the end of the road with one shilling (ten pence) to the slot machine for a packet of twenty Players cigarettes, these contained a half penny change in the packet.

He coughed a great deal and would sometimes spit onto a piece of sandpaper it was a horrible colour. To go to the toilet I had to pass his dining room window; I could see that while he was eating he took one mouthful of food and then one 'drag' on his cigarette. Looking back, despite the way he treated me I have one thing to thank him for. At a time when no body knew the dangers, not many females, but almost every male smoked, I never did. Several years after I had left his employment I heard that Mr. Brett had died of lung cancer.

I stayed at "Brett's" about one year and with Teds help I made quite a number of small patterns. Quite often unless any thing was wrong, that was it; I never saw the end result. But occasionally a sample casting would come back. One pattern that I made was for a foot for a Hanovia sunlamp. One day I saw this lamp for sale, there, for the base were three-foot castings that I had made the pattern for. The effect was, that years later when I had apprentices working for my company, I made an effort to see that as often as possible they should see the end result of their work.

Fortunately, while cycling the three miles to work one day I started chatting to another lad about the same age as my self, by the name of Harold Bonnet, the said he was also an apprentice pattern maker and that he was working for the only other 'Master Pattern Maker' in the area. He told me every thing that he was doing, including going to night school three evenings a week. I decide then and there to leave 'Brett's and go to 'Wagstaff's'. I had an interview with Mr. Wagstaff, who said he would take me on but not straight from Mr. Bretts. He told me that that would not be right. I had to get another job for a few weeks and then go to him. I discussed all this with Ted who told me that although he could teach me to be a good pattern maker, he was not allowed to spend the time with me. I was doing all these other jobs that I hated, and I needed to concentrate on my craft. This was the time coming up to the start of the war. I was made to dig a large hole in his garden; this I found out later was to put black market petrol in, as it was about to be rationed. Ted advised me to leave and go and get a job at Machine Pattern Co. One thing that has always stuck in my mind, I asked Ted, 'what was the difference between Refugees & Evacuees'?. The year was 1939. When Mr Brett died Ted also came to work for Mr Wagstaff.

The final straw was when my grandmother died. She had lived in the same house with us as long as I could remember and was as much a mother to me as my own mother. I asked him for the day off to go to the funeral, He said, 'Oh that's an old one, people always use the death of a grandmother when they want a day off'. In other word he didn't believe me. I was furious and gave him my notice. I got a job the next week at 'Woodrims' making furniture. I was only there a few weeks, but during that time I realised how lucky I was to have chosen the job I had I found the work there so boring and repetitive. When I started at Machine Pattern Co. I knew I had made the right decision for my future.

There were about ten good craftsmen, a great deal of machinery and one other apprentice younger than I so that I did not have to do any 'shop jobs' such as sweeping up and making the tea. I started attending night school three nights a week to study English, Maths and Technical Drawing. I studied hard, did extra work at home and in the next three years learnt more than in all the years at the village school. The war started in the year that I was sixteen. I enjoyed my job very much, but during the next year things became very unsettled and uncertain, yet at my age very exciting. Most lads of my age were joining the forces, flying in aeroplanes, going overseas. At seventeen and a half one was allowed to enlist; I thought I would volunteer since I thought I would be called up at eighteen anyway. I was interviewed at the Reading recruiting office and accepted. The following morning I gave in my notice to Mr Wagstaff, whom I though would be proud of me for wanting to 'do my bit', instead he was furious, telling me that I was in a 'reserved occupation'. (Pattern Makers were in great demand for the war effort). The end result was, he contacted the RAF, I got a letter confirming what he had said cancelling my enlistment telling me that they could not accept me while still working as an apprentice pattern maker, but that if I left his employment they would reaccept me after three months.

This time I was furious, I still gave in my notice, left and got a job at the 'Hawker Aircraft Co' at Langley three miles the other side of Slough where they were building and repairing crashed Hawker Hurricanes from the Battle of Britain. Ever

Me in my RAF uniform   **Me on my horse**

Black Pool 1942   **&**   **On Oscar**

since then they have always been my favourite aircraft. People think that the Spitfire won the Battle of Britain, but there were four Hurricanes to every "Spitfire". I worked in the repair department where crashed planes and those that were damaged were repaired or rebuilt. It was a six-mile bicycle ride to the factory so, when they asked for volunteers for "fire" "watching" I jumped at the chance to stay there at night three times a week and also some weekends. There were about six of us all about the same age who took it in turns to patrol in pairs. All the offices were left open, in case incendiary bombs fell in them, so I spent many hours on the typewriters and became quite good I thought, but only with two fingers of course.

There was a Rudge Whitworth motorcycle and an old Armstrong Sidley Car with 'pre-selector' gears; these were used on the airfield. Several of us taught ourselves to ride and drive these. Looking back there was surprisingly little adult supervision and boys will be boys. The inevitable happened, I had a collision with a girder, fell off the bike and broke an aluminium chain cover. Being a good Boy Scout I owned up and said I would pay for a new one. But I discovered it was a foreign make. I was unable to replace it, so with the help of a friend and his workshop I made the broken pieces into a pattern, made a core box, had a casting made at a local foundry by a friend, another friend in a machine shop machined it for me. And in a couple of weeks the bike was back in as good a condition as before. I left the bike alone after that. But I did teach my self to drive in that car. Then I enlisted in the Royal Air Force Volunteer Reserve.

CHAPTER 4

<u>In the R.A.F 1941 - 1946</u>

In the September following my eighteenth birthday I received a form from the recruiting office at Reading, saying that I had been accepted as a trainee wireless operator air gunner In the R.A.F. volunteer reserve. I was to report to a station at Warrington Lincolnshire. During the short time I spent there I was issued with the a full set of flying equipment, flying suit, fur lined boots, fur lined gloves, with silk inner gloves, helmet and goggles, also a small white flash which fitted into my forage cap, indicating that I was trainee aircrew. When it came to being issued with shoes, we were told to line up in order of foot size. I found myself 5ft 9', standing with all those that were six foot tall and over. The sergeant shouted at me, 'Montaeg! What are you doing there?' "I've got big feet serge I am size $10^1/_2$"; and my name is Mon-ta-gue (It's a wonder he didn't tell me I must do some Fat-a-gue). There were no half sizes. I had to have size 11.

We were eventually posted to Blackpool to do our square bashing (foot drill). We were all billeted in one of the small three or four storied guesthouses the town is full of them. I was in No. 42 Lord Street. The landladies were very strict and very stingy with the food. They gave us very thin slices of, (supposed to be), ready buttered-bread; they spread the butter on then scraped it all off again. We had to spend some of our very small weekly pay packet on fish and chips. Drill was done in the street in squads of about 24, each under the instruction of a master instructor. Three of these were very well known in the entertainment world and became even better known after the war. I was in Max Walls squad. Max Miller was in charge of another both were well-known comedians. Sydney Torch the organist was also there. I had seen and heard him playing one of those very colourful Organs that come up from the depths in front of the screen at our local cinema. I expect they were all at Blackpool because of the facilities at the Winter Gardens, where they all performed evenings and weekends to entertain us.

Every weekday, after about an hour's drill we were marched into the town to the huge bus and tram sheds. These were set out with tables and chairs to seat twelve, each with headphones and a Morse tapping key. The instructor would tap out sets of four digits and numbers at an ever-increasing speed that we then had to write down. I thought I had a head start on most of the others for I had learnt the Morse code in the scouts. The qualifying speed was eighteen words a minute, which I could just about managed to achieve. But before the exam they increased the rate to twenty-four words a minute. I think they had too many applicants for aircrew. Despite practicing more than most of the other lads, my poor old brain and concentration was unable to cope. I was taken off the course. It was a very big disappointment to me, I had to leave all the friends I had made, hand back all my flying kit, take out the special white 'aircrew trainee cap flash' and think about what I was going to do now.

At the time it was a bitter disappointment to me, but looking back had I been successful I might not have survived the war, like my school friend Peter, a large percentage of Air Gunners and Wireless Operators were killed even when their aircraft managed to get home. I had always been interested in sport. So I applied and was accepted for training as a Physical Training and Drill Instructor. I was posted to Arbroath on the east side of Scotland for training and for the first few days we were polished up on our parade drill. Then we were instructed how to command and control a squad of 20 men in complicated drill manoeuvres. Unlike the streets of Blackpool we were on a huge parade ground, when it came to your turn to take control we had to march the men several hundred yards away while giving them audible instructions to, move to the left, to the right, double march, slow march, about turn and many more commands.

Just like children at school we were not very kind to each other; we played up and made it as difficult as we could for anyone who did not do very well, or who did not shout loud enough even if we could hear him. The most important asset of a good drill instructor is voice, (the archetypal sergeant major). If one is nervous then this shows, the voice becomes a squeak with no volume. I know those who know me now will find it hard to believe, but I was a quiet, shy country boy in those days. My squad was a complete shambles, I knew exactly what I should be doing and how to do it, but I was a bundle of nerves. I was the worst of the lot, the lads were laughing. Then something happened that made that day one of those that changed my life, I got mad. My eyes were full of tears, but I had a very loud and clear bass voice. We were permitted to make them do any drill manoeuvres we wanted. The Staff instructor was standing just behind me, so I had them double marching up and down right to the other side of the parade ground. I knew all their surnames; so many of them got a good personal ribbing in typical sergeant major style language even if they were doing it right. That was a very good day. That was the day I found my self-confidence.

Professional boxers were my hero's, so imagine my pleasure, when who should I find sleeping in the next bed to me, but Jack'e Patterson, the contender for the world flyweight title. We became good friends. It was a long walk down to the pub where we often met for a drink. Most of the time he would have admirers around him. This time we were walking alone and chatting, when we reached the pub he was again immediately surrounded by his admirers several of them offered to by him a drink. I was left standing on my own to buy my own drink. I remember feeling a little lonely at that moment wondering if I would ever be famous.

We were together for the next four months. Unlike many who became famous Jackie never became spoilt by the admiration. I worked with him, helping him with his training, running with him, even getting into the ring as his sparing partner. On returning from a training run we would pile a dozen blankets on top of him, to make him sweat. (He had a problem with his weight). Jackie was only five foot three, but with the shoulders of a six-foot weight lifter. The biggest chap in the hut was a bit of a boaster and a trouble- maker, he was envious I suppose. One day he picked Jackie up so that his feet were a foot from the floor, with their faces level with each other, he made some sarcastic remark. Jackie drew back his right hand just six inches and then hit him on the jaw. He knocked him out. Peter Kane was the fly-weight Champion Jackie was training to fight. I listened to the fight on a wireless speaker, standing on a stool in the corner of a noisy pub, He won and became British & Empire flyweight champion.

The first hurdle was over; those of us who had passed the course were posted to St Athens in South Wales for a period of three months on a Physical training course. This involved eight hours a day of intense activity and gymnastics in a very large gym. We learnt how to layout, control, judge and referee all field, track events and sports. We had to run two five mile, and one fifteen mile cross county race most weeks. In the evenings we were given lectures on anatomy and physiology. Then with what time was left of the day, we had to write up notes on all of it.

When it comes to preparing one self for a healthy, well, but not over developed body. I think the best years for that are eighteen to twenty five. During which time a large part of each day should be devoted to exercise. Not the sort that anyone wanting to be an champion must do, this almost always results in injuries of some kind eventually. But the sort that I did, teaching and making others fit. At the same time keeping your self in tiptop condition. I did just that, for exactly those years. During which time I'm sure the foundation of my health, my fitness and my energy was laid. I consider my self-lucky to have been born at the time I was.

One of the proudest days of my life up until then was the day I was told I had passed. I was immediately promoted to full corporal and given a small special badge showing that I was a PTI (Physical Training & Drill Instructor). We were then all given leave and told that we would be reporting back to Liverpool. So we guessed that we had an overseas posting. Mum and Dad were proud of me, but worried. The whole family went to a professional photographer for a family photograph. During this "over seas posting leave", mother and I both went to Maidenhead for some reason on the bus. Mother was pregnant at the time with my sister Margaret. We were both standing, when a gentleman got up and offered me his seat for "my wife". We smiled and said thank you. It was not that I looked older than I was, but that Mother looked so young and beautiful for her age.

On arriving at Liverpool we were embarked on to SS Orduna which was a converted meat refrigeration ship, about four thousand of us in all. I was detailed to be in charge of one table of about 25 men, mainly to control meal times. The first meal was no problem we were still moored up to the quay, but by the next meal we were at sea. I sat down in my seat at the end of the table and then I noticed that some of the men were missing, others had their head in their hands on the table. The meal arrived and was put in front of me to dish up, as I did so most of them just groaned and said, 'not for me corp.' Most of them were seasick for several days. I was not. I put it down to the fact that, I up on the deck was taking squads of twenty-five men at a time on PT. all day. We were not told where we were going, but those 'Scouts' amongst us knew we were going west, we thought this was strange surely we're not going to America. But after a couple of days we did a large half circle and ended up heading east. We had done this (we were told later) to avoid submarines in the Bay of Biscay. Going through the Mediterranean (we were the first convoy to do so) following the defeat of Rommell in North Africa, we were dive-bombed and one of the ships in the convoy was hit, but not sunk.

We arrived at the Suez Cannel Cairo where we stopped for a while and were surrounded by small boats trying the sell us souvenirs. They would throw up a rope, then we would pull up a small basket into which you put the money, then lowed it and then pulled it up again with the goods. Not many of us bought anything. But just over three years later, when we were on the return trip we did. The trip down the cannel was very interesting. But it got so hot in the Red sea where we had a following wind that they had to turn the ship around to cool it down for a while.

We had left Liverpool on Aug 14th 1943, and we arrived at Durban on Sept. 14th. For ten days we were put into huts, (if you could call them that), four walls made of sacking with large holes but no windows Two more large doorways, but no doors. When it came to bed time I noticed that the lads had put their shoes one under each of two of the bed legs, their kit, they had put into the kit bags, locked them and put the handle under another leg. When we enquired why, we were told that during the night black youths completely naked and covered in grease would run through and pick up any thing not fixed down. Several times some of the chaps had laid wait for them, they had managed to grab one of them, but could not hold on to them, because of the grease.

At last we were on the way to our final destination. The journey was a very long one, 1700 miles from Durban to Bulawayo, then on to RAF. Norton. The camp consisted of a large airfield, about 100 aircraft, Tiger Moths & Harvardís, about 150 trainee pilots, a total of 1500 men on camp. The sporting facilities were excellent; a very large well equipped gym, swimming pool, tennis courts, sport's fields and squash courts. The following morning I reported to the sports office and discovered that I was the third member of the sports team, the officer Oscar State, Sergeant Tribe and myself. In those days almost everyone smoked, perhaps one in one hundred did not. Even those who had not smoked before found that, whereas in England a packet of twenty players was one shilling (five pence), here, they were nine old pennies (three & a half pence) but for a packet of fifty, the smallest packet you could buy.

The first thing Flight Lieutenant State asked me was, 'do you smoke?' I don't think he believed me when I said no, for he said, 'if ever I find out you do then you are off my team'. With all the ribbing and teasing I got from my mates because I did not smoke, but for Oscar, I might well have started. Beer was also very cheap and very good; I had my full share of that, some of the chaps thought that if you didn't smoke, you would not drink, or go with girls either. (How wrong could they be?) So I have two people in my life to thank for not being addicted to the nicotine 'weed'.

My day would start at 6.30 am before breakfast, with the first squad of twenty-five trainees in the gym, or on the sports field. Their minimum rank was sergeant; most of them were flying officers (one thin ring). Even through I was only a corporal, I had complete control and could report anyone who did not "toe the line". The new recruits were mostly reluctant to start with, but after a few days they would often come up to me and say they enjoyed it and how much better they felt for it. I told them a fit pilot was a much better pilot. I took one squad before and three after breakfast, what Sgt. Tribe and Lt. State did I never knew, I didn't see them till later in the day.

The rest of my day was spent looking after the sports office and store, issuing equipment, planning the sporting fixtures for mainly cricket and football, both of which were played all the year round. Twice a week I would have an afternoon off and would often go down to the flight path, where the trainees were taking off and landing. The more experienced were flying solo and would offer me a flip, as we called it, I think some of them tried to "get their own back" by putting me through the hoop, ('more accurately 'the loop') I loved it. The Tiger Moths were very easy to fly, they would sometimes let me take over the controls, but not when it came to landing.

The nearest town was Salisbury (now called Harare) one hour's drive away on what we called 'the liberty wagon', a typical army type canvas backed lorry with bench seats, 'not fixed', in the back, so you had to watch not to go round corners too fast. The road consisted of two concrete strips about a foot wide, just about right for the four wheels of an average car. The lorries two front wheels were just about on these strips, but at the back, only one of the double wheels was on. When a vehicle came from the opposite direction, each would have to drive off to the their left, so that the off side set of wheels were on the nearside strip, this would not have been so bad, if the rains had not washed away the earth in many places, so that there was sometimes a six inch drop off the strip.

On one of my trips into town, I saw a notice offering driving lessons and the issue of a Rhodesian driving licence. I went in and found that the one person there was the instructor and also the examiner. I told him that I could drive, but did not have a British licence. For an extra fee he said I could use his car, a very old Morris. I expected him to close up his office and come with me, but no, he just stood in the doorway and said. "Keep driving around the block till I call you in". This I did about four times before he signalled me to come in. There was very little traffic and the road was very wide, that was, I was told, so that in the old days an ox cart and twelve oxen could do a U turn. I got my Rhodesian licence that I still have today. On my return to the UK all I had to do was show it and they gave me a British one. I never did take a British driving test, except that years later I took and passed the Advanced Drivers test, similar to that which the police drivers have to take. I took it in my Alfa Romeo.

Hiring a car was very cheap, this I did many times. Several of us would get together, share the cost and go exploring. Then I saw on the camp notice board a card, asking anyone with the rank of corporal or above with a driving license who might be willing to be a driver of the liberty wagon to let the orderly officer know. On applying I was asked if I drank a lot. I said, "rarely more than two pints". There was a great deal of cigarette smoking and there was also a great deal of drinking. Apparently the regular drivers had been getting drunk and there had been a couple of accidents. So I got to do what I enjoyed very much, drive into the town, sitting on a comfortable seat with a couple of whoever were my best friends at the time sitting next to me The only inevitable problem was rounding up the lads when it was time to return to camp. On the drive back to camp in the dark, I always saw a few animals and snakes on the road, these soon moved quickly out of the way. But I had to watch carefully for the elephants, these would appear suddenly from the bush and just stand in the middle of the road and look at you.

The sports officer (my boss Oscar), was a well-known weight lifter and body builder before the war and a regular writer in a magazine for that sport. He ran weight lifting training sessions in the very well equipped gym. They would train for one off maximum lifts like the "snatch", where you pull a bar from the floor with something like your own body weight on, duck under it, then stand up holding it at arms length above your head. The 'clean and jerk' is a similar lift, but with an even heavier weight, this is done in two movements, one up to the chest, then finishing with the weight at arms length the same as the snatch.

I watched this and saw how much they had to strain, that every now and then they would hurt them selves. I decided this was not for me, so I started a class of my own. This did not involve any of these lifts, but a series of exercises for 'arm and shoulder', 'trunk' and 'leg', with no less than 10 repetitions, with a weight, heavy enough, so that how ever much you tried you could not do more that ten or twelve repetitions, In this way, so long as the correct body stance was maintained it was impossible to hurt your self. This method gave an all over good body tone and a build up of muscle you had to decide just how far you wanted to go. Nowadays, almost all athletes use this method and most gyms have very sophisticated equipment, where, instead of putting weights on to bars, you adjust a pin into a numbered hole according to how much weight you require. Many years later my company was to make the pattern equipment for many of the leading manufactures of this equipment.

I considered my self so lucky that I was living the life I was. I enjoyed every minute always up early, yes, even at weekends when most of the lads would stay in their 'wank pits' as they called their beds, some of them till lunch- time. I would go for a game of Squash, almost every day. All RAF. Stations have Squash Courts, this became my favourite form of exercise and it was to remain so for the next forty years, until problems with my eyes prevented me from continuing. It's a game one can play at any time of the night or day in any weather, even on your own to practise if you are not very good at it and I was, many times beating youngsters forty years younger than I. I would also try to fit in a swim every day. This was the pattern of my life, for the next three years. Many times in my life people have said to me. 'Where do you get all your energy from'. The thought has often gone though my mind, It sounds like boasting and an exaggeration, but I have 'lived life to the full' and probably had twice as much 'out of life' than the majority of people. I put it down to three things. Energy Inherited from my Mother, the very best of food in my formative years and many hours exercise every day, from the age of eighteen to twenty three.

Almost every game you can think of was played on the camp, cricket and soccer all the year round, tennis, hockey, water polo, even baseball; the only exception was ice hockey. Rugby was not very popular. This is the only game I have never been keen on It doesn't allow the same scope for skill as football or hockey. It depends on brute force, with grunts and bone crunching tackles. If you don't have brute force what possible pleasure can you take from such an activity, it will only give you an inferiority complex in relation to people who do have it.

I was ill just the once. Like nearly everyone else I got Malaria which knocked me down, I was in the camp hospital for a week, then sent to Umtali, a very beautiful mountainous area in the north west of the country for convalescents. It was much cooler there. I was billeted with a very kind, motherly Rhodesian lady who fed me very well and helped me to completely recover.

My best friend was a chap named John Smith; we played Squash together most days. In the following April we planned our first two weeks leave together. This was to take a bus, (more like a lorry really); with a compartment with soft seats just behind the driver for about eight passengers, these were for whites only. The natives sat in the hard seats in the canvas covered back. The bus did a round trip, covering about two hundred miles every day passing many hotels and places of interest. We would stop off for a day or two and then catch another bus. Zimbabwe ruins were our main objective, from which many years later the country took its name. Very little is known about the origin of these ruins. They were discovered in 1868 by a wandering hunter, very impressive and beautifully built, but certainly not by the local natives. At one of the hotels we stayed at for a few days there was a hot spring, where the water came out of the ground it was boiling, the water flowed into the swimming pool that was at body temperature.

My second leave was with a friend named Reg, who like myself was a real countryman and liked camping. He had an old motorbike and a twelve-bore shotgun. He liked to explore out of the way places and invited me to go with him. We travelled north one hundred miles to Senoia, where we stayed the night, then on for another hundred miles, to the border with Northern Rhodesia, (as it was called then). The border was the Zambezi River, where we set up camp for the night in sight of the Otto Beit Bridge.

This was a large suspension bridge. There was a man in charge of it with whom we became friendly; he showed us exactly how a bridge of this type is made. I had always thought large cables supported them. He showed us into one of the four large triangular blockhouses, where there was what looked just like a very large harp, with hundreds of strips of steel fanning out from a single point on the roof, down to the floor where they were fixed. Each one had a fixture where by it could be tightened or loosened. He told us to pluck one of these strips and each one made the same note. Just then a lorry went over, he told us to pluck it again, it made a slightly higher note. So instead of cables, there are independent strips of steel inside a tube going from one anchor point on one bank, to another on the other bank. Each strip could be adjusted to give the same note so that the tension on each strip was the same.

We pitched our camp, but not too close to the river, as there were many crocodiles. Reg said the next thing was to find something for our dinner. It always got dark about the same time at six to six thirty. We waited until then, when we saw quite large birds coming to roost in the trees nearby. Reg let me have the shot; I got two with one barrel while they were sitting together on a branch. They were Guinea fowl, it may not have been very sporting, but we were hungry. We built a fire, prepared the birds, covered them with thick mud rubbing it well into the feathers. We then roasted them in the middle of the fire. When cooked we cracked the now hard baked mud and away came all the feathers and skin. That was a meal to remember. We slept under the stars but kept the fire going in case of marauding animals.

It was RAF policy to move us around after about a year on one station. I was posted to Induna, a camp only a mile away from a town in the centre of Rhodesia called Queque. It was from here that I went on my third leave; to a place no one should miss visiting if they are ever in that part of the world, "Victoria Falls". As I got off the train, there on the platform was an RAF sergeant in uniform. He called me over and informed me that a few weeks earlier there had been an accident, where a young RAF man who, like myself was on holiday there, had fallen off the cliff into the water to the bottom of the falls and killed. They had only a few days before recovered the body, which had been in the water for some time. He detailed me to be one of the pallbearers at the funeral. My memory of this is not a pleasant one; I was the shortest of the four, my corner of the coffin must have been the lowest; water leaked out on to my shoulder.

The Victoria Falls is twice as high and one and a half times as wide as the Niagara Falls. The flow of water at it's maximum in April and May is 691,000 tons per minute, the minimum flow in October-November is only 18,000 tons. Just below and close to the lip of the falls is a 500 ft long dual rail and road bridge, which includes a footpath. The views from all around the falls are spectacular, but especially from this bridge. Just near and overlooking the falls is the five-star Victoria Falls Hotel that is where I stayed. The first time in my life I was in such luxury. I wondered why there were shoes outside the doors of the other guest's rooms, so I put mine out and in the morning they were back, beautifully polished.

My third posting was to Heany, about twenty miles from Bulawayo, the second largest town in the country. I found this camp was larger than all the others having many more facilities, one of which I found was a horse riding club. I had made an allowance, sent monthly to my mother, but she said she did not need it and that I would need it when I returned to Civvy Street, so she put it in the bank for me. I wrote to her and asked her with out any explanation to send me a certain sum. She told me later that they all thought I had got a girl into trouble. (As it happened I had I but I never did tell her), I bought a pony from a local farmer and named him Oscar. (Perhaps that choice of name was something to do with my first sports officer). So instead of playing squash at six or seven in the morning, we would, at the request of the commanding officer go galloping around the perimeter of the airfield, scaring away the birds which were a danger to the aircraft when taking off.

At certain weekends we would ride the twenty miles to Bulawayo, ('Bullafoo' as we nick named it), where all the hotels had stables. There was a race track there where they held gymkhanas and race meetings for all class's and types of horse's. Although small, fourteen hands, (an average racehorse would be seventeen hands). Oscar was very quick and very good at jumping in a steeplechase. Several times I was asked to ride one of the proper racehorses. (In those days I was only just over

10 stone) when they were short of a jockey. The best place I ever made was third. But I got my name printed in the results card.

Two places that I managed to visit was Mafeking on the way up from Durban, where the train stopped for an hour. This was of particular interest to me with the close association with my hero Baden Powell. Also the Matopos hills, to the grave of Cecil Rhodes the founder of Rhodesia, where years later Baden Powell was also laid to rest. I visited Kneotze Bay on the east coast in South Africa. Having always been most interested in all types of wood, I found this was the only place in the world where 'Stink' wood grew. It is the most valuable of all woods, even in those days it was very rare and only used for wooden brooches and small souvenirs. I visited one of the small workshops where these were made and I was given a small piece, large enough to make an ink stand this I still have. This wood will only grow on the side of a steep gorge where the sun cannot shine on it.

As I recall we were unable, or rather we did not bother to follow too closely the progress the war and what was going on in Europe or Asia, there were no radios or television. We got to know the major happenings through what we called the 'grape vine. We were to busy enjoying ourselves in the sun. Playing sport at every opportunity during the day and when not on duty drinking in the NAFFI (we called it the 'tank'), or in the town if we had the money. The trainee pilots concentrated on their training, they were only interested in passing out and getting their 'wings'.

Then in May 1945 it was V E day. The very next day it was announced that all training would cease. That Day the trainees went mad. They didn't want the war to be over, they rampaged around the camp burning some of the huts all of which had thatch roofs and they threw toilet rolls over the electricity wires all around the camp. The cricket pitch sightscreens were made up of three large wooden aircraft packing crates at each end. These they set alight, as they were all wood and full of black greaseproof paper they burnt very well. Within a month two thirds of all those on camp, including all the trainees had been sent back to Blighty. All according to their enlistment number, the earlier you had joined up the lower your number. Those with later numbers and that included me watched with envy as the 'on the boat' parties left the camp.

We that were left were the 'care and maintenance' and 'closing down' party. There was very little to do for most of the men. But I was even more busy than usual arranging more and more sporting events for the days, housey housey (bingo) as it is now called and snooker competitions in the evenings. One good thing was, that with so many fewer on the camp, but with the same facilities things were better in some ways, you could get a game of squash or snooker much easier, and as I discovered later with large stocks of beer in the canteen, the price was reduced.

In August of that year, at only one weeks notice I was informed that I was to be posted yet again, not to the boat, but back to the middle of the country to a place call Gwelo and a camp called Thornhill close by. So I had to hastily sell my beloved Oscar, cheaply to a local farmer. I was to be at this camp for another year.

In the centre of most of the camps there would be four buildings in a square with a quadrangle in the middle. Three of these made up the canteen for NCOs and other ranks. The other one was for The Sergeants. The sole use of this building was for recreation, mainly drinking, table tennis and snooker. With only about two hundred men left on the camp, as well as my job organizing all the sporting events, I was put in charge of this building including both bars. I found I had to keep records of the money and the stock. I needed a ledger; there was no way you could get anything new, I found one where the first few pages had been used for something else so I tore them out. When the auditing officer next came round I was put on a charge, but managed to convince the officer that I had been thrown in at the deep end and knew nothing about accounting. I learnt from that you never tear pages out of an accounting ledger.

The centre quadrangle of this building was used as a secure store containing the stock of drinks for the bars. There were large crates all with quart bottles of the local brew from South Africa called Castle Larger. Who ever had run the place before I took over had not reduced the order as the camp reduced in numbers. I could see from the dates that as the new deliveries came in, they were the ones that were used, and those at the bottom I could see were a year or two old. I cancelled further deliveries. Some months later when we were getting down to these old deliveries the chaps were remarking that the beer was getting stronger; it was. Unlike the beers of today, which I believe have a sell-by date? All this meant was, they did not have to drink so much to get just as drunk. There was a great deal of drunkenness to which the officers turned a blind eye, every one was home sick and just living for the day their name would be on the boat list. I was too busy to be able to get drunk, except on my day off. When I would go into the town, to get away from it all.

There was an arrangement, whereby we were able to send back to England, black tin boxes containing our civilian clothes that we had been able to buy and wear for some time and other items, once we had our embarkation date. I discovered that some of the lads did not want or did not need to do this and would sell you 'their box'. If the box had the right name on, then it could be sent to any address. As I was running the housey housey, I took a percentage of the takings and found that I could afford to pay the going rate for a box, then fill it with things like sugar, cooking oil, biscuits, and non perishable items that were so short or on rationing at home. So that the boxes were not too heavy, I put in tennis and squash rackets and balls, plus any thing useful that I could find around the camp. I then addressed it to the right name but 'care of' my home address. Sergeants boxes were half as big again, I managed to send home four boxes, two airman's, one sergeant's, plus my own. They all arrived safely and Mother was 'over the moon'.

At weekends the sergeants mess would be very busy, many of the local civilians would be invited. Some of these would be South Africans we called them Yarpey's (I can't remember why), we did not like them very much, they had no manners and would talk very loud in Africarns even though they could all speak English perfectly. They would get very drunk on Brandy Lime and Lemon, They would buy rounds of drinks, but before they had finished what was in the glass they had, they just handed us the glass and said 'top it up'. When they were getting merry we just put half a measure in, they never noticed. When we came to cash up and take stock we had a nice little bonus.

The lads on the camp had very little to do and got very bored, I was busier than ever trying to keep them occupied with sporting competitions, soccer, cricket, tennis and swimming were the most popular with snooker and darts in the evenings. There were two other camps in the area, so many exchange visits were made; I had to organize it all including transport. Then instead of being able to enjoy a game my self, I had to umpire or referee.

At long last my name was on the list. I was (on the boat!). I left the camp on Tuesday 20th August 1946. Almost exactly three years from the day I arrived in Durban. I left with very mixed feelings, sorry to be leaving the many good friends I had made, knowing that we were most unlikely ever to see each other again. When we arrived once again in Durban, we were very disappointed to be told we would be there for three weeks. It turned out to be a month. I think that was the longest month of my life. There was nothing to do, no sporting facilities what so ever. I thought why on earth could they not have left us at the camp for another month, 'just like the RAF!'

I notice from my diary I had kept for the whole of that year that we embarked on the S.S. 'Maloja' on 19th September 1946, At long last we were off; we stopped at Mombassa for a day and a night. I bought a fishing line and hook. I hooked a three-foot long swordfish, we saw it jump out of the water, but it was too strong the line burnt my hand, so I had to let it go. The next stop was Port Said, where this time we did buy a few things from the many little boats that came along side. Our last stop before Southampton was Naples, where several hundred Italian prisoners of war were disembarked.

When we woke up on Monday 7th October we were off the Isle of White. What struck me most was how green the grass was. As we docked in one of the large quays at Southampton, the dockside was deserted except for a small group of people and a small child. As we got closer I was amazed to recognize my sister Betty, my Mother, the small child I knew must be my new sister Margaret whom I had never seen. Also there was Ken Wright, a long time friend of mine who had some how managed to find out what boat I was on and the arrival time. He had brought them all down in his car. I rushed to the gangway, but they said I could not go ashore. All those lining the side of the ship shouted, 'let him off'. I saw an officer who said 'go on then, ten minutes only', Mother, as usual was at the back of the group so the first one I embraced was sister Betty who was holding little sister Margaret's hand. When I got back on board I discovered that they all thought my two sisters, were my wife and small daughter.

It was Friday the 11th October 1946 before I got home. First we had to go all the way up to Worton in Lancashire to be 'demobbed', hand in our uniform and be issued with a 'demob' suit and eighty pounds. It was just over five years from the day I joined up, I arrived home and I had no regrets. I would not have missed it for the world. I found that I was sorry for those friends whom I had left at work, who had done what I was supposed to have done. Had not joined up but stayed and worked in a 'reserved occupation', even though I found that they had made plenty of money.

My Vellocette

CHAPTER 5

Back to work 1946 to 1996

I spent the next week visiting old friends and catching up on what had been happening over the last five years. One thing I found was that about ten of my friends and others that I had known had not made it. Killed in action, most of them R.A.F. aircrew. I remember thinking; I had been lucky to fail my Morse exam and to be sent far away from all the action.

At this time I had no transport, not even my trusty old bike my brothers had worn it out, so I was walking and bussing everywhere. It was while I was walking near to where I had been serving my apprenticeship that I saw my old employer, Mr. Wagstaff. He greeted me very warmly and asked if I was coming back to work for him. I told him I had not decided, but had seriously thought of applying for a job as a P E instructor . He talked me out of that idea; I put down my meeting up with him again, as another piece of good luck. If I had not done so I think I would have applied at one of the local schools, I've often wondered if they would have taken me on.

I told him I could not afford to take on the job with the wages of an 18 year old. So he told me that the government would make up the difference to what it would have been if I had not joined up. Ah! I said "But I joined up against your wishes and that of the government". He said. "Leave that to me", he was not only successful with a grant to make up my wages, but got me a ? 100 grant to help me buy the tools I needed. I must say I felt a bit guilty. But I picked up where I had left off five years earlier. I also went back to night school.

With the eighty pounds "demob money" I was able to buy a motorbike. This made life a great deal easier, but I found I missed the exercise that I had become used to. I found a couple of squash courts in a most unlikely place, a small back street near the castle in Windsor. You never saw anyone there except for other players. You had to put two shillings, (twenty pence), in a slot machine that gave you an hour's play and covered the cost of the shower. I usually managed to fit in three games a week, often not until quite late in the evening.

Three years went by and I was by then what was called a journeyman. A fully qualified craftsman, we were always very busy, we being the only Pattern Shop in the area with quite a number of Foundries on the Slough Trading Estate, who in those days were the main customers. We rarely did less than sixty hours a week. The working week in those days was forty-eight hours. Overtime was on Saturday mornings and evenings. I knew a couple of friends who were starting up their own business in a garden shed, who asked me if I could make them a few small patterns. They said that my boss was very expensive and his deliveries were too long. Without giving much thought to what I was doing I said yes. It meant that I would be working for a couple of hours till at least midnight, Saturday afternoons and Sundays Working with out any machinery or many of the special tools. Being a good Boy Scout I stole nothing from work, wood, screws, glue or pattern paint, although I think I would have been quite justified in doing so, for I found out from the office girl that Mr. Wagstaff had been paying me short, from the money that the government gave him to make up my wages. When I had finished the equipment that my friends required, they took them to one of the local foundries to be cast. Mr. Wagstaff, who called at all of these places, saw them found out that I had made them. He sacked me on the spot.

I was devastated the next nearest Pattern shop was at Reading, fifteen miles away. In those days I would have had to have a reference. Also I'm sure they would not have employed me if they were told what I had done. I went home early, mother knew something was wrong, but I did not tell her. Then in the evening there was a knock on the door, mother said. "George! There's a gentleman to see you", it was someone I had seen many times in the pattern shop, an important customer of Mr. Wagstaff's. He had been told what had happened and had come to see me with a proposal. He said it was about time there was some competition in the local Pattern trade. He said Mr. Wagstaff had the monopoly; he over charged and was late with deliveries. He would give me what work of his that I could handle. I don't remember what I said to him, I must have said I would, but when he had gone I thought how can I, I have no workshop, no machinery and no capital. If there had been another Pattern shop near I would have gone there and begged for a job.

CHAPTER 6

I start my own business

    Being self-employed had never ever crossed my mind. Fortunately as it turned out there was no alternative. I spent my savings, borrowed some money from mum, cleaned out a corner of dads coal shed, scrounged some scrap castings, made a treadle lathe out of an old treadle sewing machine and got started. I had no electricity or gaslight only a paraffin "Tilley" lamp that had to be pumped up. A great deal of the work involved machinery and electric hand tools. Every thing took me twice as long to make, than it would have back at work. I had to do my own running around, quoting on jobs and delivering, all on my motorbike. Then I found nobody pays you for six weeks or maybe ten. I ran up a debt on my house keeping with mum and spent no money at all for weeks. I worked fourteen hours a day; I had no social life and no more games of squash for a long time.

    After about six months I found a man whose name was Jack Fellows. He had a fair sized workshop in his garden from where he had been running a small business. But he was ill at the time suffering from TB. We came to an arrangement, where by I rented it from him. We became good friends and as he got better he would help me. He became very useful. The big benefit was electricity. For the first time in my life, in fear and trepidation I made an appointment to see the local bank manager expecting my request for an overdraft to be turned down. To my delight he offered me more than I requested. He said he was quite impressed with the copy of my accounts, drawn up for me by one of the few school friends who had gone to grammar school and become an accountant. What I did not realise was the difficulty in paying off the loan as well as the interest. I was to be saddled with an overdraft for most of the next 47 years. I dread to think of the amount of interest I have paid. The very first machine I ever bought was a small band saw.

    Fortunately for Jack, but not for me he got completely better and needed his workshop back. I then moved to another premises, which was very nearly my undoing. It was the outhouse of one of the local pubs called the Mile House. The problem was, that once the pub was open at 10.30, the landlord who was also a friend, having no customers at that time would come across the yard to talk to me. Then he would "say come across and let's have a drink". Also, as I worked late into the evening friends would see me through the window and they would try to persuade me join them. Fortunately, I then found a builders workshop which was quite large, that had every thing I needed, three phase electricity and a lot of medium sized wood working machinery, with a tortoise stove in the centre, just like the one in the laundry at home. In the summer we saved the scrap wood and shavings, then we burnt that in the winter, giving us free heat. In five years I had taken on a partner and was employing eight men and an apprentice. But not without building on two large extensions, plus digging a very large hole for a toilet. We were not bothered too much with planning permissions in those days.

We were now doing quite nicely and thought about renting premises on the Slough Trading Estate. But again one of the best things I ever did regarding the business was to listen to my accountant. He strongly suggested that we try to purchase our own freehold premise. So we took on an even larger overdraft from the bank and bought a piece of land in Cippenham. It was another two years 1963 before we could afford to get the builders in. I designed a purpose built building with three bays, one for the handwork and one for all the wood working machinery so that unlike all the other pattern shops I had been in, the men had a quiet and dust free place to work in. The third bay was let and then some years later used as a metal machinery shop, I did a lot of the building work myself. One night we were working late, doing the finishing touches. It was an evening we all remember where we were. We heard on the radio, President Kennedy had been shot.

Six months before we moved into the new premises I got a phone call late at night to say the workshop was on fire. Fortunately the good old Burnham fire brigade had got there in time to save most of the building and the office was OK, but every thing was saturated. There was a great deal of water damage with holes in the corrugated roof. I got home in the early hours of the morning feeling very down. But in the full light of day as they say things never look so bad. We got out the insurance policy, which again, I must thank our accountant for, I often grumbled about the cost of the premium, but thanks to him we were well covered. An assessor turned up very early and asked us to estimate the cost of the damage. We quite honestly told him what we though at that moment the cost would be and how long it would take us before we could get back into full production, but as it turned out, being craftsman out selves we managed to get back into production very much sooner than we thought and ended up doing very nicely out of it financially.

Following our move into the new workshop we had plenty of room, we were able to take on more men and in a few more years we were employing twenty men and three apprentices. We had become larger than Mr Wagstaff's Machine Pattern Co. which I noted with some satisfaction, but it took us twelve years to pay off the over draft. Many times over the next thirty-five years we found ourselves needing another, or a bigger overdraft. Due to the several recessions we went though and to pay for the extensions. But because we had a valuable asset in the building, with the bank holding the deeds, we never had a problem. If I had rented premises on the Trading Estate for 47 years I would have ended up with nothing but my pension and that was nothing like large enough, for I was only able to put money into it when we made a profit. But thanks to the property boom, when I eventually sold the freehold of the 6000 sq. ft. of industrial premises, that over the years it had become. It gave me enough for a very comfortable retirement.

Good pattern makers were like gold dust and never unemployed, so we had to take on apprentices and train them. This was one of the main reasons for my success. I advertised in the local press and gave details to the local youth employment office once a year. The youth employment officer that I saw was the every same one that I had seen all those years before when I was fourteen. He helped me a lot by vetting the boys him self and only sending me the most likely ones. I took on one every year. I would interview four or five, then I would visit the home of each one talk to the parents telling them that if he was chosen, Pattern Making was a very exacting craft and it would be a long time before their son would be able to call himself a Pattern Maker That both he and I would need their support. It was important to me what their hobbies were and of course how they had done at school. And so I visited the headmaster and the woodwork teacher. All this I found paid dividends, for I was choosing those that would lay the golden eggs for the company. I had very few failures. Most of them stayed for many years and even if they left they often came back again.

My most outstanding success was Tony, he was the one chosen soon after moving to the new premises. At that time I was a member of a small bodybuilding club, there were only about 30 members in all. On the very day that I had told Tony he had been the successful applicant, I was in the changing room, which had a large clothes rack down the centre. I could hear some lads talking on the others side of this rack but could not see them when one of them said "I got my first job today, I'm going to be a Pattern Maker"). It was Tony. He eventually became my Manager and by the time I reached the age of 60 he was running the practical side of the company making my life a great deal easier.

As mentioned earlier I did have a Partner, Billy Toll, in 1972. While we were going though one of the worst recessions, he dropped a bombshell telling me he wanted to sell the Company and was going to immigrate to Spain. I had a word with my advisers who told me I would have to buy him out. Based on the company accounts, the future prospects and the value of the property at that time. We came to an agreed figure. We were already running on an over draft. I went to my Bank, which in those days was Barclays; I had been with them since starting the Company in 1949. I asked to borrow £12.000, despite owning the freehold of the workshop he said no. I had resigned my self to letting the company go and the prospect of getting a job working for someone else was depressing.

At that time I was in the Burnham Village Choir, where the organist was a friend of mine, (he used to accompany me some times on my singing engagements). I told him of my problem for I knew he was an assistant Bank manager at a National Westminster Bank. He said, "Go and see Mr. Evans at the Slough Estates Branch". This I did and straight away he said. "Yes, and was £12,000 enough", (another lucky break) I was left with a largest overdraft I had ever had during a slump. These were the days of boom and bust that affected us directly. Fortunately soon after this for the next few years we were on a boom.

We had a very good customer in Aylesbury called New Holland Sperry Rand an American Company that built agriculture machinery. It was quite a large concern with their own design and drawing office. In the old days any apprentice "budding" designer-draughtsman would have had to spend some time in a Pattern shop and a Foundry to learn at first hand the problems of each craft, but none of these had. I would be called in to the drawing office to quote for work. One day I was given a Drawing of a simple casting where the pattern would have been difficult and expensive, because it had three ribs, (strengthening pieces). We have to make it possible for every thing to leave the mould in the sand, which usually requires the item to be split into two. With three ribs this becomes impossible. We would have to make prints and a core box and that would have trebled the cost. I pointed this out to the chief draftsman and asked him could it not have four ribs, as that would make it stronger and so much simpler and I explained why. From then on I was his "blue eyed" boy, he insisted that I see every job at the design stage.

They had a great many patterns made the drawings being sent out to several Foundries, some of these had their own Pattern shop, but my now new friend insisted that I be given the orders for the patterns, which gave me an introduction to several new customers; one of these was W. Lucy at Oxford. The manager there was Barry Newton. At first he was not too pleased with this arrangement. Most foundries had their own "pet" Pattern supplier; it was always difficult to get in with a new foundry, but he was pleased with our service. We started to become his No.1 supplier. It was often necessary for him to visit my works to sort out production problems. On these occasions I would take him out to lunch. Then we discovered that we both played Squash. He would then arrange to come later in the day and we would book a court for a game. By this time there were squash courts all over the place. Then he invited me to his home where he had a large Koi Carp pond. I was hooked by this and took up the hobby and so we always had other things to talk about other than just business. He became my very best customer responsible for one third of my turnover.

I still took on one new apprentice every year. But they now worked in the shop for just a few months and then went on an, "off the job" training scheme for one year run by a government sponsored Foundry Training Committee. We paid the lads wages and his keep at the live-in hostel. They spent three days a week on practical work, which included making a casting of the test piece that they would have made and two days on theory in the classroom. I would visit several times during the year and often take my family down with me to the college at Stroud in Gloustershire.

When my sons Martin and Edward were coming up to school leaving age, we had talks as to what they wanted to do. I told them there was a job for them at the works if they wanted it, but that they must decide if that was what they wanted to do pointing out that it would be nice if one day, one, or both of them were to run the company. Martin was just over one year older than Edward and he decided that was what he wanted to do, he was academically very bright. His teachers at his grammar school wanted him to stay on, go into the sixth form and then to university. I made him think very carefully about it, but told him that to run my company he would have to train as a pattern maker and that he should start at sixteen. I think he wanted to leave school and was also influenced by the prospect of getting away from home for a year and going to Stroud, so this is what he did.

We then, as a family visited him regularly and found that he was very happy there with about twenty other lads of his own age, who apparently had a very good time socially. Edward was very envious and couldn't wait until it was his turn, when that time came he was very keen to do the same. I thought he would make a better craftsman than Martin, but no, Martin turned out very well. Edward seemed to take more to the foundry side of it. That was why, when some years later a small aluminium foundry wanted to sell up. I bought it and put Edward there together with the two foundry men that came with the deal. We used a great deal of castings in the Pattern shop and frequently customers would give us an order for the castings they required as well as for the patterns.

This meant that the company now employed thirty-two altogether, the largest Pattern Shop in the south of England at that time. Every job was the result of a quotation, then an order. Nothing could ever be started with out an order and every job was just a one off. This took a lot of work on the administration side to keep the workshop busy. The men regularly did ten hours or so overtime and were very unhappy if this was stopped when we slackened off. These were still the days of boom and bust; a bad year would follow two good years.

The larger foundries were becoming more automated and the smaller ones were closing. We had to look further a field for work from the customers that required high production equipment, which meant cast iron patterns capable of producing up to half a million castings. This still required a wooden "Master Pattern", from which, if it was large one a casting would be made, or if small several. These cast iron patterns would then have to be machined by metal cutting machinery, which we did not have. I had to tour the auctions buying what we needed. We could not have afforded new ones. Not only did we need different machinery, we needed different Pattern Makers, "Metal Pattern Makers". But we still needed our wood working equipment and woodworking Pattern Makers. It was a time of great change and a bigger over draft!

We won an order for a full set of all metal pattern equipment for the left and right hand axles for the Massey Ferguson tractor; to give you some idea of the size of the job it kept two men busy for ten weeks. It was by far the biggest job we had ever handled. We made very little profit on that one but we learnt a lot, and we must have done a good job, for from that, came another order for an identical set of equipment.

A company in Islamabad, Pakistan was producing the same tractor on licence; apparently they could make all the parts of the tractor themselves including the castings but not the patterns. There was no Pattern shop in a country of one hundred and sixty million people. We quoted the same price, including the cost of the wooden master patterns, which of course we already had in our store. There was a clause on our quotation forms, where by we retained ownership of all master patterns, but it was very rare that we were ever able to use them again. So this time we made a very hansom profit. Then as luck would have it and owing to our good reputation, soon after we had finished that order we got a third identical order from another foundry, this time in Karachi. Since we were dealing with letters of credit we got paid as soon as they were put on the aircraft for delivery. I then went to Pakistan, met the owners of both foundries, following this we did more work for both firms for many years.

One of my several trips to Pakistan was in 1986. This was the year of the America's Cup twelve-meter sailing race, which had been lost to the Australian's by America for the first time ever four years earlier. I wanted to see this race, the test Cricket and all my Australian relations descended from my Fathers sister Auntie Vi. So I booked a round trip Via Hong Kong to Perth, to Singapore, then to Lahore. That was where they were machining the castings of the Massey Ferguson axle castings. I spent Christmas and the New Year staying with my cousin Joan, seeing quite a bit of my Aunt Violet who was 92. I wanted to ask her if she knew about my parents not marrying until I was three. But for some reason I could not bring myself to ask her.

I quite liked Hong Kong, but I doubt if I shall every go there again. Singapore I did not like too much, maybe it was because it poured with rain the whole time. I just spent the one night and one day there. Then had to be at the airport late in the evening. We flew during the night; I have never had such a bad flight. Quite naturally I suppose it was full of Pakistanis, mostly women all of who seemed to have babies. Now as most will know they don't like flying, something to do with the air pressure and their ears popping I think. They all cried the whole journey.

When we arrived in the early hours of the morning I was very tired. My bag was about the last one to appear and then I had to walk some distance through a large hanger like building with glass doors at one end. I could see a large crowd just the other side of these doors, as I walked though they all seemed to pounce on me, hustling me to take their taxi. At that moment I wanted the earth to open up and swallow me. My chin was on my chest as I tried to force my way through, then I lifted up my head and saw a fellow holding a large card with my name on it I have never been so relieved. My Customer had sent a car for me.

I didn't get time to see much of Lahore I was too busy at the machining works sorting out their problems. But what I did see was very old, unlike Islamabad, which was a completely new city built after the formation of the country fifty years earlier. I told my customer about my exhausting journey and then later he asked for my passport and ticket. I thought nothing of it, but when he gave it back the next morning I noticed a different ticket. He had 'up graded' it for me to first class. Islamabad is laid out just like a chessboard, with nine squares, three on each side and one large square in the centre. The centre square is the city-centre; the other eight are like small towns, each with their own administration. On the outskirts was the largest mosque in the world, at that time still being built.

1984 saw yet another slump, the U.S. dollar was almost equal with the pound at the time, so through a marketing agency I went to St. Louis, where there was a foundry exhibition. It must have been about October for I remember the clocks went back on the night of the day I left. I left London about midday, arriving in New York in the afternoon by the clock there. Then I caught another plane to St. Louis and during the flight the clocks went back another two hours. So I arrived by my watch, that I had been adjusting, only two or three hours after leaving Heathrow. I 'did' as much of the city as I could. I went up the famous arch over the Mississippi River. I was talking to someone for a while and then when I stopped speaking a typical, large, middle aged over dressed American lady standing near me, whom I noticed had been listening to me, said in a loud voice with a broad southern accent. "Oh don't stop". I couldn't think what she meant and then she said. "I just luuve your English accent'".

I got to bed that night about midnight, not feeling at all over-tried, even though I had by then been up for over 24 hours. My first meeting with prospective customers was an eight o/c breakfast one. I was not at my best. But I got the promise of enquires from two of them. We did a fair number of jobs for them over the next year or so, but then the dollar got stronger again and we were no longer competitive.

When we bought the site for my works there was a sitting tenant in about 1000 square feet of our premises, Rogers Auto's repairing cars. We didn't mind at that time, as we needed the rent he paid. But as time went by and during one of those rare occasions when we did not have an overdraft and there was money in the bank, we wanted him out. Mr. Rogers was five years older than I and fortunately unlike me, he wanted to retire at 65. This worked in well with our plans for the extension. It was a red-letter day for me when he moved, out and the builders moved in.

They pulled down the unsightly tin building that was right in the front of us and a two-story block in smart red brick was built, giving us another 1500 sq. feet of working space at ground floor level and a smart 1000 sq. feet of office space above. Together with the architect (one of my now grown up Scout Gang Show Boys) I had a great deal of pleasure at the design stage. The final touch was putting up the name of the Company in large wood block letters, which of course we made our selves, also a bracket, a pole and the union flag. We then had an open day inviting all our friends, customers and families to call. Most of our suppliers put advertisements in a special page of the local paper congratulating us.

A write up in the 'Buckinghamshire Businessman magazine. Jan 1988

A Proven record of steady progress   A £125,000 Extension
The realisation of a dream

From a one man business in Dad's tool shed in Burnham, with no electricity or gas, (just a Tilley lamp and a treadle lathe-cum-sander, made out of a couple of scrap castings and Mum's old mangle) to 6000 square feet of freehold property in Slough, full of both wood and metal-working machinery and 32 employees including five apprentices. That is the proud record of Montague Pattern & Casting Co. Ltd. who started in the modest way mentioned way back in 1949. Today six of the patternmakers have been with the company since leaving school and together they aggregate more than 100 years of service

The company has progressed even if slowly, each year, with just a couple of exceptions, using the wide scope of their craftsmen's skills and serving a wide range of customers with orders ranging from £5 to £50.000 A full range of production and prototype equipment in wood, metal and resin is supplied and the fully-machined iron equipment side for the automated foundry is increasing all the time and some 20 per cent of their turnover is for exports to Asia and America.

Everything they make is different and individually ordered, from a pattern for a cast-iron kitchen saucepan to 29 segments of an eight-meter satellite dish, all in aluminium castings. This was for the GPO and was the largest dish ever made in this way at that time.

In these days of automation most of the skills required to produce a casting lay with the pattern maker and despite some modern aids and skills (which take at least five years of diligent apprenticeship to acquire) are the same as they have been for hundreds of years.

Basically, anything made in molten metal as opposed to a fabrication, has to be poured into a cavity, usually in sand. This may sound simple until one thinks of a vehicle engine, with four or six cylinders each surrounded with a water jacket. The pattern that looks just like the engine is spit down the middle into to haves, so that it will leave the mould, forms the cavity. Then cores, which are a solid replica of the Holes required, are suspended with-in this cavity, using the core plugs for support.

The recent completion of the £125,000 extension to the premises - a new workshop with first floor offices - was the realisation of a 25 year dream of George Montague Managing Director, Tony Hunter Works Director, John Furlong Works Manager and all members of staff, welcomed customers, suppliers and friends to an open day to celebrate the event.

Just about this time a large well-known ship building company in Southampton closed down and held an auction. Almost all the equipment and machinery that I had bought over the years I had got from auctions, so I received all the catalogues. In this one there was a lot of office furniture. I was down there a couple of hours prior to the sale and saw in the managing directors office a whole set of beautiful items, a large very attractive curved oak desk and swivel chair, filing cabinets, a board room table and chairs to match. I marked these but thought there was not much chance of this entire lot going for the price I was prepared to pay. They were all separate lot No's so I thought I might get some of it. When they came up the whole lot went for "song". When years later I sold the property and I advertised it all, I sold it for twice what I had paid for it.

I had hoped to be able to pass on the whole business to my two son's Martin and Edward who were both working in the company. A few years earlier Martin had broken his ankle at a motorcycle race and was sitting at home doing nothing. I told him to come down to the office and start getting used to the admin side of the business. I left him to it with my secretary and was out for an hour or so. On my return he was not there, Joyce said he had just gone home without saying anything to her. When I challenged him he said, Dad I'm not a "work-a-hollic like you, I don't want to do it, I want to write play and entertain with my music.

Over the next few years problems arose that I was unable to do any thing about, a good Pattern Maker was like gold dust. But I started to lose some of mine some though retirement and some, who did what I had done, picked up their toolbox, went into their garage and started on their own. No longer could I put an advert in the paper for an apprentice, for I got no replies at all, or those that were just not suitable. Boys wanted to straight away earn good money, which they could do, often with out getting their hands dirty. Half of all the work we did now was with dirty cast iron. We advertised up north where there was unemployment, even Pattern Makers. The type of man we needed were those with some experience, which meant that he was older, married with a mortgage. So there was no way he could sell up and move south with the price of house's being four times more in the south. So there we were with plenty of orders, but not enough men to justify the size of the premises we were in. Tony my Manager was seriously thinking of emigrating and I was over seventy.

With very much regret, I started to think of selling our 6000 sq ft of very valuable free hold industrial property and moving to smaller premise. I could quite easily have closed down altogether, but I was still enjoying it all. Then with many of those men I still had, having been with me for so many years 25, 20, and 15 years the redundancy pay would have been very great. I contacted an estate agent and when he told me the figure I could expect was twice what I had thought, I started to think seriously about it.

But first I had to find new premises; this I found was very difficult, the economy was booming, with little business's starting up every-where. There were units on the Trading Estate, simply because of their high rents and conditions. You had to put down a bond of several thousand pounds, but we had no alternative. The freehold premises, (as it turned out,) were sold, at the height of the property market. Those of us that were left after weeding out some dead wood moved into 2000 square feet. We sold my beloved industrial workshop the address of which had always been 2a Bower Way. One of the directors of the company that bought it thought the building should have a name. He had a relation whose name was George. He knew my name was George, so he called it 'George House'. That eased the pain of selling and I felt very proud. It is a very well built and will stand long after I am gone.

Tony Hunter had been with me for over 33 years, he was responsible for the successful introduction of the all-metal side of the business. He was just as much at home with metal work as he was with the wood working side, which was very unusual. He was totally committed, to running the company for the last 10 to 15 years as if it was he own. He would come into work on a Sunday, finish off a job that was promised for first thing Monday morning and then drive all the way to Oxford to deliver it. He became totally indispensable to the company. Our customers all thought very highly of him, it was him they all wanted to see and speak to. We spent a great deal of time on the telephone; with pattern making there are always a great many problems and quires. Written on many of the drawings were the words, "if in doubt ask". His telephone manner and the way he was always totally polite to the customer contributed a great deal to our success.

Foundries are places where there is a great deal of stress, if things don't go right they will blame the pattern maker if they can and the managers were always under pressure. On these occasions they would want to speak to me not Tony, I would get a good 'ear bashing' so I held the phone away from my ear and listened politely. I could often tell that there were others in the office at the other end and the words were for other ears as well as mine. More often than not the problem was not ours at all, but the way they were using our equipment. But our motto was 'the customer is always right even if he is wrong'. When they were rude to us we, just like Liberace, cried all the way to the bank. During all the years that Tony was a director, he and I never had a serious disagreement.

1988 was a year I had looked forward to for many years. It was the year in which I was 65 and should have retired and drawn my pension. I did draw my DHHS pension and my company pension. I was able to pay off the mortgage I had on 24 Westfield Road. Once again, (and nothing to do with me, just pure luck) I found years later that I had drawn my company pension at the best possible time for many years. Why it is I don't know and to me it does not seem fair. But the rate of interest one gets on the annuity that you are obliged to buy, depends on what the bank interest rate is at the time. It was $15^1/_2\%$, so that I receive an increase of $8^1/_2\%$ each year and will do until the day I die. But when the interest rates are low, as they are as I write you would get less that half that amount.

The slump of 1995/6 hit us very badly, we had lost another couple of men though retirement. I could not persuade them to stay after they were 65. I was 74 and still willing to carry on if it had been practical. After much consultation with my accountant, (but not with the bank manager this time), we decided that because of our lease with our Landlords to go into voluntary liquidation. But this was not so easy. Most that do this do it because their assets are less than their liabilities, but we were not bankrupt. With the help of our accountant and liquidator we managed it. Several time's different companies had gone bankrupt on me, fortunately never for any great amount. I was friendly with most of my suppliers, so I asked them to let me have an up to date invoice, then on "the" day I went round and personally gave them all a cheque telling them to pay it in straight away, I could not tell them why, but I expect they guessed.

I gave the company to John, who had been with me for 30 years, and Andy, together they took over the company employing one other. If you go into liquidation the government pay all the redundancy. So the only one that lost out was the greedy Slough Trading Estate. Unfortunately the name of the company had to be changed. They moved into premises just next door and are as far as I know still going. I can't help thinking that if we had stayed where we were, we would have had to cease trading anyway. And by then the bottom would have fallen out of the property market, I would have got at least one third less for the business property.

I was disappointed not to have made the 50 years running the company. I was $2^1/_2$ years short. I started work at aged 14 years. So I worked it out that including my five years service in the R.A.F. I had worked for 60 years with not one day being unemployed and very few days off sick in all that time. The best decision I made was to have my own freehold premises. It would have been so much easier to have rented, like the majority of small companies do and not struggle for years to pay off the overdrafts, but although for the last 30 years I had a good income, with new cars every two or three years, when we closed down I would have had nothing but my small Company and state pension. My good luck has been to invest in property, both Industrial premises and private housing.

rom

MONTAGUE PATTERN & CASTING CO. LTD.

EST. 1949

GEORGE HOUSE

CHAPTER 7

SINGING

As mentioned previously I joined the local church choir at the suggestion of Mrs. Hanbury at the tender age of seven, to cure the stammer that I had. I couldn't read very well and the shortest cassock was far too long but I enjoyed the ceremony and the ritual of the services. Christmas was always exciting, on Palm Sunday and Easter Sunday we had processions and on Armistice Sunday the service was held around the cenotaph. Also I got paid and was able to join the choir club where we played games such as rounders and cricket in the summer, table tennis and indoor games in the winter at the vicarage before choir practice on a Friday evenings.

I probably memorized the words of the hymns and the prayers rather than read them. Before joining the choir. Sunday had been something of a boring day, when we had to wear our best clothes, in which we were not allowed to play. But now Sunday was a very busy day, there was "Said" Holy Communion at seven o/c, the same service only sung this time at eight o/c. Matins at eleven, Sunday School at three o/c, then Evensong at six thirty. We looked forward to weddings and funerals when we got paid extra, then sometimes we were invited to the wedding reception.

About the age of ten I was allowed to join the bell ringing team, I had to stand on a box to ring the lightest of the six bells. We rang the bells for about half an hour before Matins (that's the morning service), and Evensong, then those of us that were in the choir had to run quickly to the vestry to get changed into our cassocks and surplice's. Once a year there was a choir outing when we all went by coach usually to the seaside. Also once a year we would take part in a Choir Festival. For a few weeks before we would rehearse several pieces of special music, then on the big day we would all go to St. George's Chapel Windsor Castle, where there would be many other choirs including the St. George's Choir and the Eton College Choir

There were so many of us that we filled more than half the Chapel. A rehearsal was held first. Then we would have half an hours break before putting on our Cassocks and Surplices that we had all had to remember to take home to be washed and ironed and take with us. Being a professional laundress, mum would put some starch on my Surplice I thought it always looked the best. We then processed right round the chapel then up the step's, just like the Knights of the Garter do. Our parents and members of the public were invited. We very much enjoyed the sound of this mass choir in the magnificent surroundings of St. Georges Chapel, where the acoustics were perfect. It always inspired me to sing my best. There was always several solos' for which there was an audition. I decided that one day I would audition.

I sang my first solo at eight and a half years old it was a verse from "Away in a Manger" during a carol service. From then on I often did solos not only at the church service's, but also at weddings and funerals. A friend of my family lost a tiny baby, she made a request to my Choir Master that I sing a verse from the hymn "Love divine all love excelling". At the age of ten I was put forward for the Audition at St George's Chapel. My Choir Master gave me several lessons. There were nine boys competing, I was not successful, the three boys that were, were aged twelve and thirteen. The judicator had a word with my Choir Master and said I hope he will be here next year. He told me that he probably chose the older boys as their voices could have broken by the next year. I was chosen the next year and the year after that.

My voice did not break until I was nearly sixteen; I had been head boy of the choir for three years by then, boys younger than I never did get to be head boy because of me. I followed with great interest the career of Alled Jones, the finest treble voice of all time; I noted that his voice did not break until he was sixteen. I think that perhaps the more you use your voice as a boy the later it breaks. When you are as interested as I was in singing as a boy, you wonder what voice you will have when it does break. My Choir Master made me have a years rest before he would let me join the men of the choir. The organ we had did not have electric bellows, so I did the pumping. I did experiment and was a bit disappointed when I knew I would be a Bass or Baritone I dearly wanted to be a Tenor. I have never understood why it is that Tenors are always the most popular. They have most of the best music written for them and are always the most popular and in great demand. My favourite Tenor aria is Handles "Every Mountain shall be exalted".

I did join the men as a Bass Baritone and found I had a very good range, so when we were short on Tenors, which happened when the war started, I was able to sing on that side of the Chancel so long as the tune did not go too high. It is not well known that a bass or baritone voice can also sing in falsetto. (alto Alfred Delar). Who sings Elizabethan songs is the most famous alto, sometime called counter tenor. So if several bass's turned up I would cross to the other side of the Chanceland sing alto. At the age of eighteen I joined the R.A.F. where many times I would sing in the canteens, but only after I had a few beers. "Ave Maria" was all the rage at that time; I would sometimes sing this in alto. Then the boys would cheer and ask me to drop my trousers to prove I was a male.

The very first Sunday I was home after the war I visited the church again, but was very disappointed at what I found. The Choir Master I had known had left, there were hardly any boys in the choir and no men. I did what I could, but the old Vicar Cannon Evans had died; the new one was not very interested in the choir and was talking of have girls to make up the numbers, that was the last straw. Then I was "head hunted" by the Choir Master of Burnham Church, where there was a very good

Choir. I left Hitcham and joined the Burnham church choir. Mrs. Handbury who had all those years before suggested I be put in the choir, now suggested that I have my voice trained. This I did.

I started with a Mr. Cooke in Slough; I was with him for about six months, towards the end of which he took me to the Slough Grammar School to sing before the sixth form there. One of the several songs I sang was, "Drink to me only with thine eyes" by Roger Quilter. Fortunately this was in the days before "pop" I am sure he did it to put me before one of the most difficult audiences. Soon after that I found I was in a concert with several other artists, one of whom was a brilliant pianist, Mr. Harold Mead who played among other pieces (The Rustle of spring). I had a word with him and complimented him on his playing. Then I discovered that he was a singing teacher, an L.R.A.M. A.R.C.M He was also a professional tenor. He had some kind things to say about my singing but added some constructive criticism and suggestions. The end result was I left Mr. Cooke and started having lessons with Harold Mead, even though he lived at West Wycombe the other side of High Wycombe about ten miles away. That was the start of a very long relationship. One of the first things Harold did was to enter me for Music festivals. In those days all the large towns ran one even Slough. That was the first one he entered me for.

Two test pieces were set for each voice; sometimes he would enter me for both the Baritone and the Bass section. Usually there were four or five competitors. A well-known musical adjudicator would listen to each artist; this took place in the afternoon, then later on he would read out his judgment on each one, which was always part critical and part praise. Then he would announce the winner. In the evening there would be a concert of all the winners, these were always very well attended, with not only the friends and relatives of the soloist, but music loving members of the public.

We would get about two months notice of the date of the Festival, then the first thing I had to do was to buy copies of the music. Often the local sheet music shop was sold out, I had to write off to London for copies. Harold always came with me to the festivals and accompanied me. This was a very great advantage, many of the soloist had to have a strange accompanist with whom they had had no chance to rehearse. I won my Class at Slough, Maidenhead, Reading, and Wembley for which I have all the certificates. For some reason unlike Slough, Wycombe and the surrounding area was very musical all the churches and chapelís had adult choirs. Harold was, in some way or another connected to most of them. Handles Messiah was a great favourite with them; they were always looking for soloist. After a few years I could sing all the solos of this wonderful Oratorio without the score. Easter was another very busy time when I was in great demand to sing the solos of Stainers Crucifixion, also the St. Mathews Passion by J.S. Bach.

Harold wanted me to turn professional and for a time I did seriously consider it. That was why I took on Billy Toll as a partner in my business. We did a few professional engagements for annual dinners such as a Masonic Lodge, Toc H and an ex serviceman's association, usually in London. I remember we got five guineas a time. Harold was a fine Tenor who often sang professionally. We would both sing solos, then a duet and then he would play some piano pieces. Unfortunately at times I found it difficult to be professional. I sang, with Harold accompanying me, this was after the dinner when the audience had had a few drinks. They were usually pretty good when I, or we sang. But when Harold played they would talk and make a noise. Once they did not listen during my song, so I just stopped, walked off the stage and told them to keep the fee.

I decided that fifty years earlier, I would have been able to make a go of singing as a career. But television was coming in fast and these were the days of Cliff Richard, Adam Faith and Tommy Steel and then the Beatles the type of Music that I sang was getting less and less popular especially with young people. Any way I only wanted to sing to those who wanted to hear me. We all know how much pleasure there is in listening to good music, the sort that makes the small hairs on the back of your head stand up. Then just imagine the pleasure one gets from performing that music your-self, to an appreciative audience if you are fortunate enough to have been blessed with a talent.

Harold was disappointed I think, he kept telling me that I had got what it takes. He persuaded me to visit a friend of his who was one of the top singing teachers in the country. His name was George Parker. He had taught Joan Southerland, Isabel Bailey, Heddle Nash, Norman Walker and many of the top soloists of the day. He listened to a couple of my songs that we thought I did best. He said, "Yes I had the voice but it needed more work done on it, preferably at one of the music academies and after that it would mean, just like top sportsmen and ballet dancers, many hours singing practice every day for the whole of my singing life". I gave the matter some more serious thought. Had I not got a promising business that needed me, or had I been a Tenor I would have given it a go. I would carry on having singing lessons as long as was possible, but with Harold, deciding to sing for my pleasure and the pleasure of an audience that wanted to hear me sing and not to sing for money.

I joined the Windsor and Eton Coral society, where we did many wonderful works. At the performances there was always some of the top soloist in the country. Our conductor was Dr. William Harris, who was the Presenter of St. Georges Chapel Windsor; he was to have conducted his own work, "Praise The Lord." We had the final rehearsal of the choir in the afternoon, then the choir left, so that the orchestra could go over the piece they were going to do. When we arrived in the evening for the performance there seemed to be some thing wrong, people were all talking in a worried sort of way. Then it was announced that there had been an accident after the choir had left. Apparently Dr. Harris has stepped backwards and fell off the stage, he was not going to be able to conduct. Then we saw Dr. Sydney Watson, (Presenter of Eton College) he was going to take over, but told us he was familiar with the work but had never conducted it before, but with our help he would do his best, he did very well.

Soon after this Dr. Watson took over as our permanent conductor. Some time later after a rehearsal he called me to one side and to my surprise asked me if I would like to do the solos of work that was coming up. It was just before Christmas 1953; the piece was called "a Christmas Carol" he said he would like to take me though it himself and would I go to his chambers on a certain evening. I was thrilled and flattered, but wondered how he had known that I sang solos, he told me later that some one had told him. I had several rehearsals with him and some with Harold. He told me that I should wear evening dress "tails" he assumed that I had some, but I didn't I had to quickly guy some. The big day came, I was singing from the score so I was not too nervous, despite the fact that it was the first time I had sung with a large orchestra and with a choir of 80 that were one of the best in the country. I received a letter from him that I have kept to this day.

My dear George
To thank you for your singing last night and to congratulate you on it, it was the best I have heard you do, to give of one's best at a public concert is an enviable quality.
All best wishes, Watson.

The 2nd of June 1953 saw the coronation of the Queen and a very busy time for me, I sang at the High Wycombe football ground to a crowd of about 5000 on the Saturday afternoon the 30th of May. Then the same evening, I led the community singing, with several thousand in the Gore, (a large natural hollow) in Burnham Village. On the 20th Of June The Burnham Dramatic and Orchestral Society, put on a concert where I sang four songs and the solos with the Towns Women's Guild Choir.

Harold organized a concert party of about thirty of us. We all blacked our faces, wore very colourful old clothes and straw hats, we sang about twenty Negro songs. We called it the Darky Show. We sang most of Steven Fosters songs, Ole Man River, Way Down upon the Swaney River, Uncle Ned. That one probably would not be allowed today. It would be classed as politically incorrect. The song includes the word Nigger. In all we probably did about twenty shows over a five-year period.

I now had a repertoire of about thirty ballads, any one of which I could sing at very short notice. The next thing I was told that I must do a recital; I would sing sixteen songs in one concert. Four sets of three with an encore. This was to be done at the Wigmore Hall in London. It was something that every budding artist had to do, if he wanted to be known and accepted. At this concert there would be critics whose opinions would decide my immediate future as a Bass Baritone.

We decided we would do a trail run locally in the village hall at Burnham. Charge a small entrance fee, the proceeds of which would go towards my Scout group at the Canadian Memorial Hospital. 100 tickets were sold and on the night we were sold out. We invited along a critic and this is what he wrote in the local press.

"On Monday evening the inhabitants of the Burnham Locality were entertained and edified by an unusually well arranged Concert in aid of the Handicapped scouts

The principle artist was George Montague Bass Baritone who sang well-varied groups of operatic and oratorio arias, lieder and folk songs. The weakness of the translation from Italian and German were most marked, but singers are always faced with the dilemma of choice, between indifferent translations of the original tongue.

Mr. Montague was adequately equipped and obviously well prepared to sing the programme, his efforts were ably supported by Mr. H. Mead. Supporting artists gave readings from the classics. The acoustics at the hall were not good; much of the excellence was lost. About 100 people attended and the organizers are to be commended for their enterprise ..."

Joan Boddy was another unforgettable character. I considered my self very privileged to have known and worked with. She was a real bubbly person full of energy, she played the piano as an accompanist for me. She was always gathering amateur artist together to put on a show for some charity or other. I always took part if I was free, for the rehearsals and the shows were always so much fun. She frequently entertained at several old peoples clubs, she would play to them, tell them funny stories and get them singing all the old songs that they loved. Then she asked me if I could possible spare the time to go along to sing a few songs to them.

This was on a working day afternoon. She would ring up and tell me what time to appear. I would leave my office, drive to the hall and arrive exactly at the time arranged. I would go in quietly and stand at the back of the hall. She would be playing the piano and she or the audience would be singing, but she would be looking out for me. As soon as she saw me she would finish off the piece she was doing. Then play the introduction of one of my songs (as arranged), some thing like "Scotland the brave", I would walk down the aisle singing, then up onto the stage and sing another couple of songs. Joan would introduce me, telling them I was a very busy man. Then I would sing another suitable song like, "Goodbye Dolly I Must Leave You," whilst walking back to the door and out. I would only be away from my office for less than an hour. This went on for most of the late 50s and 60s. Then Joan tragically contacted breast cancer and we lost her. They say nobody is indispensable; but there was no one to take her place!

Lillian Good was a housewife and mother of a school and scouting friend of mine; she was also a very find actress who could have graced any London stage. The Taplow and Hitcham Women's Institute was quite large, it had it's own drama section; they regularly put on very good plays with Lillian as the producer. There are of course very few plays with just women in. So she would gather in local men as honorary members. She approached me and asked me to take the part of Jasper, in Noel Cowards Musical, "Family Album," and could I find another three males for the cast amongst my many singing friends? This I did, one was Harold Mead. For those not familiar with this work, it is a very funny musical that takes place in Victorian times. Four offspring, their husbands and wives of a middle class family, plus the butler, are gathered in the drawing room, reminiscing about their childhood following their father's funeral. I think we did about six performances. It was great fun. But of course Lillian didn't stop there, she pleaded with me to appear in many other plays that were not musical. She was one of those that it was hard to say no to. So I got to enjoy acting as well.

One of the highlights of my singing career must be when I sang under the baton of Sir. Charles Macakerras the famous conductor. Harold, a Soprano and I as the soloists, with a very large choir sang a "Festival Concert" somewhere near Watford. I don't seem to have a souvenir programme and I can't remember the pieces we sang. My Aunt Violet was in England on a visit from Australia. She and My Mother both came, I was very proud.

Many times I have been asked to sing at wedding receptions, pubs, parties, even karaoke's. "Come on George give us a song", but unless it was planned and with an accompanists I was never tempted, even when I had had a few drinks. I think it went back to the days of my few professional engagements, where the secretaries of clubs thought they were giving their members a treat, when all many of the audience really wanted to do was drink and talk.

I made one exception, at my sailing club annual dinner. In nearly 20 years as a member I had never heard any thing other than course jokes and speeches by those who were, by the time they got onto their feet, a little the worse for drink. There was never anything with any culture. But one night quite early in the proceedings there was, by the Commodore, a reading with a nautical flavour that was very good, it held every body's attention. I whispered to the M.C. that I would sing a song to follow that. I had always thought that with a room full of about 150 sailors, John Masefield's song "I Must Go Down To The Sea's Aga'n" should have gone down well so long as they were quite and listened to the words. I had to sing it unaccompanied of course. Only one or two in the audience, many of whom had known me for many years knew that I sang, it went down well; Even though many there had plenty of drink. They were quite, they listened then they clapped for an encore.

I must go down to the seas again to the lonely sea and the sky.
And all I ask is a tall ship and a star to steer her by.
The wheels kick and the winds song and the white sails shaking.
And the grey mist on the Sea's face, with the grey dawn breaking.

I must go down to the seas again, for the call of the running tide.
Is a wild call and a clear that may not be denied.
And all I ask is a windy day with the white sails shaking
With the flung spray and the blown spume
And the seagulls crying

I must go down to the Sea's again to the vagrant gypsy life.
To the whales way and the gulls way where the winds like a whetted knife.
And all I ask is a merry yarn from a laughing fellow rover.
And a quite sleep and the sweet dream when the long tricks over

John Masefield

The last time I ever sang in public was at a party to jointly celebrate, my 70th birthday, a farewell to Tony (my works manager leaving for Canada), my secretary and works foreman, both having been with my company for 25 years. My son Martin who takes after me in one respect, writes his own songs and accompanies him self on the guitar, he was the other artist. For the last five years or so before that I sang very little, not because of my voice, Norman Walker (Bass) with whom I closely identified sang professionally until he was 80. But It had become harder and harder to find any one like Joan Boddy or Harold. Or for that matter, any one that can even play the piano, let alone accompany a vocalist. The sheer pleasure of singing the wonderful songs, most of which one rarely hears now a days, I still miss it, the pleasure I got from the rehearsals, giving pleasure and yes the applause, a little addictive really. You wait in the wings for your introduction, always a little nervous. Then you walk out onto the empty stage with nothing. Your only instrument your voice, all on your own except for the accompanist sitting at the piano. You see the pleasure you are giving in the faces of the audience, if you dare to look down. Then they clap and you hope they will carry on long enough so that it will justify you doing the encore you have prepared. At the end you mix with the crowd and enjoy the complimentary comments. I think I understand a little of the loneliness of artists, who are no longer in demand. I never did get to the Wigmore Hall, but there are no regrets.

One of my favourite radio programmes is Desert Island Disc's. I have often thought about what I should choose if ever I was asked (which of course I never will be). Here is a list of those that I am sure I could never get tired of listening to:-

Kathleen Fierier.	Contralto	"Blow the Winds Southerly"
Ronald Binge.	Orchestral	"Sailing By" (from the shipping forecast)
Edith Piaf.	Singer	"Non Je Ne Regrette Rien".
Aled Jones.	Treble	"Where E'er you walk (Handel)"
Peter Piers.	Tenor	"Any thing that he has ever recorded"
Joan Sutherland.	Soprano	"I know that my redeemer liveth" (Handel)
Elton John.	Crooner	"Composer of Sacrifice"
Alfred Delar.	Alto	"Where the bee sucks" (Elizabethan)
Paul Robson.	Bass	"Ole Man River" :

At Twinches Lane School under the baton of Dr. Sydney Watson from a christmas card painted by and sent to me by Harold Mead

CHAPTER 7

SCOUTING 1931-1941 Wolf Cub, Scout, Patrol Leader, Rover, Assistant Scout Leader

At the age of nine I joined the Wolf Cubs of the local scout group the 1st Hitcham. I gained many of the badges. I did best on those connected with wildlife and camping. I became a sixer (that's one who gets to lead five other cubs). I remember the excitement of my first summer camp that was held at Wantage in Oxfordshire. It was there I learnt to swim when my "second hand", but proudly owned scout hat was thrown into the swimming pool. The very first letter I ever received with my name and address on it was handed to me at the morning assembly following flag break. In it my mother told me that my pet budgerigar had escaped from his cage.

I owe a great deal to the quality of the Scouters of this group who were, (I think it was Ralph Reader who said) 'not only mindful of the rightful upbringing, of their own, but also of other men's sons". Too many today are not mindful of the rightful up-bringing of their own, let only other men's sons. Regrettably as time has gone by there have been fewer of this type. Car ownership, television, D.I.Y., over-time, more money, all this has led to a lack of leaders for the most important age group, 12 to 18, with many groups closing for lack of leaders and others who have a shortage of leaders of the right quality. This means boys lose interest and leave. I think one of the major causes of juvenile crime is boredom. A measure of the success of my leaders could be judged by the number of their boys who, after the war stayed in the movement to become Scout Leaders themselves. I must admit I took some pleasure in visiting the founders of the group, Mr Norman Wallis and his wife who by then were in their 70' 's, telling them I had been appointed an Assistant County Commissioner and thanking them.

I particularly enjoyed the camping and did so as often as possible at week-ends and holidays, as well as the annual summer camp. Things like the smell of burning wood, cooking over an open fire, sleeping outside the tent under the stars on a fine night. The organising of camp life, the wide games, tracking, pioneering, working on the proficiency badges such as knots and whipping, points of the compass. I am constantly puzzled at the number of mature people who are at times not sure which is their left or their right and have no idea which is North South East or West, let alone the other 32 points of the compass. Forestry, Axemanship, fire lighting, cooking, first aid, signalling, swimming, estimation, map reading, the character training, all have stood me in good stead through out my life.

On leaving scouting in 1974 I took up sailing, which requires knowledge of the weather, navigation, cooking, knots, rope work, leadership, observation, (and in those days) Morse and Semaphore. Also how to live comfortably with a minimum of possessions and equipment, getting on with people, all this I learnt as a boy in the Scouts when later on I was to become a scout leader myself, running my own group. This knowledge was then extended and ingrained in the best way possible, by planning and preparing a programme. Then seeing how the boys enjoyed playing and learning the game of Scouting,

In 1936 we put on the first of three pre- war Scout Gang Shows, (little did I know then how much of my life would be taken up by this). With the small profit made from the first show we bought a brand new trek cart from the Scout shop; it all came to pieces for easy transport. It was very well made, for 20 years later, when I was running my own business that involved woodwork; I made a new handle for it. The 1939 show although we didn't know it at the time was to be the last for ten years.

The war took away what we thought was our indispensable Scout Leaders and the Rover Scout helpers. The troop was full with six patrols of eight, but there was a danger that it would fall apart without a proper programme and continuation of the discipline. Further more we had a fair number of evacuees down from London, some of who wanted to continue with their scouting and others who wanted to join.

At a Patrols Leaders meeting, (I was by then Leader of the Ravens) we decided that we must keep things going. The talk then, was that the war would be over by Christmas! It came down to four of us running the troop. The Group Scoutmasters wife ran the Cub pack, but she had lost one of her male Cub Scout Leaders, so we found ourselves helping out there as well.

We were asked to give a demonstration of first aid to the local A.R.P (air raid wardens). These were mostly older men and included my father, most of whom were too old to be called up; on arriving home he congratulated me. He had been particularly impressed by my demonstration of the firemen's lift, where I had lifted one of my friends about the same size as myself who pretended to be unconscious, on to my shoulders from the prone position. Until then I can't remember my father ever giving me much praise. Being the eldest of four, with my brother Edward being somewhat delicate, the next one down being my sister I tended to get the blame when we got up to mischief, which of course we often did. How ever on this occasion he said he was very proud of me. I grew up a little extra on that day. I have a letter from my Scoutmaster that I have kept all these years, dated 25.xii.39: -

Dear Monty,
I really must thank you for all the marvellous work you have done for the troop during the past few months. You have done splendidly. You cannot realise how pleased I am that the four of you were able to keep the "flag of scouting" flying without the aid of the officers. Don't be discouraged if a few of the youngsters drop out, remember 12 good Scouts are worth 80 who treat Thursday night as a club.

The future is difficult to foresee, but what ever happens I feel sure that you, Arthur, Ray, & Dolly will make sure that Scouting continues along the right lines in Hitcham.

Best of luck

Arthur.

PS The scarf is a present for passing the "Kings Scout Badge."

We older boys did our national service and proudly wore the red N.S. badge over our left pocket. We provided a telephone answering service and did fire watching duties. At the age of 17 some of us also joined the Home Guard. I was at the time, serving my apprenticeship cycling three miles to work on a 48 hour working week, then cycling four miles to night school at Slough town centre. All along the side of the Slough Trading Estate were barrels of old oil that gave off a choking black smoke, which was to hide the factories from the bombers. All this time I was still very much involved with the Church, in the bell ringing team, the choir, the Choir club, a Server assisting the priest at Holy Communion. But we kept the troop going, also organizing the main after scout activity, "waste paper collection", the trusty trek cart was worked very hard.

National Service 1939.

RAY   ME   ARTHOUR

1941 - 1946 A ROVER SCOUT

Soon after my 18th birthday I joined the R.A.F., but kept in touch as much as possible during the next year prior to my posting overseas. At which time things were still going strong, lead by the next generation of patrol leaders with the help of a few more adults that we had managed to rope in. I spent the next four years in Southern Rhodesia (as it was called then), as a Physical Training & Drill Instructor training aircrews. The four different stations to which I was posted all had Rover crews, these I always joined. I was able to use my skills as a woodworker on such projects as a Toc H. hut, which we then used as our Rover Den, also a 25-yard bowling alley cum small-bore rifle range.

I was "demobbed" in 1946. On the first Troop night I went along to the old H.Q. and was disappointed and surprised to see it was empty and partly derelict, but the small house that was attached was still occupied by the same caretaker and his wife. They were in and were very pleased to see me once I had reminded them who I was, they then told me that the old hall had been sold and would eventually be turned into a house. They were as disappointed as I and we reminisced about the pre war days, then they told me that the troop was still going, but that they now met in a scout hut in Burnham, but knew no details.

Now Burnham was the next village and one of the largest in South Bucks. There had always been rivalry of a mild nature between the Groups, the Choirs and the Schools. I very soon found out that the 1st Burnham Group had closed during the war. There was a Scout HQ, quite a good one, on it's own piece of land with equipment and some money held by the vicar, but no Scouters or boys. Then there was the 1st Hitcham, still a flourishing Group, but with no HQ, meeting in an old dilapidated barn, so the inevitable had happened.

The vicar of Burnham insisted (and I suppose it was only right) that the amalgamation of the 1st Burnham, who had no leaders or boys and the 1st Hitcham with no Head Quarters should be call the 1st Burnham and Hitcham. We "old boys" were horrified at the time and vowed to see the re-establishment of the old Group. About this time we formed a branch of the B.P.Guild of Old Scouts. At the very first meeting about 20 turned up.

1946 I Join the Baden Powell Scout Guild

We did quite soon get together all the makings of another group, but when we tried to get the old name back, we had not realised that those running it had by then been doing so for some time and had built up the very tradition and pride that we had done. They were not going to give up half their name. So we thought about it and came to the conclusion that it was Scouting that mattered most and the best thing to do would be to form another group. This was done with Scouters from the Guild and called the 1st Lent Rise. They are still going strong to this day.

Before the war I don't recall there being a "Local Association". We were an island with no contact that I can recall with any other Troop or Group. Now we became the Burnham & District Local Association with a Chairman, Secretary, Treasurer and a committee with four Groups, a Rover Crew and the Guild. It was decided by the Guild to put on a district show, Ralph Readers "We'll live forever". I had been "roped in" a couple times by the local Women's Institute Drama section when they needed male players, they knew I was taking singing lessons, so I was put forward as the producer. Reluctantly I agreed. We put on two shows and a matinee making the princely profit of £30, not bad in 1949.

We then had a request to take the show up to the local hospital called the Canadian Red Cross. This was in the grounds of Lord & Lady Astor's estate at Cliveden Taplow. The first four wards were a special unit for the research on rheumatism in children. Wards 1 & 2 were for boys and girls ages up to 12 years. Ward 3 was for girls 12 to 18 years and ward 4 was for boys 12 to 18. Each ward was full with some 36 beds in each. The show was staged in the small hospital theatre. The audience were made up mostly of the older children who were well enough to attend from the unit, some still in their beds, some sitting on the beds and some in wheel chairs. A few of the boys were wearing odd bits of Scout uniform, when the show was over we talked to these boys while taking them back to their wards, they told us that there had been a Scoutmaster who used run a meeting in ward 4, but that he had stopped coming some time ago.

At the next BP Guild meeting I mentioned this, pointing out that we ought to do something about getting things going again. The outset was (as has often happened in my life) they said "Yes George what a good idea" and so I was handed a scoutmasters warrant. Six months previously I had started my own business and was at that time, still the producer of the district Gang show.

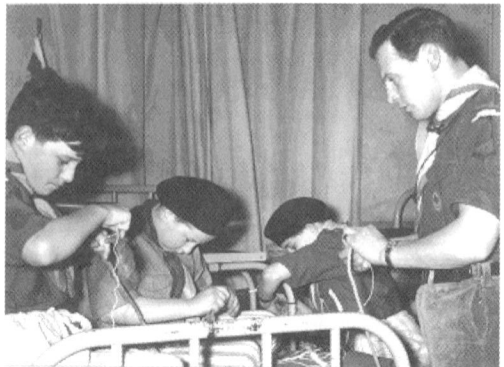

Learing the knots

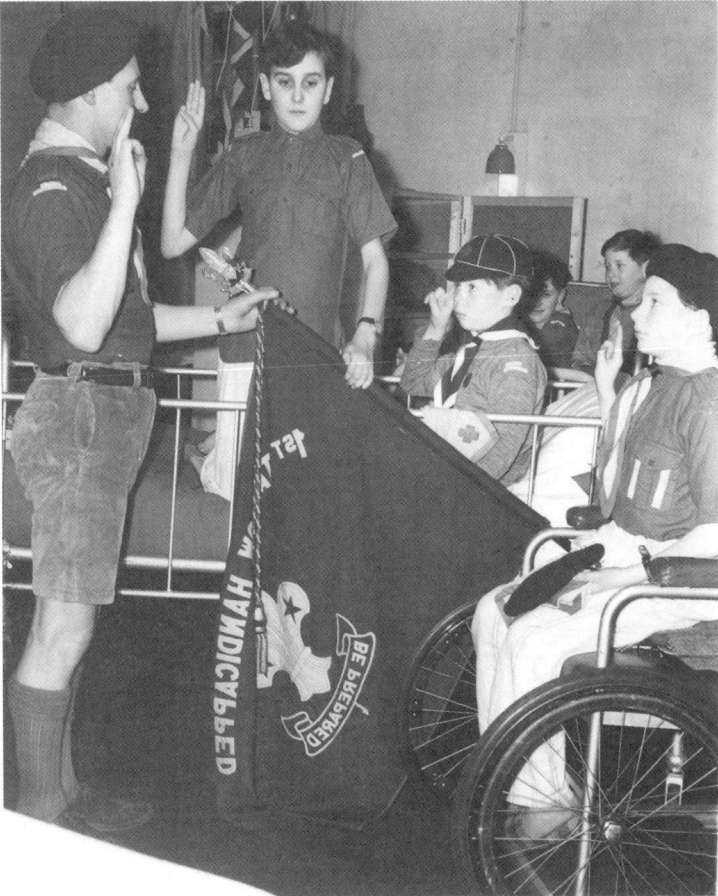

The Investiture

1949-1963 SCOUTMASTER OF THE 1st Taplow (Handicapped) Canadian Red Cross Memorial Hospital Taplow Bucks.

My first task was to learn as much as I could about the conditions that had bought these lads to this special unit. Rheumatic Fever that can severely damage the valves of the heart was caused mainly by neglect or poor social conditions. At the first meeting out of the 36 boys in the ward who came from all over the South of England, one had been sent from Borstal and one from Eton College. On admission they were put on to stage one, that required that they lay flat, not move, not even feed them selves. This job of feeding them being very time-consuming for the nurses was one of the first jobs we helped out with before we could start the meeting. So we right away became popular with the nurses and the Ward Sister. I recall having to be careful. Never having fed anyone before, if one did not concentrate you found yourself from force of habit, about to but the food into your own mouth.

The co-operation I received from Dr. Ansell, who was the senior medical officer in charge of the unit, the Matron, ward Sisters and nursing staff was total. They realised that Scouting was, for their patients therapeutic. Boys were there for a minimum of three months, most for much longer, many for several years. This was the same year that I had started my own business; people asked how do you manage when you work 60 hrs a week?

At first I did wonder if I had taken on too much, but I soon realised what I came to be very certain of and continued to be certain of for the next twenty-five years. That if you do it right the more you put into it the more satisfaction, peace of mind and down right enjoyment you get from it. This is true for those working with the able-bodied; most of the boys I worked with would never be fit and well, some would not live to reach adulthood. How could I, as fit and healthy as it was possible to be, with seemingly boundless energy (inherited from my Mother), not do what I could to make the lives of these lads a little brighter?

I would walk into the ward and 30 smiling faces would look up and shout "ello Skip" my tiredness and worries would drop away, my cares and problems were nothing compared to theirs. I was told whilst doing my "Wood Badge" (Scouter Training) that if you got to the stage where you said in a tired bored voice, ("Oh dear Scout night again!) Then you were not doing it right and it was time to retire. That never happened in my case, but I think it might have, if I had been working with the able-bodied. But not the lads I always "played the game of Scouting" with. There was constant admiration for their cheerfulness, their zest for life, the acceptance of their lot, they had a lot to complain about, but never did, I gained I didn't give!

One of the first items of equipment I built out of the many that were custom-made was a double-sided cabinet on wheels with four compartments one for each patrol. On the top of which was a removable flagstaff. It was the job of the Troop Leader to see that this was brought out, the flag raised and rolled ready for breaking and the boys wearing what items of uniform they had, before I and my assistants arrived. A lot of thought went into the design of the neckerchief. It was a bright orange colour with a green border and in the centre at the back was the Canadian Maple leaf on a red cross.

There was very little of the Scout Training programme that could not be carried out once the boys were on "stage three". Then they were allowed to sit up and to feed them selves; they could also be wheeled outside in their beds. We constructed a special "tray" to enable them to do the "fire lighting" test on the bed in front of them. We had an altar fire made out of welded steel with a spit so that they could cook from their bed. They enjoyed stoking the fire and turning the handle. If the other lads enjoyed the extra meal then he'd passed his cooking test.

Camp Fire in the Ward

Pioneering was done in miniature. They particularly enjoyed the knots and I put in fun ones like the highwayman's hitch, the hangman's noose and the thief knot. They learnt surprisingly quickly, probably quicker than most in an able bodied troop seeing that they were all together all the time, which of course they had plenty of. A spirit of competition was introduced between the patrols. On reaching stage six & seven they were able to come out in our cars. This was when they did map reading, points of the compass, tracking, collecting leaves and tree study, sometimes having a treasure hunt. One that they enjoyed the most was a "wide game" where Morse signalling was used between two groups using an Ald's Lamp. This could be seen during the day; since we were never able to be out with them during the hours of darkness. When ever possible we visited able-bodied scouts in camp at the local campsite.

Many of the lads came from deprived back grounds and some from many miles away so they often had no visitors. Sunday was the only visiting day. After we had a word with the parents that did visit, we, my assistants and I either stayed with those that had no visitors, or took those who could go out on these trips. I was never short of helpers. At Christmas the whole ward was transformed with a different theme each year. Extra visiting days were allowed and we made sure that those without a visitor had one from the "Friends of 1st Taplow (H)". This was a special group of supporters set up to help in all the ways that a parents association would do for an able bodied group, particularly raising in funds, since we did not charge a subscription as other groups do.

During the time of the "Festival of Britain" we built a model Skylon in the ward. On another occasion a working model railway ran down the centre of the ward. For the Queens Coronation the first edition of the "Group news letter" was produced, with a picture of Her Majesty on the front, the boys made contributions, it was printed by the boys themselves in the ward on an old duplicator. Yes, we had by now become a Group with approximately 30 Wolf Cubs in wards 1 & 2, and before very long with a few hints and a bit of help the Brownies in 1 & 2 and Guides in ward 3 became established. Guy Fawkes night was one of the "high lights" of the year. There was a large grass area at the back of the wards and beyond that a wood, so we were able to build a real fire complete with a Guy Fawkes, which of course the lads made themselves.

In 1959 on the 10th anniversary of the formation of the troop we had a party in ward four. There was a large cake with ten candles made by the "friends". The County Commissioner and the Assistant County Commissioner for the Handicapped attended. By this time, due mainly to successful research the introduction of

The Tenth Anniversary

"Cortisone" and other drugs the numbers in each of the wards were down by about half. The length of stay was very much reduced from some time's several years to several months. I said at the time, (what might seem a strange thing to say), "that hopefully we may have to close the group down due to lack of boys". About this time two of the wards of the special unit were changed over to being general wards for adults.

Rheumatic fever could severely damage the heart, on which more strain was put as they got older, quite a number would not have reached adulthood. At least five died at the hospital during my time there including one who was the Troop Leader at the time he died at the age of 17 years. Brian Walker was with us for over three years, my nomination for the award of the Cornwall Scout Badge. (An Award for outstanding fortitude and bravery) to him was successful, but unfortunately he died before it could be presented. I have a letter of thanks from his mother to whom his badge was sent. Brian Dilly was another who was so honoured with this badge; I had the great pleasure in 1959 of attending the troop to which he had returned in Newbury Berkshire after over two years with us, to present it to him in the presence of his new Troop.

By 1962 there were only about a dozen boys of Scout and Cub age left on the unit. Rheumatic fever, like Polio had been virtually eliminated, those lads remaining had rheumatism related problems, such as "Still's Disease" and "Chorea". In December 62 I was appointed Assistant County Commissioner (Extension Activities) Buckinghamshire i.e. for Boys with a Handicap. I handed over to my senior assistant, who carried on for another six years, until the unit closed. I estimated that during my time there, over 500 boys either joined, or continued scouting at Cliveden. On four occasions we had a representative in the corner of the quadrangle at the St Georges Day Parade Windsor Castle. This is where all those boys who have passed the Queens Scout Badge, are inspected by and then march pass a member of the Royal Family. Most often this was Her Royal Highness the Queen.

It was there for the first time, at that Scout HQ at Newbury, seeing a boy in a wheel chair in an "able bodied" Troop, completely at home and accepted, that started the driving force with in me to do more for "the Boy with a Handicap", particularly those in wheel chairs. Nationally it was policy for kids with a handicap, particularly those in wheel chairs to be sent to special schools. I thought that was in many cases wrong and I could see no reason why many Boys with a handicap in wheel chair should not attend an ordinary school, or participate in the weekly "able bodied" Scout Troop night.

CANG SHOWS 1934 - 39.

1952 TO 1964 Producer of Burnham District Gang Show

The district was comprised of seven Groups, totalling some 350 Scouts ages 11 to 14, Senior Scouts 14 to 18, Rovers 18 to 24 (some of whom were also Scout Leaders). Following the success of the first show that resulted in my taking on the Hospital Group. I was unable to get out of the post of producer. We started in a small way with approximately 50 in the cast.

Each year I attended Ralph Reader's London Gang Shows at the Victoria Place Theatre in London, at least once, sometimes twice together with Avril Lyford a stenographer, not to take down the script, for we always bought those, but to take notes about the staging and the costumes etc. I interviewed all the potential cast making sure that they were not tone deaf and made a card record of all their details including a photograph which helped a great deal in the casting and getting to know their names, for as time went by we had at least 80 in the cast.

The first show was held in the largest Scout HQ, which was also the local W.I. (Women's Institute) hall. It had a small stage and two small rooms used as dressing rooms. Rehearsals were held once a week for two months with several each week as we got near to opening night. To start with I found myself involved (lumbered) with arranging, organising, everything. Planning the programme, auditioning the cast, printing scripts, getting the wives to make costumes, designing and making the scenery, designing and producing the tickets and programmes, booking the hall, finding a pianist, a stage manager and stage staff, plus front of house staff, even publicity and selling tickets. But each year as we got bigger I delegated more and more to different committees.

We graduated to the hall of a small school, then a large school and then to the very large stage of The Maidenhead Town Hall. Ralph Reader attended our Silver jubilee show. We had a cast of 120. Many of the boys who came from all the groups in the district, were in the shows as boy and man, some becoming stars of the show. One thing I was often surprised about, for I re-interviewed each one again every year if only to change the record of their height, was how much some of them grew in one year, some of them as much as four inches.

In the early days we did every thing that was Ralph Readers, not always from his latest show, for we could pick and chose from many of his earlier productions. Then I began to tire from the same old stuff rehashed. So I began to put in ideas of my own, much to the dismay and with protests from the RR devotees. In those days not every one had a television, it was about this time that we got our first black and white set. I very rarely had time to watch, if I did sit down and try to watch something I found that being hyper active I could never sit still long enough to see a programme through. Late at night I would watch what ever happened to be on, just to relax before going to bed. I often found the adverts the most interesting. It seems strange to say so today, now that we have been "eye bashed" with so many mindless spectacles constantly repeated, but in those days I found some of them very funny and found that they were often talked about.

We were sometimes short of ideas for (what we called "a tab" item) something lasting just a few minutes performed in front of the second curtain, while a longer sketch was being prepared on the main stage. Late one night I saw the advertisement for a well-known beer where the tune they played was one of our scout campfire songs. It was (There's a hole in my bucket "dear Georgie dear Georgie" It went, A double diamond works wonders, works wonders, works wonders, a double diamond works wonders so drink one today. We wrote to Double diamond telling them our intentions and then along came a large crate full of bottles of DD, with their compliments. They went down well with the adults of the cast.

To start with the profit, which was always very good went to buy equipment for the groups who needed it most. But from 1961 it went to finance the District Camp site Dorneywood, the site for which I personally negotiated with the then owner, Lord Courtold Thomson.

Silver Jubilee show Maidenhead Town Hall

1960 - 1974 CAMP WARDEN Burnham Dist Camp site DORNEYWOOD

When during one weekend district camp, his Lordship paid us a visit. I noticed that he was beginning to look quite old and frail. He told me that when he died Dorneywood House and the estate would be left to the National Trust" and used by senior government ministers. I then said "I hoped that day would be a long way off" and "that we very much hoped to be able to continue to use his lovely site as Scouting was growing in the district" and "how important camping was as part of the training". He said "don't worry I shall see to it that you will be allowed to have it as a permanent site". I asked the Local Association secretary to write to him to confirm our conversation. About a year later his lordship died.

I was then asked by the committee to contact the National Trust agent, a Mr Rogers, this I did. He subsequently told us that there were no instructions in the will regarding our use of the site and as the house was going to be used by the Foreign Secretary he doubted if we would be allowed to use it for security reasons. He said he was worried about fire and damage to trees. I pointed out to him the importance of youth training. I told him that we taught boys about these things. I mentioned Brownsea Island that was now owned by the Trust, that Scouting was allowed there and that that, was where Baden Powell started Scouting. He said we could continue for the time being.

In the wood behind the campsite we discovered a large ring of Rhododendrons and Azaleas that in the early spring were, for several weeks were blaze of colour. On talking to one of the gardeners from the Dorneywood house we were told that his lordship had had this planted many years before, as a place where he could go to sit and contemplate in perfect peace and quite. We asked him if we could use this circle as our "Scout Own Chapel, in return for keeping it in good order (it had become very overgrown) There was no hesitation in giving us his blessing, saying that although he could no longer get up there he was pleased for us to use it particularly for that purpose.

We used some of the granite blocks given to us by the council to erect an altar on which we placed a cross-made out of silver birch. One day I had a call from a friend who said. "Have you seen what there is in the local paper about the Chapel". Apparently some one, trespassing (for it was a private wood) had seen it, told the local newspaper and a reported had written an article suggesting it was connected with black magic or a "hell fire club".

One of the first Foreign Secretary's to use Dorneywood house was Michael Stewart MP. The first weekend that he was in residence he visited us. I showed him all that we were doing and told him what we wanted to do to develop the site. He then invited my assistant and I back to the house for drinks where I asked him if it were possible for him to have a word with the National Trust. I am sure he must have done so, for eventually we got full permission for a permanent site providing that we submitted plans for anything we did. Plans went in for toilets, a Camp Wardens hut, a Providore, (scout tuck shop), also a permanent hut as a dormitory.

The whole area around the camp had, at the beginning of the century been a brick works with it's own kiln, the remains of which could still be seen. There were three very large (I can only describe them as-craters,). The largest was about 60 feet across and 20 feet deep, presumably where the clay had been dug out. This "dip" over the course of the next three years, we built into one of the finest "camp fire circles" in the country.

A couple of miles away there was a Council dump for old granite kerbstones. A letter to the right department got us full permission to use any or all of them. I wore out my little company pick-up-truck moving about 50 tons of it. These we placed it in tiers just like a Roman amphitheatre and when finished it could seat over a thousand. There were four sets of steps made out of obsolete concrete railway sleepers courtesy of British Rail. An attractive bridge at the entrance was made out of telephone poles courtesy of British Telecom. It often pleasantly surprised me, the results a letter to the right person could bring.

At the base of a very large Oak tree on the edge of the circle we placed the "Pattern" of the Bronze Scout Badge that is to be seen on the side of Baden Powell House in London. My friend with an art foundry had received the order for the casting and my company had modified the artwork supplied by the artist to make it suitable for moulding. It was made of plaster on a wooden frame, but it lasted for many years.

After three years hard work, by all that could be persuaded to help, Rovers, Scouters, Scouts, the Guild, lay people even Cubs. The camp was ready for it's opening day. Mentioning the help we got from the Cub scouts reminds me. Some one put us in touch with H P. baked beans. They wanted to make a commercial for television. They need 200 or so Cub Scouts. I contacted the producer and suggested that they do it with Cubs that I would supply at Dorneywood. He visited the site and was very impressed deciding there and then to use the campfire circle. I duly arranged it all with the local Cub packs and on the day, a film crew of at least 40 with mountains of equipment and a large catering van arrived. Then along came three large coaches and many cars packed with excited Wolf Cubs.

The producer asked that they be assembled in the campfire circle so that he could tell them what he wanted them to do. If you have ever seen 200 lads of that age together you can imagine the noise. He tried to make himself heard so that he could start, but was getting no attention. Then with my "drill instructors" voice I shouted "Pack Pack Pack". (The first thing a Cub learns is to be quite when a Cub Scout Leader shouts that). Immediately there was complete silence, the producer was amazed. "How did you do that?" he said. "I want you to stay by my side".

After they had dished out 200 plates of baked beans they started filming, but before long it started to rain, I told them I did not think it would clear up that day. This turned out to be a blessing for us for it all had to be done again the following weekend. This meant that we got the fee that I had negotiated, plus another 50% for the repeat performance and all expenses paid. £450 we received, all of which was spent on improvements and getting the camp ready for the opening by the then Gillwell Camp Chief, John Thurman in the summer of 1963. The only upset of the whole event was the tummies of some of the Cubs through eating too many beans. After a few weeks they were all able to watch themselves on television. The commercial was shown for about six weeks.

At the opening ceremony, the Camp Chief planted a Beech tree (this I note today is now over 40 feet high) and an identical one given to him to plant at Gillwell. My art foundry friend made two commemoration bronze plaques from patterns that I supplied. Over the next eleven years the camp was constantly improved. At weekends for well over half the year there were rarely less that 40 in camp, and during the summer camping season there were often as many as 200, some from overseas, for we advertised in a Scout Headquarters publication. All fees received were ploughed back for improvements. The Providore (tuck shop) made a healthy profit selling brands and badges, as well as the usual sweets and drinks. I designed the emblem of the Camp that appears on them this consisted of three of the four Oak leaves that appear on the emblem of the National Trust, fitted into the Scout Badge.

Soon after being given my first warrant in 1949. I attended Gillwell Park at North London to do my Wood Badge. (Scout leader training). It was the very first time I had been to this wonderful training centre in Essex. It is steeped in memories of my hero Lord Baden Powell. I loved the house, his old preserved caravan, his pictures, his books (I think I have read almost every thing he has ever written). Every time a new edition of "Scouting for Boys" was published I bought it, as I did most of the Scout Shop publications.

I was, over the years to go back to Gillwell many times. One of the most memorable was the "1952 First World Indaba", (Zulu name for a gathering). In the back of the Twenty-Sixth Edition of BPs book I have the names and addresses of 50 Scouters from 50 different nations, several of whom I have seen since, years later in their own Countries. When I was on holiday or business trips. Other courses I attended were a Camp fire Leaders and a Commissioners Course.

I have all my life been a great lover of trees and as a wood worker a particular dislike of any one who would damage a tree. If nails are driven in to a tree such as happens if it is part of a barbed wire fence by someone who knows no better, then the nail or staple gets grown over and buried. Timber merchants and those like myself who often "deep cut" timber find that our saws are ruined and the wood spoilt.

While I was putting up a barbed wire fence at Dorneywood it had to go around a large fine oak tree. I was unable to drive in a stake as the roots spread out from the bottom. So I put the stake up against the tree then nailed the wire to it. If I had just wrapped the wire around the tree then the wire would eventually have been grown over. As I was doing this a car stopped and a voice said. "Montague being your fathers son I would have thought you should know better that to hammer nails into a tree" It was the son of my father's employer. I did not object to his remark about the nails, an obvious misunderstanding, but that he addressed me by my surname, as he and his father had always addressed my father. I must say I took some pleasure in saying to him. Hanbury if you get out of your car you will see what I have done, as the tree grows it will only tighten the fence, but will not damage the tree. He told his father that I had been insolent.

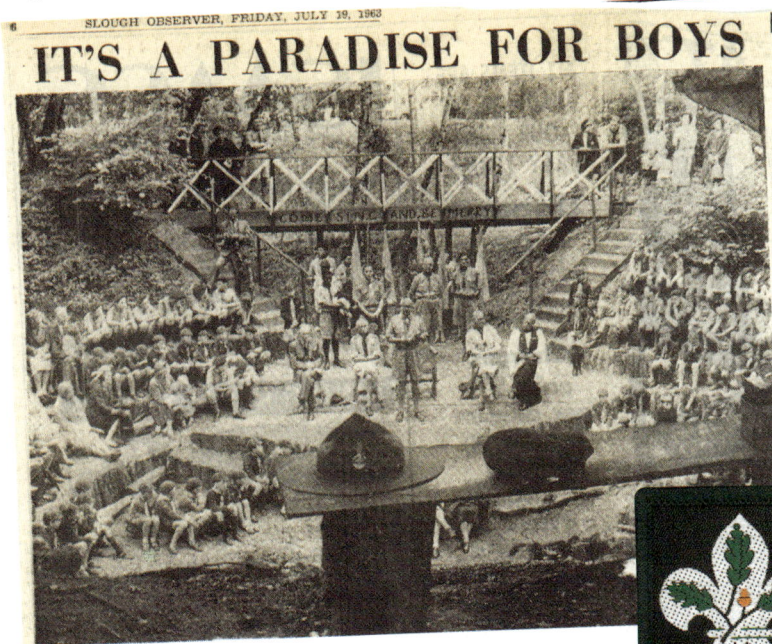

SLOUGH OBSERVER, FRIDAY, JULY 19, 1963

IT'S A PARADISE FOR BOYS

THE Camp Fire Circle
The opening of The Dorneywood Scout Camp
by John Thurman

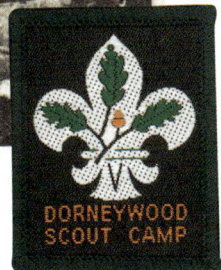

1962-1974 ASSISTANT COUNTY COMMISSIONER (EXTENSION BRANCH) BUCKS

Soon after my above appointment I visited all the institutions in the county that had "boys with a handicap" in them. There were three. One for the Epileptic and two for the deaf, one of these had a Scout Troop running. It took some time but eventually I succeeded in getting things going in the other two. But I found many districts did not have an Advisor ("for the handicapped") some one whose sole duty was to find and promote Scouting with the Handicapped. Not one Group could I find who had a boy in a wheel chair. But gradually following my visits and talks to the districts I began to be told of some, the very first was right in my own village, a boy of eleven named Roger Wild. Roger was suffering from Muscular Dystrophy.

This is one of the most distressing ailments that could befall a boy and his family. The Daikon type, that is the most common is diagnosed in apparently perfectly healthy boys from the age of four to ten years old. A progressive muscle wasting decease that starts in the legs, for which there is (even to this day as far as I am aware) no cure. It affects only boys. The mother is the carrier and there is a 50% chance that any of her male children will develop it. Any female child could be a carrier and I have known several families who have lost more than one son. Life expectancy is about 18 to 20 years.

Roger had an older brother who was not affected; he was in the local Scout troop. But nobody thought it would be possible for Roger to be a Cub or Scout. At first the local Scout leaders were concerned about taking on the responsibility of a boy like Roger in a wheel chair. I found out all I could about him and his handicap mainly from his parents. I then managed to convince those in doubt that he was, in every way an ordinary boy, except that his legs were not strong enough to support him. He was my first success.

For the first few meetings I went along to see for myself how things were going and to learn how he would fit in. To see that he was not just put in a corner to watch, when there were games and certain activities where he could not join in. There was not one, he was made the scorer or judge. There was however one problem and that was the forthcoming summer camp that would involve hiking and wide games some times at night. By this time he had been completely accepted and the boys all assumed that he would be going to camp with them. But attending a troop night for a couple of hours and going away to sleep in a tent when the weather could be bad was not at all a good idea. Boys in wheel chairs catch cold easily then there was the question of the changing of the colostomy and catheter bags. I also told them that it would not be fair to the other boys, or the leaders to plan the camp activities around Roger. Scout summer camps should be full of hectic activity.

I had heard of the "London Agoonoree" run by Leonard Robinson (now O.B.E.)

the then Head Quarters Commissioner for the handicapped. It was run for boys from London just like Roger. I wrote and asked if I could join his 1964 camp as a helper and bring Roger, this he agreed. The Camp was held at Norfolk and was the first of four camps that I was to attend. The 1966 camp was held in Scotland and the outstanding memory of that camp was when we were all in a large hall, about 200 of us. At least 60 were in wheel chairs watching the football "world cup". I shall never forget the cheer that went up when England won. By the forth-camp 1967 that was held in Belgium, I was taking six lads along from Bucks. During this camp at which there were a few problems due to sheer numbers, Leonard took me to one side and told me that the camp was getting too big and that he could no longer take boys from outside the London area. He suggested that I start my own camp.

I had gained a great deal of knowledge at these camps, but being in charge of a patrol of eight severely physically handicapped boys with eight other able bodied boys of about the same age as "buddies" (helpers'), for eight days was, I found very demanding even though I always had an abundance of energy. Now, to think about starting and running my own Camp! With a dormitory, at least one S.R.N (state registered nurse), transport, a bus with a tail lift, a mountain of equipment, a central kitchen, trained staff, not to mention funds.

To make a camp of this nature viable, the number would need to be about 60, 25 of these would be boys with a severe physical handicapped. I had taken six from Bucks to the London camp, all I could find. These were those where it was not advisable for them to attend the annual summer camp with the able bodied. So that meant we would have to amalgamate with other counties. I wrote to five neighbouring counties and got favourable replies from all of them. I was daunted at the thought of the organization involved. But if I did not follow it up. No camp for my boys.

Founder and Camp Leader of the "Six Counties Scout Camp"

Two months later after much travelling, talking, phoning, burning the midnight oil and writing letters we held our first meeting at Bletchley in Bucks. At this meeting were the representatives of the Extension Branch of six Counties. Buckinghamshire, Berkshire, Bedfordshire, Hampshire, Hertfordshire Oxfordshire, a Field Commissioner from Scout Headquarters and Leonard Robinson. I set out my plan, the aims, the constitution, and funding, potential size of the Camp and the training of helpers. I came up against some "political red tape" in that I was told that at least two of the County Commissioners were concerned that we were undermining their authority.

I had some difficulty in convincing these Commissioners. I pointed out that with no more than six to ten boys of scout age with severe handicaps in any one county. A camp for them was not viable. They would most likely not find the right professional help and the camp would end up consisting of boys who were not so severely disabled such as amputees, the deaf and blind. For all of whom it was most important and perfectly possible, that they should go to camp with their own able bodied troop members. I did point out that we should welcome such lads as these to our camps, but they would be classed as "helper buddies". I had found that it was a great help to this type of lad, who often had a chip on his shoulder and thought that life had given him a raw deal, to look after some one so very much more disabled than they. By "look after" I meant dress and undress, take to the toilet, feed, look after all their clothes and belongings, put them to bed, get them up in the morning, lay out both his own and his charges kit for inspection, to virtually be with them or near them for 24 hours a day.

There was a lad in my district aged 14 who, when on a scout camp outing on a canal barge, had his arm hung over the side. He lost his arm at the elbow when the barge touched the side of a bridge; he naturally went though a very difficult time, his character changed very much for the worse. I suggested to his Scouter that he come to my camp, not as one of the disabled but as a helper. We got him to come and the verdict was it did him a world of good. The thanks I got from him when he said to me at the end of Camp, "I know why you wanted me to come", made every thing worthwhile.

An example of about the most severe case in my experience would be Stephen Argyle, from Kennington Oxford. Stephen was aged 11, when I first met him, in a wheel chair, very severely spastic, unable to speak clearly, totally blind, but very intelligent and always cheerful. He was the chess champion of the camp. I had done a great deal of the "spade" work, in promoting the idea of a new camp. I in no way assumed that I would be the leader of it. There were many others at the meeting more capable than I. For I had left school at the age of 14 and had always been a "hands on person" personally looking after my boys, with others doing all the administration. I would have been very happy to have come away from that meeting, having been asked to be, maybe the deputy leader, or camp advisor.

When I was nominated I resisted the proposal. I told the meeting of my doubts and limitations, but once again no one else volunteered or was put forward. They said. "We will give you our full support; we want you to be the leader". I thought about my family of three children, 7, 6 and 5 years old, all perfect physical specimens. Then I thought about Roger, who by then only had another two or three years to live and the others who did enjoy and look forward so much to the summer camp, so I accepted. On the way home I had this strange feeling, a mixture of destiny and heavy responsibly and a realization that this was something that had to be done and at that moment I was the only one who would do it.

I have always believed in delegating where possible, but I found this very difficult to do to start with. The first thing was to find 30 or 40 people from the age of 12, who were, as far as the adults were concerned Scouters with at least some experience, able to spare the time from their own Group, who would accept that the boys did not need or want, sympathy or pity, but just to be involved.

The Deputy Camp Leader, Qualified Medical staff, Treasurer, Quartermaster, Transport, Catering, and Dormitory, all of these except the Deputy Camp Leader could be lay people. They all had to be brought together for a training day. The area these would be coming from was approximately 150 x 75 miles. Of the 30 boys with a handicap that I had approved as eligible, 20 were in wheel chairs; the others were delicate, (with weak hearts), asthmatic and epileptic.

I say "approved as eligible", for one of my most difficult tasks as ACC (H) and as Camp Leader of the Six Counties was to deny membership into the movement to those that were severely mentally handicapped, not the ones with learning difficulties, or slow learners. But those who would find it impossible to even begin to understand the "Scout Promise", we would be unable to teach them the "game of Scouting" I had to explain to parents and well meaning Scouters, that we were an educational movement. All one could do with a boy aged 12 with a mental age of 3 or 4, would be to use valuable resources just looking after him. This would not be fair to those who could be taught.

Our first camp was at "Woodlarks" in Farnham Surrey, in 1968. The reason being that this was a permanent site, tailor made for the handicapped, with lots of equipment, a dormitory for those unable to sleep on the ground in tents. But every boy had at least one night in a tent, even though some had to be in a proper bed. The swimming pool was excellent, heated to 70% (at enormous cost) with every facility, a ramp, with a special wheel chair and a winch with which one could lower the heavier lads straight into the water. There was also a small crane with a harness, so boys could be lifted straight out of their chair and lowered into the water. Other boys were so small, like Timothy who suffered from fragilities (Brittle bones). He had a normal sized head, was very intelligent and sharp as a new pin, (he was the camp jester) aged 15 but with a body the size of a four year old. His 15-year-old "buddy" just picked him up and walked down the ramp into the water.

I had always been interested in cine photography and filmed on most occasions. This was a great help in fund raising and training. One of my best shots I think was one of a row of empty wheel chairs with just the towels draped over the seats. All the boys were in the pool; some of them could not even operate a "joy stick" of an electric chair. There they were in the pool, moving themselves along with just an inflatable aid under the ever watchful eye of their able bodied buddy.

A great deal of thought was given to detail; I was personally responsible for the change in terminology. Instead of "handicapped Scouts" it became "Scouts with a handicap" and "Scouting for boys with a handicap" this was adopted on all literature and letterheads etc. and is now universally used. The London camp accepted that we were an extension of that camp and allowed us to use the Stile as our emblem.

The late Lord Somers, a former Chief Scout wrote. "To help a" lame" dog over the stile is considered to be one of the primary virtues, but to teach that lame dog to climb over the stile by him self -particularly- if the "lame dog" happens to be a boy with a handicap, is even better". Our stile was on a green background to show we were the country cousins of the London gang.

The motto of our first camp was "doing". It was important that these lads, who had become used to just sitting and having every thing done for them, should be doing for themselves not just watching, so we trained the helpers to be on constant watch and wherever possible (and even if it was impossible) that they should be "having a go". There were two lads who were the victims of thalidomide one of whom had no arms. I saw him watching the potatoes being peeled and I knew these lads could do a great deal with their feet. "Had he ever peeled one I asked"? No he had not and although it took a lot longer he did it and enjoyed his meal that much more.

Some years later, there was a programme on the Radio called, "Does he take Sugar". This reminded me that we had always told our staff; when shop assistance's speak to you and ask you what he wants, tell them to ask him. For even those who could not speak could indicate what they wanted.

At the end of the camp each boy was presented with a Certificate of Attendance and a record of the tests passed. This included the able bodied "buddies". A plaque made out of a slice of wood with a leather bootlace was branded with the year and the name of the camp. I made these at my works by making a pattern in wood of a block. Getting this cast in iron, then mounting it in a bench drill. Heating it with a blowlamp, then branding the wooden plaque. Being a Pattern Maker I was used to putting letters on patterns, which were reversed in the mould, then reversed again on the casting. But when I used the iron block casting as a brand I was reversing it once again, so the letters came out reversed. I had to buy special reversed letters and start all over again. We live and learn as they say.

We all learnt a great deal at this first camp and each year we had a training day and a Reunion. The 1969 camp was at "Hill End" Oxford, where the Lord Mayor visited us. The third Camp in 1970 was at Winchester where we had a special service in the Cathedral. It was in that year that we adopted our theme song, "if I can help somebody as I pass along". It was pointed out that this was the theme for everyone on the camp. That however bad a hand life had dealt you, there was always some one worse off than you and you should always look out for the chance to help others where possible. I sang the first verse. The acoustics in the Cathedral were perfect.

If I can help some body as I pass along
If I can cheer some body with a word or song
If I can show some body that he's travelling wrong
Then my living shall not be in vain.   *Music by Alma Androzzo*

The 1971 Camp was at Tewin Water, Herts. The 1972 Camp was held at Sandhurst (the army officers training camp). The "highlight" on this camp was the "assault course" and the very high, very long aerial runway. Almost everybody on the camp had a go watched by the lads in wheel chairs. Then I thought "this won't do", so later that day I called a meeting of the service crew. That evening they were missing from the Camp Fire. When we all went to the aerial runway the next day, a hoist had been built next to the ladder that one had to climb to reach the start and on the platform was the camp spare wheel chair attached to the hoist. One of the lads not in a wheel chair, who had been so disappointed not to be able to have ago, because we told him he would not be strong enough to hold on to the bar, was strapped into this chair, then hoisted to the platform and down he went in complete safety. While the chair was being returned over land another lad went up in his own chair, many of which were custom made to suit their owners, I think every one on the camp who had not been down the day before had a go, including the ladies on the staff.

A typical Patrol one of six on each camp

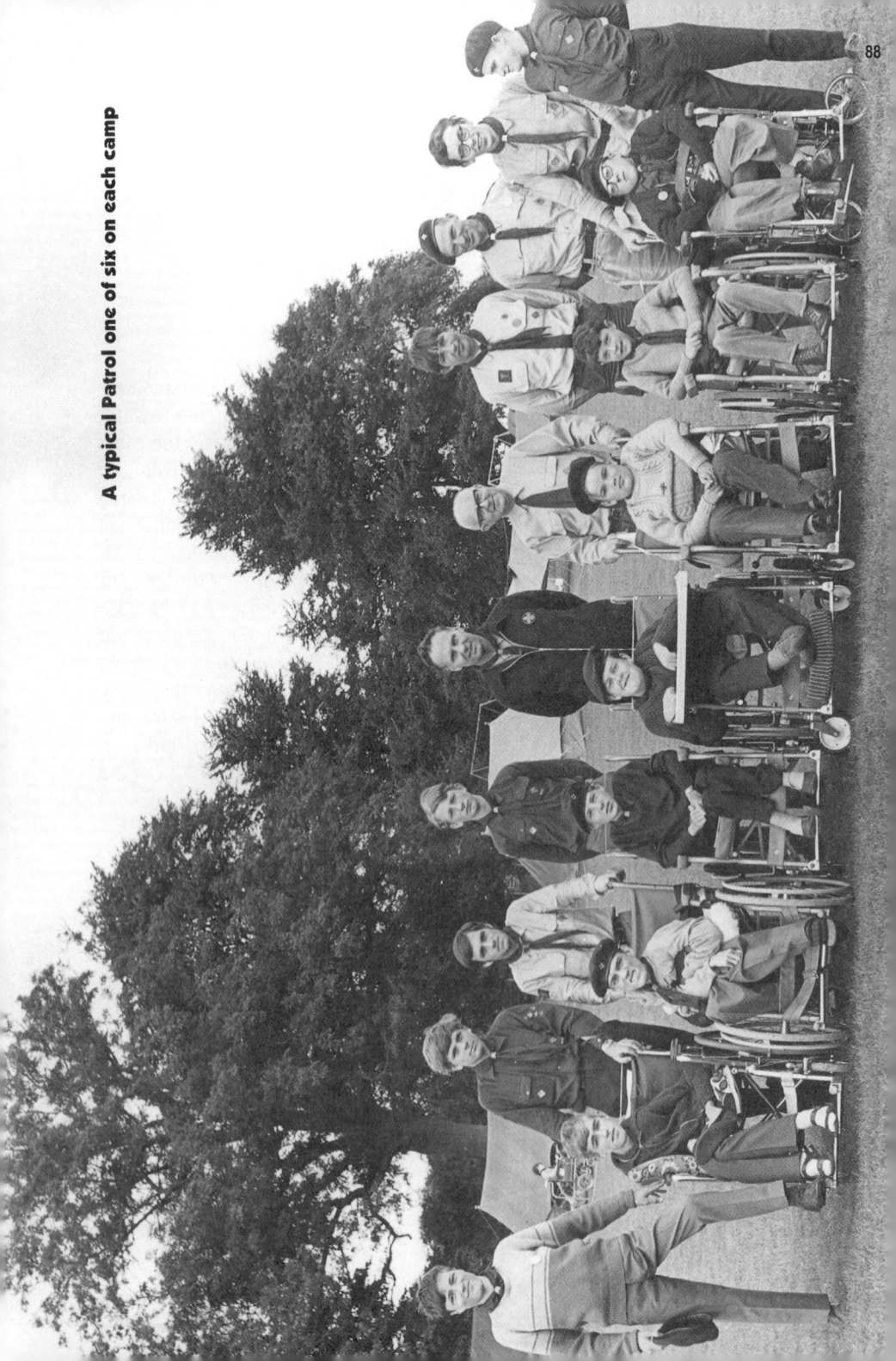

The 1973 camp was the big one. 120 in total, 50 handicapped, 40 in wheel chairs, all in a chartered aircraft from Heathrow to a place called Ommen on the other side of Holland. This excellent permanent Scout camp was called Ada Hoeve "the Gillwell of the Netherlands". The Camps took almost a year to plan. Soon after returning from one, the next one was "on the drawing board" but this one took two years.

All the camps held in the counties were subsidized by approximately fifty per cent, so that every one paid a very modest amount the same for able-bodied "buddies", handicapped and staff. But the subsidy on this one had to be seventy five per cent. I remember my dismay when during the two years in planning, the Pound devalued by about thirty per cent against the Guilder. All the counties ran various events during the year to raise money. At this time there was an economic slump and extra funds were hard to come by. I was told that Eton College donated to a charity once each year. The boys, (following a talk from several different organisations) decided whom to support. I put together a cine film of the previous camps, gave the talk and Five hundred Pounds was donated.

At long last we were all at Heathrow Airport counting heads. One hundred and ten all present and correct what a relief! A large fully laden lorry, a bus with a tail lift, two cars and 10 adults had gone on a few days before as an advance party to set up the camp. This was the time of the "hi jacks of aircraft" and the security was very tight. When we arrived at the checkout the man in charge must have been new at the job and had not handled wheel chairs before because he started putting them through the metal detector, they went berserk.

Although I didn't know it at the time, this was to be my last camp. The Camp Chief of Ada Hoeve, his staff and the local Dutch people could not have been more helpful. In one of the many letters that were sent in both directions during the planning, I asked about a "chip fryer" for the kitchen large enough for the numbers on camp. In his reply he said he had been able to arrange for us to hire a large cooker for the "frightened" potatoes, (apologies to the Camp Chief who's English was very good) At the closing ceremony a budding artist drew out on very large sheets of paper, cartoons of the highlights of the camp, the trips to Delft, Amsterdam and several other amusing incidences that had occurred. Another was a picture of a chip fryer with all the "frightened" chip potatoes running away from it.

On the last day before setting off for home about a hundred local people came to the camp, all those who had helped us in some way. For a couple of days I tried very hard to learn my closing speech in Dutch but had to give up, most other European language's I think I could have managed but not this one. But it didn't matter for they all spoke very good English. The very high regard they all had for British people was very evident. Oh! I have nearly forgotten we had a film crew with us for much of the time paid for by the publicity department of Scout Headquarters it took a long time to be finished and I never did get to see it!

Following this over seas camp I did nothing about the 1974 camp until after Christmas although the site had been decided as Bedford. I realised that the Holland camp had been a climax and for the first time I found I had lost some of my enthusiasm and drive. I had, by this time been on four annual camps with the London Agoonoree and had almost single headedly organized and lead the Six Counties Camps, for the last six years. There was a movement afoot coming from some of the County Commissioners that the Liaison should be split up into smaller Camps. I disagreed most strongly and knowing much more than they did about it, said so. Following the Bedford camp and my departure from the Scout Movement it was split up and with-in a couple of years, there was no longer a Six Counties camp.

In 1970 there was very little Headquarters literature on "Extension Activities" (giving advice to those in the districts who's job it was to find "Boys with Handicaps" and integrate them into the Movement). What there was, was very basic and so I wrote one. It was a 22-page quarto size closely typed booklet with the following 10 Sections :-

To locate, To make contact, To advise, To give reports, To liase, To keep records, To undertake training, To publicise, To promote support.

At the back, were three pages with advice on "Scouting with the Mentally Handicapped". The existing small and very basic H Q leaflet stated the there was a leader in every district to advise. I made the mistake of pointing out that this was not so. This upset Leonard Robinson and Scout Headquarters. I sent a copy of my handbook to several of my follow ACCs (H) in other counties, two of whom Essex and Sussex, both asked my permission to reproduce it for their own use. The Scout headquarters did eventually produce a handbook that contained much of that which appeared in my booklet.

The Dorneywood camp was just about as fully developed as it was allowed to be by the National Trust, it was being very heavily used and was too small. I obtained permission from the tenant farmer to use another 3 or 4 adjacent acres. But our Mr Rogers who was still the agent of the National Trust refused my request. I had always had to fight for every improvement I wanted to make So I put it to the Local Association Committee that we write to Scout Headquarters outlining the problem we were having and ask if they could apply some pressure. The answer we got back was that on no account must we do any thing to upset the National Trust and certainly there must be no adverse publicity between them and us. Just one year later when I had left the Movement and Rogers had been replaced the camp was extended.

For Twenty-five of my adult years Scouting for me had become a vocation and almost an obsession. For several hours every day often until the early hours I would be in my study planning, writing letters, telephoning. My customers were spread all over the south of the country and I would spend hours going miles out of my way to see a member of staff or a potential new member for the camp. At weekends I would be at Dorneywood summer and winter. Much of this time should have been spent concentrating on my business or with my family. I could not see any one taking over from me and being able to afford to spend the time and energy that I was doing.

During the early 60s there was a craze on walking started in the states and encouraged by President Kennedy. This was taken up over here and a Dr Barbara (her surname escapes me) walked from John-o-Grouts to Lands End followed by many others. Then there was a London to Brighton mass walk organized, starting from one of the bridges in over the Thames. Two of my friends and I decided to have a go. We had about six weeks to get ready, so we walked where ever and whenever we could. I was living in Beaconsfield at the time with my wife only having got married some eighteen months before, so I walked the six miles to work and back very day.

We enlisted another friend who would accompany us with a mini van containing refreshments spare footwear and "Sped" (a powder to put in the shoes) We were all Scouters so we decided to go in uniform, a mistake as it turned out (long trousers did not come in till years later). All went very well to start with, leaving about midmorning with the prospect of a minimum 24hrs walking. By the early hours of the next morning we had reached Gatwick still going strong. But there was a strong wind, it was February and the temperature was down to 15 degrees below freezing. Our knees froze. Despite warming up in the mini van and having leg massage We only managed to walk on with stiff legs as far as Popham where we just had to give in. We had walked for 24hours 55 mile's, just 15 miles short of our target. I was feeling very down and completely exhausted totally unable to walk another step after stopping at a local pub for a drink and a rest, when quite unexpectedly a car drew up with another friend who had brought along my wife a baby Paula

CHAPTER 9

Charged with Gross Indecency

Looking back I can see that for me Scouting was a sublimation for I had not come to terms with my sexuality. There is no doubt that I was going though a difficult time both with Scouting and my marriage, when I was charged with and convicted of "Gross Indecency".

The facts were these: - One evening in July 1974 I was in one of a two cubical public toilet. In the other was a man, married, with children in his fifties (I learnt later). In the wall between the two was a hole through which I could see him masturbating I was doing the same. He then put his penis through the hole. He did not have an erection. I did not touch it but continued what Baden Powell called "self abuse". Then there was a very loud bang on the locked door and a voice shouted, "open up Police!" and we were both arrested. One policeman only with the help of his colleague had looked over the top. He was young, obsessively Homophobic and lied in his evidence against me.

Through my solicitor I briefed Council who informed me that before a Magistrate I took a big risk of being found guilty. But that I stood an excellent chance of a not guilty verdict if I went before a Jury seeing that it was just one policeman's word against mine and although we were in a public toilet, we were in separate cubicles with the doors closed and locked, "in private" in fact. (A debatable point). I gave this matter a great deal of thought. I came to the conclusion that if I went to trial before a Jury there would be a lot of publicity, even if I was found not guilty It would be very bad publicity for the Scout Movement. Mud sticks as they say and what was I doing in a public toilet about a mile from my home anyway.

My entire scouting career I had believed in good publicity and was very well known to the head reporters of the two local newspapers. I had given them both a great deal of material on all my Scouting activities over the years. I talked to them both and explained the whole story. They were very sympathetic. I admitted, that whilst I was dreading the publicity for my own sake and that of my family I was most concerned for the good name of Scouting. I decided to go before the Magistrates. The other man pleaded guilty and so his case came up a week or so before mine. There was a full report in both local papers that just said "with another man". I felt very sorry for him.

The solicitor who represented me did not do a very good job of it I thought; he did not challenge the police officer on his lie and obvious homophobia. He did not call the other man as a witness. He could not understand why I refused to have any character witnesses appear on my behalf. As I was pleading not guilty my case came up very late in the afternoon. I walked into the courtroom and noticed there were no reporters there. As predicted I was found guilty.

The following day I went to see Bernard Frost the county commissionerI who for very many years had been a close personal friend. Both of us having lived a secret gay life stile before we got married I made it very clear to him that it was an unofficial "off the record" visit. I had known him long before he joined the Scout movement as an adult. He had at one time helped me as a layperson with my troop at Cliveden. We were then both unmarried. The irony is that at that time he and I were both having problems with our sexuality.

I recall that on the first night that Bernard came to my troop meeting at the hospital, he sat on the side of the bed of one of the older boys holding his hand for some considerable time. I told him I thought he ought to be careful about that. It was in the capacity as a former gay friend, rather than that of CC that I went to see him. He made a grave mistake and I was very deeply hurt that he should have made the matter of my private visit to him and my trouble known to others without speaking to me first or waiting to hear from me whether or not I had been successful in avoiding publicity. I can only assume he thought that there was no possibility of that, so he rang his mentor, Bill Paine a former retired County Commissioner of Kent, who lived nearby and informed him.

The result was, that instead of resigning quietly at the most opportune time if that is what he thought I should do after the Bedford camp. I was not allowed to film the Chief Scouts visit that weekend that I had undertaken to do, just as I had done some years previously. All the most senior Scouters in any way connected with me were informed. I had to hand over the leadership of the Bedford Camp at very short notice; I had to return my warrant book to Head Quarters and the leave the Scout Movement. I had to cut my self off from all members of the movement both men and boys which is what hurt the most. I also heard through one of my closest friends that because there had been no publicity giving out the facts of the case, when they were told about my sudden and totally unexpected departure it was assumed that boys were involved.

There was nothing I could do except to cut myself off completely from every one who had any thing to do with Scouting. Fortunately with the exception of my wife, the rest of my family, my parents, my children, my employees, my customers, as far as I am aware never knew of my conviction. For that, at that time I was very thankful.

Bernard Frost betrayed me even though I had assured him that I would ring him and inform him wether or not I had been successful in avoiding any publicity. I offered him my resignationhim and said I would leave it to him how and when I was to leave the movement. Although it would have been on my police record, "because there was no publicity", no one else would have known or found out about my conviction. That was why I had not asked for any character witnesses, which would not have helped my case anyway. In fact had my position in Scouting been put before the court then they also would have assumed that I would have been a danger to boys, which is what most people though in those days and many still do today.

Had I gone for a trial by Jury, I was told I would have had an excellent chance of an acquittal; I did not do so for one single simple reason to prevent the adverse publicity. The words "Gross Indecency" and "a very well known "Scout Commissioner" would have been the headlines. Not only locally probably but nationally, even if I had been found not guilty. "Mud sticks" as they say and "there's no smoke without fire". That was 1974, since then I have never mentioned to a single person not even to close mutual Gay friends that Bernard and I had at the time what he did and I have never put it down in writing until now.

After a time I began to see that what had happened to me was not all bad. I bought a 28.ft Sailing Yacht in kit form. With the help of my wife and three children with whom I was now spending much more time, we spent three years fitting her out. We have had great times sailing the South Coast of England and the north coast of France. I was fifty-one at the time and I would probably have carried on in Scouting, until the age of sixty. (At which time they kick you out anyway). For I'm sure I would never have been able to give up, or to continue to fight for what I though was best "for my boys". There is a saying that says "no one is indispensable". There's another that says "there's an exception to every rule". "There is no longer a "Six Counties Camp"!

There were repercussions and disappointments. I would love to have been allowed to help out on the Sail Training ship for the handicapped. "The Winston Churchill" or her Sister Ship the "Henry Miller". My experience with the handicapped and that which I gained after leaving Scouting on sailing would well qualify me, except that my "criminal record" that I had "accepted" in exchange for no publicity would have disqualified me. I was at the time nominated for the "Silver Acorn Medal". It is the second highest award in the movement I would have been very proud to have received It. I should like even now to see the film that included the "Ommen" Camp. Even if the structure of the "Six" was changed, as I'm sure it probably was due to my departure. I would still have loved to able to attend the camps, visit reunions, and continue to see my many friends.

I must say I was most pleasantly surprised to read that the Scout Movement has allowed Homosexuals to be members of the movement. I would wish that, whoever the most enlightened and intelligent person or persons it was who put this forward and got it accepted, could know how much that means to a person like me. Some time ago I saw the film about the life of Baden Powell. (I would wouldn't I) and I was not surprised nor was I in disagreement at the suggestion made in the programme that he probably had problems with his sexuality. In fact, had he not had the complete self control that I am positive he did have, he would probably have been a paedophile. I could not help feeling this when I saw the picture over the fireplace (it is where one hangs one's favourite picture) at Gillwell Park, of a group of pre-puberty boys bathing naked on the banks of the serpentine some of them pictured full frontal.

I have never been sexually attracted to boys, but I was very well aware that Scouting is a very big attraction to those who are. At first I had some doubt about the sexuality of some of my adult unmarried male helpers. Without letting any one else know, I kept a close eye on them. Most of the boys with a handicap on my camps needed some help or were completely helpless when it came to dressing and undressing, washing, helping with toilet. It would have been a very great tempta-tion if they had been that way inclined or had not had complete self-control. But to my knowledge I was never let down. They were some of the very best and most dedicated of my staff. I can't help having the thought that if what some feel about BP and his sexuality is correct, then had it not been so we might never have seen the formation of such a wonderful world wide Movement as the Scouts.

I think it was Ralph Reader was said:- "To be commended are they who are not only mindful of the rightful upbringing of their own but of other men's sons".

I'm adding something here that unless you think carefully about it might shock or disgust you. But I feel it needs to be said, or if not perhaps said then written down and read.

When you look after the very severely physically handicapped, doing all the extremely personal things for them that have to be done and here I have in mind those with cerebral palsy, where they are totally unable to use their hands. You realise that unlike some disabilities and I think I'm right in referring to paraplegics they (and you may think it ironic) do not lose their sexuality or erectile function.

Although even now, rarely discussed in "straight society" masturbation is a fact of life. From the age of puberty frequently practised well into adult life even after marriage by some. Now-a-days there are wonderful inventions to enable those who can only move a finger, a toe or even just an eyelid to deal with the many tasks that were frustratingly beyond them. But have you ever thought of what to me anyway in my younger days would have been the ultimate frustration, if we were totally incapacitated ?

Most of us would do what we could to help a disabled boy or young man if we saw that they needed help. But what if the help he desperately needed, was something that if we were seen to be giving it could result in catastrophic repercussions. I know that the adult disabled do sometimes use prostitutes, but that option is not likely to be open to a boy or very young man. - If cows are not milked they suffer pain and distress and the farmer would be punished. -Such is the taboo that society imposes.

Note:- It has just recently come to my notice that Bernard Frost has died. I have been titivating and polishing these memoirs for two years now. Maybe this news is what I was waiting for.

As I go to print, it seems that part of the reason for this book has been pre-empted in the recent Queens speech. (November 02) They are at long last going to remove discriminatory victimless Victorian crimes from the statute book. Such as Gross Indecency, and Soliciting of men by men. The Home office have said that the bill would "modernise the laws on sexual offences 'so that they do not discriminate on grounds of gender but provide protection for all'. It added that the law should not treat people differently because of their sexual orientation.

The bill is expected to sweep away the "cottaging" laws but will not legalise gay sex in public. Authors note:- We don't want that any way, just that the law should be equal for all.

CHAPTER 10

A Labour of love.

When one door closes another opens. Very soon after I was forced to resign from the scouts, a friend of mine approached me and told me he had bought a sailing yacht in kit form (that's where you buy all the bits and put it together yourself). He knew I was a woodworker and asked me if I would help him with the tricky woodwork involved. Nothing on a boat is straight or square, very thing has to be fitted. This I found a complete relaxation from work and the family. I enjoyed it so much, that I started to seriously think about fitting out a boat of my own.

Living near the Thames I had, as a boy and young man done a lot of "messing about in boats", but my only experience of sail was in a "pram dinghy" from a Norfolk Broads launch, on my own, just for half an hour whilst the family were off shopping. It had about ten square foot of yellow mackintosh type sail. After two near capsizes when I thought "the boat will sink and I'll have to swim for it" I managed to get back to the shore. It gave me my first lesson, on the effect of a light wind on a small sail.

Following the launch of my friends boat I had got the bug. Not for sailing one but for fitting one out. This time I knew I had to involve the family. My daughter Paula was thirteen Martin twelve and Edward eleven. We decided we would buy one, fit it out and then if we didn't like sailing we could sell it at a profit. We all went down to a marina to look at boats. Paula said she felt seasick on the pontoon. My wife did not say much, but the boys were all for it.

We were invited down to a friend's boat that was moored some way out on a swinging mooring in Langston harbour for the weekend. My wife and Daughter were relieved that the boat was only big enough for four. We loaded up every thing that was required; (I was amazed how much). We all got into a small Avon dinghy and rowed out to the boat, no outboard motor yet. The two boys had life jackets on and before we got half way I wished I had one too, it was very choppy.

The only pleasant part of the weekend was the Friday evening, still on the mooring, with us all well fed, the boys in their bunks asleep and my friend Richard and I having "sundowners" in the cockpit". That night the wind got up to force eight and stayed there for 30 hours. With no possibility of getting ashore and no way to contact any one, "we were stuck". We did manage to put the nose of the boat just out side the harbour entrance, but it was far too rough. Fortunately the wind calmed down by the time we needed to row back to the shore.

I decided that if we were going to take up sailing it would have to be in a boat that I could stand up in, in the cabin, fully equipped that we could afford to keep in a Marina on a pontoon, so that we could step on and off with all the facilities and that I would have to learn all that I could about it.

After visiting many boat yards it came down to a 26 ft Westerly Centaur, or a 27 ft Marcon Sabre. I visited both yards and was shown all stages of production. I was impressed by the sturdiness and the layout of the Sabre. It was more expensive, but as luck would have it they had one that they had had for some time. The person who ordered it didn't like the colour - Phantom Grey—. I thought the colour was about the least important-I liked it-but said I didn't, I got five hundred pounds off.

My parents had moved into a smaller property on the same estate. Adjoining their house was a barn with a hayloft and a door ten feet from the ground, into which the hay was once unloaded straight from the horse drawn wagons. A chat with Mum and Dad. Dad was not too sure - but - Good old Mum.

The budget kit was delivered in December 1976, on a trailer towed by a Land Rover. The keel was only about six inches from the ground. Two lorry jacks lowered her on to a piece of two-inch thick plywood. I realized the weight of the boat when this bent and sank into what was my Dad's lawn. We put some wooden props around to hold her up. The U shaped trailer then pulled away, the whole operation only took half an hour total cost thirty five pounds and there she was with the cockpit level with and a couple of feet away from the loft door. (What a contrast to what had to be done when she was completed). The loft was already set up as a workshop, a frame, a polythene cover and we were ready to start.

During the next two and a half years I spent on average twenty hours a week working on her with help from family and friends. During the two winters I attended a Yacht Masters training course. Then two annual holidays in chartered Sabres. What I learnt from them proved invaluable in the fitting out. The whole of the inside of the boat was a not very pleasant yellow fibreglass; I would have loved to have had a wooden boat, but that would have meant buying an old one and the maintenance would have put that out of the question. So I decided to make her look as much like a wooden one as possible. Every inch of the inside was covered in very thin Mahogany panelling and as much of the deck as I could I covered in thin Teak.

The first year was spent fitting all the bits and pieces that came with the kit. Sometimes this involved drilling a hole in the hull. I made the measurements, thought about it, made the measurements again, said a little prayer and then drilled it. Then I could see the grass (that my dad still mowed where he could under the boat) through the hole. I was impressed by the thickness of the plug I took out of the tank cutter, it was over half and inch thick. Six holes in all had to be drilled below the water line! What a worry that was!

The Samson post (like a small bollard for towing the boat) has to be very strong hence the name, this has been known to break away taking some of the foredeck with it, if for instance, when the boat has gone hard aground and has to be towed off. So I bolted a piece of one-inch thick plywood right across the foredeck under where the post would be, then bolted it to that. Where did I get all my tips? I read every thing I could lay my hands on, Yachting magazines, books, talking to other Sailors and I visited the London Boat show every year. More information, although tragic, came from the inquiry into what is known as the Fastnet Disaster, where quite a number of Yachtsmen died in a very bad storm during the race of that name.

The toilet compartment (heads we call it) on some boats tend to become in bit smelly and difficult to clean when the surface is left with rough fibre glass. So I completely covered mine with white Formica, which is stuck in place with Thixofix. Now this is the stuff they do not put on the shelves in the ironmongers or D.I.Y. stores you have to ask for it over the counter or at the check out. It is what some kids use, or did then, to get their kicks "glue sniffing". I came over all dizzy and very nearly passed out, calling for the use of a powerful fan.

My sons came and helped and they came in very handy with the many jobs where more than two hands are required, such as holding the nuts on down below while I screwed them down from the top. Edward the smallest got down into quite small lockers to do this. The problem was, fibreglass when cut or drilled is a skin irritant. I got into hot water over that from his mother. It was now May 1978, well into the sailing season, there were many other jobs still to do but I was now impatient I wanted to get her afloat. I wanted my Mother to name and launch her but she was to be put in the water by travel lift. There would have been a lot of waiting around and travelling, so it was decided we would just have the naming ceremony. A half bottle of sparkling wine and Mother standing on an up-turned crate as a podium. Then she named her Woody. I had spent a very long time thinking about a name, but when she was finished the name became obvious.

During the time I was working on Woody regulations came into force; where by a towing vehicle must be at least as heavy as the trailer and it's load that it is towing. So this meant that a Land Rover was out. It meant hiring a large mobile crane and the boat being loaded onto a low loader lorry. It took half the day to load and then there was great difficulty driving the vehicle out. I can't think why because it backed in OK. Dad was looking very worried about the corner of a listed building. Woody was finally delivered and launched in Brighton Marina, that had only just been completed, having taken as long to build as I had taken to fit out Woody. I was one of the first to take up a mooring and was made a founder member of the marina.

For the two winters that I was working on Woody I attended the adult evening class's on the Yacht Masters course, where we learnt all about navigation, seamanship, the weather and the many other things that one needs to know before taking a boat out to sea. I found that many of the things I had learnt in the Scouts the knots, Morse and Semaphore, that in those days before Satellite Navigation we still had to use. At the end of this course many of the others in the class went on to do the Ocean Yacht Masters this is the highest qualification. But I found it involved a great deal of mathematics so I "chickened" out on that one. My excuse to myself was that it was mainly for blue water sailing, where you sail for many days out of sight of land. I have never thought I would like to sail the Atlantic. I liked a good all day sail then a comfortable marina for the night.

Having done all the theory one then had to do the practical course and I found this was usually done at a Sailing school. But I decided I wanted to do mine in Woody if possible. So I wrote to all the sailing schools and advertised for a "Master" Yacht Master to come with me and use my boat for the course. I only received one suitable reply; it was from a Colonel Kemer, who was the Principal of the Calshot Sailing School. So together with another friend who had been on the evening classes with me, we sailed all the way down to St Malo, calling at Guernsey on the way down and Jersey on the way back. We both passed and we became qualified Yacht Masters

I take a Cooking course

During the winter following the two that I had spent at evening classes I found my self at a bit of a loss for two evenings a week. So I went along to the local school and picked up a syllabus. I looked at all the courses offered. Thought about photography, but there was too much theory and too many exams for me. So I decided on Cooking, after all I should be doing plenty while on board. I signed up for the winter's course. At the first lesson we were told that each week we would be given a menu and a list of ingredients for the following week. I bought a wicker basket, bought all the items on the list, covered them with a clean cloth and along I went. There were about twenty-five women and four men to start with, but as always on these courses many of them dropped out. I was left as the only man with fifteen ladies. At the end of the course we had to do a test piece consisting of a three-course meal. Then the next week we had to sit a written exam, I was proud to pass and receive the only City & Guilds certificate I ever got.

I sail Woody to the Scilly Is.

Two great friends of the family, Joe and Joan had taken early retirement and moved out to the Scilly Islands. As soon as they heard that I had a boat they said Oh! You must come and visit us. I don't think they realized that it takes a good four days and three nights to get there from Brighton and then when you get there if there is a strong northerly wind blowing you can't stop without getting blown on to the shore. The anchors will not hold there in the stony seabed. I had mentioned this to the colonel and my friend while sailing to St Malo. When we got back to port they both said how much they had enjoyed the whole trip and who was going to be my crew for my Scilly Island trip? I said my family was too young and too inexperienced for such a trip. The end result of that conversation was, we got together again the next year. Only this time instead paying for the Colonels keep and fee's he paid his way.

That same year (1979) I took the family to Ramsgate by car, put them in a hotel and then drove back to Brighton. Then together with a friend who lived in Ramsgate sailed Woody around the south coast to drop off my friend and pick up the family. This took two days and a night, with a stop off for a rest at Folkestone. I told the family that I had no idea what time we would arrive, that it could be early or late on the second day. We arrived in the afternoon and there they were on the wall of the harbour entrance waiting for us, they said they had not been there very long. The next day with just the family on board we set off for France.

We sailed down the coast of France to Fecamp, where I had been many times before, sailing straight over from Brighton. I took them to see the monastery where they make the Calvados wine, they gave us a little to try and it was vile how anyone can drink it I don't know. The family spent one of the days exploring the town, while I took Woody out for a sail on my own. The next day we set sail for Brighton and home. I listened to the midday shipping forecast it was fine. I told them we would be having an all night sail back. Then when we were about fours hour out I, (very fortunately as it turned out) listened to the six o/c forecast. I was horrified; it said storm force nine increasing severe storm force ten imminent in sea areas Wright exactly where we were. That was the "infamous Michael Fish" weather forecast. We "came about" and headed straight back to Fecamp.

We found a mooring for Woody for a week at Fecamp. We spent that night on the boat. Then in the morning set of for Boulogne to catch a ferry back to Newhaven. Very many young French students came on board, they were all in holiday mood laughing and making a lot of noise. I settled the family right in the middle of the ferry on a lower deck and told them to stay there. As soon as we passed through the harbour wall we hit the rough seas. The ferry was pitching so much that sea spray was covering the ship from stem to stern. The stabilisers helped but she still rolled a lot. With-in a very short while there was not a sound coming from the students they were all huddled on the seats looking green, or hanging over the side being sick. I was enjoying it walking around the decks. I had my sailors cap on and a group thought I was the captain and asked me if every thing was going to be all right.

We arrived at Newhaven then we had to get a taxi to take us to Brighton

Marina where the car was. At that time there was a Hydrofoil running a service to Boulogne several times a day, it has a top speed of forty knots. The following weekend a friend and I went back to bring Woody home. We had one of the best sails ever using the spinnaker all the way, (that's the large very colourful parachute like sail that you use when the wind is astern). That storm cost me about two hundred pounds, but if I had not listened to that weather forecast I dread to think what might have happened, we would have been in the middle of it long before we reached Harbour. I have several times been out, or caught out in a force seven gusting eight (that's about forty miles an hour) but always with an experienced crew. Woody being very sturdy and heavy, was not much good in light winds, but good in a heavy seas. Instead of bouncing on the waves she just ploughed though them.

During the next twenty-five years I spent a great deal of my time on the boat, if the weather was not suitable to sail then I would be working on her. There is always something to do. It was best to moor her "stern-to" on my berth. It is not the easiest of things to do to get on and off a Yacht from the side, especially if one is carrying something. So I incorporated a gate in the transom (stern). Several times it was necessary to tow another boat all yachtsmen help each other. Sometimes it would be some one who had gone aground, or another where the engine had broken down. There was no way the towing line could pull from the centre of the transom Woody would slew round to one side and not give a direct pull. So I made a "fairlead", somewhere for the towing line to pass through. I made a Pattern, had it cast in brass and then fitted it in the centre of the stern. Problem solved.

A major improvement was the Jib, (that's the fore sail) winches; these usually have a handle on top and are two speed. But with the Sabre the guard rails and the spray dodgers are in the way, so that the winches you have to have are very slow. I made two six-inch tall, very strong cylinders with flanges top and bottom, on top of which sat the new winches. I discovered a newly formed Sabre society, who by then had a membership of some fifty. At the first rally I attended there were about twenty boats. As the "new comer" they all came to look at Woody. They had heard about the Sabre covered in wood to look like a wooden boat. I was very highly complimented on the modifications and improvements I had made.

The first Log I had (mile-o-meter and speed indicator) stopped working after a few years, I still have it as a souvenir and it reads 4772. The next one I bought had a trip which you reset each time you left the pontoon, so I can only estimate the total distance I sailed. I would think it would be at least 30,000 miles. That may not sound a lot compared to a car, but when you consider that the average speed would be about 3 Knots, (less than four mph.) that is a lot of hours. My dream for many years was to sail Woody down to the Mediterranean, through the bay of Biscay, but to do that would need at least two others who were experienced sailors, so it just remained a dream.

I sold Woody when I was seventy-seven, to a man who lived in Southampton who was self employed, whose work included metal and wood. I could have got a much better price, but I could see that like me he was in love with her and would keep her in the condition to which she had become accustomed. Where-as I had got to the stage that I could not. I miss sailing I miss being out on the wide-open sea. Even in the English Channel once past the separation zone (the shipping dual carriageway) four hours out. You can sail for another four or five hours and not see another sail or ship or any land. I feel very nostalgic when I hear the tune they play before the shipping forecast (SAILING BY) and think about the many pleasant hours, especially sailing at night.

Woody

CHAPTER 11

My Wheels.

I have told you about my very first pair, the bicycle I bought with the wages I got before I left School. The next two or three bikes I had I didn't have to buy, they were just left lying around the RAF camps. People bought them to get around the camps that were very big and then when they were posted they just left them. Soon after I was discharged from the R.A.F., I met up with an old school friend of mine who had an old Vellocette 350 motorcycle that he wanted to sell. I bought it. I had a cousin, Gordon who was Chairman of a large well- known London motorcycle club and a very experienced motorcyclist. One of the first journeys I made was to see him and ask him what he thought of it. His first words were 'you've' got a thorough-bred there but it needs some work done on it". Knowing very little about motorbikes I had been lucky in my very first buy.

There was no chain guard, it leaked oil, but the engine was good I learnt a lot from that bike striping it down and rebuilding it just for the fun of it. Then I joined a local club who were very active, visiting all the events around the south of England. Many of the members had sports bikes for scrambles on Bagshot Heath. Also for trials at Beggars Roost in Cornwall I think it was and grass track racing at West Wycombe. I would go along to all of these events at first just to act as a Marshal. We would all travel in convoy where we were not allowed to over-take the one in front. On the way home from the trials somewhere near Salisbury Plain there is a very long straight road. There we were allowed to have a "burn up" (a race), there were no maximum speed limits in those days. The first time this happened I put my head down, twisted my throttle and found to my surprise I was not only up with the leaders but I passed them. That was when I discovered that I had the sort bike that was winning the Isle of Man races.

We all wore the same clothes, just like a uniform. Peak cap, no crash helmets in those days and what was called a trench coat and waders. The Vellocette was no good for all the sporting events it was a road racer. I wanted to get another bike and take part in the "off the road" events, but I could not afford one on my own. So I went into partnership with a friend, we bought bits and pieces from all over the place and built one. It had a Rudge Whitworth engine and telescopic forks. We had a lot of fun with that bike. I had now started my own business and needed some thing more practical. I could not afford a car, so I being a Vellocette fan I bought an LAC road bike that had pannier bags to carry things in. The timber I used was too small an order for them to deliver, so I collected it with my bike. I remember going over a "hump back" bridge and it all flew out.

I managed with the bike for nearly two years collecting materials and delivering patterns and then I got my first car. A Morris Eight four-door saloon, I got it fairly cheaply although it had not done a lot of miles it was in a bad state. One of the faults of the model was the two front wings were not strong enough, they flapped and if not strengthened would have fallen off. The solution was to fix a curved bar across the front of the radiator bolted to the wings. I patched up the dents and then re-sprayed it black. It looked good except for the spokes on the wheels they were difficult to keep clean, so I made a pattern and had four aluminium Disc's made, this very much improved the look of the car, also making it unique, they were very much admired; The very first person I gave a lift to was my Mother she was very proud. Very few people had cars in those days. I kept this Morris, for over two years before selling it to a lady friend of mine who had admired it, she lived locally and she kept it for many years.

My next buy was also a Morris eight, but this time the small shooting brake type with the ash timber trimming with two doors at the back so it was so much easier for me to load and unload. It was not new; it was a long time before I could afford a new vehicle. The first new "car" I ever bought was in fact a Hillman Husky van, the reason being it was a lot cheaper than the Car of the same make. Because of the tax difference between private and commercial vehicles, it was identical except for the windows at the side. The trick was to buy the windows and put them in your self. This of course I did.

Some years later my Aunt Violet came over from Australia and stayed with her brother in law (my Uncle Harry) in London. She got him to advise her and to choose a car for her. A larger and more comfortable one than the one he had, to enable her to travel around visiting all the relatives. He chose a Humber Super Snipe, quite a large car and he drove her wherever she wanted to go. But he also used the car as if it was his own. Then one day she said she wanted to go somewhere on her own without him and said she would drive herself. (She had her own car back home in Australia where they also drive on the right) He said, "No you can't do that?" She had been driving most of her life. She was furious; she left his house and came in the car to stay with us. When ever we all went out together she wanted me to drive. This I enjoyed very much. She stayed about three months then before she returned home she said. "Would I like to buy the car cheaply?" I needed to change my car at the time, but I felt guilty with only paying what she asked, which was about half what it was worth. She convinced me by saying that it would be so much better for taking Mum and Dad out in.

The very first accident I ever had was in the Humber; I was in London somewhere near Victoria Station. In those days many of the roads were made of wooden roadblocks. It had just started raining. It was 11.55 on Friday the thirteenth; I drove around a slight left hand bend at a reasonable speed but the car did not respond to the wheel, it just went straight onto the other side of the road and collided with a taxi. The taxi driver was very sympatric and said he quite understood and that "these xxxx wooden road blocks were a menace". I was well insured and both vehicles were drivable. So it was not as bad as it night have been. But ever since I have been very reluctant to go very far on the thirteenth and even more reluctant on a Friday the thirteenth.

Of all the cars I have had and I have had Rovers, Mercedes, Jaguars, and a Daimler Jag. The two most outstanding that I loved the most was a Ford Zephyr. In was very pale blue with an open top, four seats, two doors with an electric hood. Driving that, on a journey to the coast in good weather, I felt like a million dollars. The other was a car sold at the 1952 London Earls Court motor show. Only two others were ever imported into this country and only 100 were ever produced. I bought it from a private person who lived quite near. I saw it quite often. I found out where the owner lived, then asked him to give me first choice when he came to sell it, this he did when it was eight years old.

It was an Alpha Romeo 2500 Super-Sport. It had an all aluminium, Farina designed body, open top with twin Weber carburettors. It had two doors with one seat for three in the front and with a small platform behind. It was the only car I ever kept for four years. I had this car for about a year before I got married and to give you an idea of how big the platform was, my Daughters carrycot just fitted on it. The wheels were very large with the brake drums about the size of an Austin Sevens wheels. Soon after I bought it I took it to Germany onto the autobahns where there were no speed limits and found it would easily do 120 miles an hour. Then down to Milan just to have it serviced. At Silverstone races the car park there was, in those days a very large field. Returning to the car after the races I could see a crowd of people around one of the cars, as I got nearer I saw that it was mine. I proudly pushed my way through to put the key in the lock then I opened up the bonnet to let them see the engine and answered their questions.

My wife and I went to Spain for our Honeymoon in the Alpha. We drove down to Lydd near the south coast to a small airport where the planes carried three or four cars and the passengers. We were told to park the car near the aircraft by an attendant and to give him the keys as he would be driving it into to the plane. I started to tell him how it was started, but he said he had driven every car there was and to go and sit in the departure lounge, so we did. Then over the tannoy came a request for "Mr. Montage to go to his car, as the attendant could not start it". If he had listened to me I could have told him that the ignition key has to be pushed in not turned. For the whole time I had the car I also had a van as a run around.

During the time I had this car I completely resprayed it, striped the engine down, reground all the valve seats and with the help of a mechanic friend of mine and generally gave it a good over haul. I was very impressed with the iron casting of the engine block. It was very thin, but a very actuate 3/16th thick all over. I had a new Mohair hood made and fitted two new head-lamps as the glass of one was broken and I was unable to get a replacement. At last I decide it had to go, or rather the size of the family decided it for me, for I could not fit them all in. I advertised it and the person to whom I sold it, collected it late one evening. He then apparently drove to a local pub where he knew the landlord and he must have stayed there long after closing time. In the early hours of the morning the telephone rang phone rang. It was him, he sounded much the worst for drink he said he could not start it!

In over 63 years biking and motoring I have never caused the slightest injury to my self or anyone else. I had the inevitable spills on the bikes from wet leaves or ice and several bumps while on four wheels. There was only one accident that could easily have been fatal for me or for the driver of the other car. I was travelling on a dual carriageway; doing about 60 mph. The central reservation had gaps joining the two carriageways but these were obscured with thick hedges and small trees. Suddenly there appeared in front of me, less than a 50 yards away the bonnet of a car that kept moving slowly into my path having travelled straight across the other carriageway from a side road. There was no way I could avoid him, I struck the rear nearside wheel of his car spinning him around. My car travelled on for another 50 yards, had I hit him "square on" we would both have been severely injured or killed.

I ascertained that the other driver was OK, he was still sitting in his car just a little dazed. I went into a post office just nearby which was where this nearly eighty year-old man was headed. I explained what had happened to several people there and they said, oh! "That must be Mr.? He's nearly caused an accident several times, it's a wonder it hasn't happened before". The whole incident caused me enormous problems, added to by the fact that before his case for "Driving without due care and attention", against him came to court he died.

When I moved to London I found I did not really need a car. I purchased a residents parking permit but found that it did not guarantee me a place to park. I often had to leave it a quarter of the mile away from the flat. As I was now over 65 I had a bus pass, this I have always enjoyed using. I've always liked something for nothing. Then my friend Geoff who lived at Tooting had his car stolen so I told him. "Instead of buying another why don't you use mine"? We were always going down to the boat together or to the gay pub and I always wanted him to drive. I had long since lost the joy of driving. Using my car he acted as my chauffer picking Somchai and I up and taking us from door to door whenever we needed it and saving Somchai bus fares. This arrangement worked very well for a long time. When we bought the flat in Brighton we bought a VW Golf Polo chosen by Somchai and driven by him most the time.

When we are in Thailand we hire a car so that we do not have to use the Baht Busses and Somchai uses it for his frequent visits to see his family.

MY FIRST CAR

CHAPTER 12

I GET MARRIED

Vera was working for a customer of mine; I used to see her almost every day for several years. We had a very short engagement. As soon as people got to know about it they started to organize the wedding, I was and had been for some time in the Burnham Village Choir so the whole choir turned up and the bell ringers. Without my knowledge a large group of my singing friends got together to rehearse a piece to sing at the service. When we came out of the church there was a guard of honour with lads from the Gang Show dressed in the Gang uniform. The reception was held in a large Marquee at my parentís house. I discovered as we shook hands with the 150 guests, that many times it was possible for me to shake hands with two people at once. (Scouts shake hands with the left hand).

For the honeymoon we toured Spain in the Alpha Romeo going through places where very few tourist go returning to France over the mountains through a place called Hoesca. When ever we stopped the locals just stood in groups and looked at us. On arriving home we settled in at my small flat in Beaconsfield, which I was renting from a friend, it only had one bedroom. In just a year our Daughter Paula was born. I turned a very small box room into a nursery, it was just about three times larger than the cot. Then with-in another few months our first son Martin was on the way. Paula had been born in Hospital but Martin was born at my Parents house. Once my wife's contractions started he was a very long time coming. So I took my wife into the farmyard and walked her round and round, it worked. I was there at the birth of both Martin and Paula.

The flat was on the first floor with a large area of flat roof at the same level. The Pram had to be kept in a shed at the bottom of the steps. It was a problem for my wife carrying Paula up the steps and then returning to carry the baby up, whom she would often like to have left in the pram as he was asleep, then once again for the shopping, all up and down the same steps. At the back of the property was a piece of waste ground so I built a 40ft long ramp with small steps in the middle. There were planks either side for the wheels of the pram, the gradient worked out at 1 in 4, so taking Paula and most of the shopping up in one trip, with a bit of an effort she could then just about manage to push the pram with baby Martin in it up the ramp

With-in another few months second son Edward was on the way. Now we did have a problem, we had to find a house. This we did, it was only half a mile away from my works and just near two schools. Edward was born in our new home. I then spent all the time I could spare after the Gang shows, my troop of scout at the hospital and working at Dorneywood, working on the house. We needed somewhere to store the coal for the central heating, as well as a small workshop, a garden tool shed, and a playroom. I combined the lot in one attractive building with a pitched roof covered in cedar tiles. With the material left over I built a "Wendy" house. The next job was kitchen units, then and an extension to the kitchen for use as a laundry.

Every so often there is a debate about smacking children. All I can say is that we never found it necessary. We impressed on them if they were good in public then we would forgive them a great deal in the house. There was just the once, with each of the boys only, when they were about a year old sitting in their high chair at the table. They would throw the food on the floor, look at you in defiance and then do it again. I picked up a tablespoon and said. "If you do that again I shall punish you and you will cry" They did it again. Then I carefully gave a measured tap with the back of the spoon on the knuckles. They never did it again, and while they were very young if they ever misbehaved at the table I would pick up the spoon, they would put their hands under the table, but it worked.

I took a lot of film with my cine camera of all the family weddings, christenings, birthdays and holidays. I got fed up with setting the screen up in the lounge every time to show them. I wanted a small, cinema. I also needed a study and so I combined these two. The study was about twenty feet by ten, replacing an old much smaller shed (planning permission not so strict then), everything was in wood (of course) with a pitched roof. The beams I painted black. The windows came from my village church, left over following an extension there. A small projection room was built complete with a small window just like a real cinema. Another door was knocked through from the lounge that meant that I could go out to the garage with out going out side. I then fitted a motor and all the fittings so the I could open the 'up-and over" door with a key from the outside with out getting out of the car, then close it, or open it with a switch inside the garage. Finally I built a wall with an entrance and an exit and had tarmac put down on what had been the front garden.

When I came home from the war I saw in the estate woodshed a large pile of oak "in stick" (that is with thin sticks between each plank, so that it "air dries" thoroughly). These planks were very wide and two inches thick. I spoke to my father about it and he told me that one of the best oak trees in the park (one that we boys used to climb) had been commandeered by the government to build the "war time" mosquito bomber. The state was not required to pay for it, but once it had all been though the sawmill they returned a quarter of the wood. I asked, "what was to happen to it?" he said. "It will probably be burnt eventually but why don't you ask the Colonel". Even in those days the value would be several hundred pounds. I saw my Fathers employer and asked him about the oak, "did he want to sell it?" and "would he sell it to me"? He said. "what do you want to do with it?" I told him. "To build my own dining room furniture". He replied. "Then you shall have it my boy with my compliments".

Over the next year or so whenever I had a few spare hours out of working hours I would work on it. I first built a small coffee table and two stools as a model. Then a large "Cromwellian" style table and eight chairs, two arms chair type and six (milking stool style). These were of my own design. I saw one in an antique shop where the seat is low and has a lifting slot in the seat. The back was tall to match the shape of a body and was slotted into the base that was but was removable. The idea was, that very poor people many years ago had very little in the way of furniture. This chair had three uses. The husband used the stool to do the milking. The removable back the wife used to do the ironing. Finally in the evening, they put them back together and it became a chair. I designed the whole suite including two sideboards and when finished I engraved my own crest on the backs of the chairs, this is in heraldry terms a naked cubit arm symbolic of a manual worker (that's me!) and a sprig of mountain ash. My ancestors many years ago came from France and there, Montague means Mountain.

Each year we all went on a family holiday. In the early years we chose a place where there was child supervision in the evenings. In 1969 it was Butlins. I particularly remember this one, for I sat up all night watching the man-on-the-moon landing. Martin surprised us by singing solo on the stage. The year we when to France we were approached by a man from French television who asked if we would appear on a program depicting a "Typical British family on holiday in Paris", we spent a whole day being ferried around the city, being filmed on different locations, which ended with a trip on a boat on the Seine.

In 1980 with the children now much older we went to Malta and all enjoyed swimming in the crystal clear water with snorkels. The boys and I were swimming where there is another small Island a hundred yards or so from the main Island, the three of us went together to swim across. Half way over Edward dropped his goggles where the water was about twenty-five feet deep, we could see them lying on the seabed. Edward tried to swim down to get them, but didn't make it, then Martin had a go he came up and said no Dad it's too deep we will have to leave them. I said I would have a go. Edward was very concerned and shouted "no dad you'll kill yourself". But fifty seven year old Dad had a go and with ears popping did make it. That day I went up a little in my two son's estimation. The following year we all went to Brighton probably because Woody (my boat) was there in the Marina. By now following a few rough trips and some seasickness they were not so keen on sailing. The boys and I slept on the boat, Paula and my wife stayed in a hotel where they had insisted on a television being in their room. The reason was, the Royal wedding of Prince Charles and Diana; they spent all day glued to the screen. I went out sailing on my own. The boys spent most of the time touring the town spending their money on the slot machines. I watched the recording of the wedding in the evening.

For a long time before I got married I had been interested in cine photography. Now I wanted a complete record of the family. My first camera was a 8mm. So I started filming in earnest at the wedding and then the honeymoon. I have about half an hour's film of a Bull Fight taken at Barcelona, as well as film of our travels in Spain. As soon as the children started to arrive I took film of every event from the birth onwards. Next was the christenings, my brother and sisters gatherings, and of course my parents. Because we had the biggest house, a family gathering was always held on Boxing Day with us.

After dinner we would all adjourn to my Study cum Cinema where each year I would show the results. Since all those present were on some of the film the show always went down very well. Most of the comments were made by the females about the clothes that had been worn years earlier. Later on I bought a new camera, the latest model, which was called Super Eight. It was 16 mm film cut down the middle with a sound track; I also had to buy a new projector. I spent many hours editing and putting on more sound. I now have had this film made into a video so that it can be played on the television. If asked what would I snatch if I could only take one thing, if there was a fire, I would say this film. I have now had several copies made and given them to the family.

When the children were young I enjoyed family life very much, I took a keen interest in their schooling. Paula and Martin did very well both finishing up with many O and several A levels. Martin was a bit of a loner not joining in too easily with his contemporaries. We had to take him to family counselling sessions. But he has now turned out fine. Edward took after me not doing too well at school, but he has turned out fine also, we can't all be "egg heads". Once the children were grown up there were frictions, puberty is a difficult time for young adults but also for the parents. We no longer went on holiday together. The two boys saw a lot of me at work and I, as always, was "on the go" sixteen hours a day. Both Martin and Edward joined the choir and the scouts but their interest was not held for long. Paula was courting her school-days sweetheart, the only boy friend she ever had. I was so proud and pleased with my daughter. Unlike so many daughters these days she was never any cause for worry or concern to her parents.

Paula and David now have two lovely boys, my Grandsons Daniel and Simon I look forward to being around long enough to see them grow up. Martin is still not married but now has a girl friend again, living in his own house since his Mother died as a very eligible bachelor. Edward also is not married but it does not seem to matter these days. He is living with Carol. Whom Somchai and I met at my wife's funeral. I said to my two sons "what are the chances of perpetuating the Montague name"? They both made the comment I think we have left it a bit late dad!

Our   Wedding day

A TRIP TO NEW YORK

Ever since she was built the Q E 2 has been the most famous liner afloat even though there are bigger and better ones now. So I took advantage of an advertised offer to fly to the "Big Apple" by 747 and return on her, spending just four days in the city. All the usual places were "done", a trip to the top of the Empire State building, Central Park, Times Square. Manhattan. Including a trip by helicopter over the city to the Statue of Liberty and back. China Town I found fascinating, they always gave you more than you could eat. Spent many hours in the huge Dept stores. Bought a three candle silver candelabra for the dining room table from Mace's

One thing that amazed me was the poor state of the roads and pavements. In places the pavement consisted of sheets of steel just like you find as a temporary thing on road works, you could hear very plainly the subway underneath and in the gaps you could see the trains! The last Item on the Itinerary was a visit to the Top of one of the towers of The World Trade centre on the morning of departure, where the view was spectacular; I could see the Q E 2 in its dock awaiting the passengers. I have since Sept 11th been so glad we made the effort.

On boarding the ship the weather was quite mild. After sorting myself out in the cabin I noticed we were moving off. I grabbed my camera, and dashed up on deck just in my shirt selves. I could see the sun dropping and that it was going to be a good sunset. I wanted to get shots of the Statue of Liberty with the sunset behind it. As I waited suddenly! In just a few minutes the temperature dropped 10 or 15 degrees. I was told this often happened the wind would change to the north and we got what was coming from Canada. I have never been so cold in my life, but I was determined to get my picture. If I had gone below I would have had difficulty finding the cabin, so I froze, but got some good pictures.

The trip home took five days, after the first couple I was bored. There was nothing much to do but eat, drink, gamble or play silly deck games. In the cabin was a monitor which constantly displayed our Latitude and Longitude, I found that interesting. I spent a lot of time on deck just watching the waves. We had one severe storm a force nine; I did not think much of the stabilizers! They did not work very well. At meal times I always sat near a window. One breakfast time I noticed she was slowing down; she came to a stop and then reversed. I said to a busy waiter, why have we stopped? He said, (without looking) we never stop till we get there. Nobody else seemed to notice and nothing was said until about half an hour later when it was announced over speakers that some of us might have noticed that we had stopped. They announced that the reason was, we had hit a large whale that had become impaled on the bulbous nose and was making the ship vibrate. Apparently this had never happened before. I expected there to have been some publicity, but there was done as far as I knew.

Towards the end of the trip there was a request for passengers who had any talent to volunteer and take part in a concert. There where very few offers and they kept appealing, so I put my name down. I sang a few songs and was presented with a red Q E 2 umbrella that I still have. When we arrived in the English Channel I took great interest and was surprised when we entered the Solent by Hurst Point on the west side of the Isle of White. In all the years I sailed in the Solent I had never seen her go in that way and I have seen her coming and going many times. Maybe it was to make up the time lost over the Whale.

SHEBA

I saw an advertisement for yellow Labrador puppies for sale, so I bought one; a bitch, she was one of three that was left of the litter. I was able to take her away the same day. I sent off for all the forms and information to register her as a thoroughbred. I named her "Sheba the Captains Daughter", as her father had been named Captain. That was exactly the maximum number of letters that were allowed. In the first few days I very nearly lost her. I would let her out into the garden at lunchtime. One day when I called her she didn't come and I could not see her. Then I heard a whimper and saw her clinging to the side of the fishpond. I put a piece of wire netting over the pond to stop that happening again. I took her to the vets where she was given the first of three injections; on the second visit he said. "There was something not quite right her front legs seem to be shorter than they ought to be". He said. "We shall be able to tell on your next visit". This time he said, "Yes her legs are much shorter than they ought to be". It was a mutation and was very rare. He asked me how much I had paid for her and where had I bought her? Then he said. "I should take her back and ask for a refund of your money".

I did go back and as soon as the breeders saw her they said, "Oh! I'm so sorry Mr Montague we will give you your money back" I said. "And what will you do with Sheba?" "We shall put her down" they said. "Oh no you will not!" I said. "Give me half my money back and I'll keep her". By then I had got very fond of her, it was just right. I had spent many years working with a boys with handicap. Now I had a dog with a handicap. They were reluctant to grant my request, but did so if I did not breed from her. The vet had said that her condition was very rare. I was to learn how rare and unique she was. She was about one third smaller than she should have been and her front legs were four or five inches shorter than they should have been. Every time I took her out, I was stopped and they said. "Isn't she beautiful what was she crossed with?" Most of them didn't believe me when I told them she was a thoroughbred. I got fed up with the same comments, I thought of getting a small card printed to give them. But I was very proud of her really.

Some years later when I lived in London near Hyde Park there was a rally of country folk, a protest mainly over the proposed Fox hunting ban. Hyde Park where

I regularly took her for her walk was thronged with thousands of farmers and country people most of whom would be dog owners and lovers. I was besieged with the same enquiry all the time I was there. During her lifetime I had taken her to many vets and she was seen by a couple of Crufts dog judges. None of them had ever seen one like her. I lost her at the age of ten. She became ill with cancer. When it became time for her to be put to sleep I was in Thailand and a friend was staying at my flat looking after it and Sheba. We arranged every thing by telephone and fax; he did everything including the cremation. I was very grateful to him for I could not have done it. But I was so sad not to have been able to say goodbye to her.

The next time I went to Thailand I took with me a photograph of her. There are very many talented artists in small shops where they mostly paint portraits for customers from photographs. My oil painting of Sheba that is exactly like her and cost me £20 is one of my most treasured possessions. The flat I bought in London was a basement, just because of Sheba. She used to come sailing with me but not if there was someone to look after her, she did not like it too much. She only ran off once. I think she got lost in the wood at my house in Farnham Common I was very worried. She never wore a collar her neck was as big as her head and she just slipped out of it. I didn't hold out much hope when I rang both Beaconsfield and Slough police stations. But success! There she was in Slough, I could see her in a kennel before she saw me she looked so forlorn.

About two years after she died I saw a full-page picture in the Daily Mail of a dog that looked exactly like Sheba being taken for a walk by Jimmy Hill (The famous Footballer, Football commentator and now Chairman of the football association.) The article described how they also had a "dwarf" yellow Labrador (a dog) with a very rare condition   called Chondroplasia and that every body thought how beautiful and rare he was but that many did not believe it was a through bred. It said that some one had offered them one million pounds for him. So I wrote to him enclosing a photo and my story of Sheba. His wife rang me and said how thrilled they were to get my letter and that Sheba looked exactly like their "Charlie" She said they would not sell him for all the money in the world. She was also so pleased to hear Sheba had lived to the age of ten years. She had been told that Charlie might not live for too long People might not believe me but I also would never have sold Sheba. Something completely unique is priceless.

Less than one in 10,000 dogs
of all breeds is born with chondroplasia

SHEBA

CHAPTER 13

<u>I BUY WOODSIDE</u>

By 1989 House prices were starting to fall. I had the money sitting in the bank from the sale of the works. I viewed about six properties and then returned to the first one I saw. It was fully detached with three bedrooms and a large secluded garden. But so had most of the other properties I had seen. The thing that attracted me to this one was a large workshop. It was bigger than most lounges. It also had a private entrance to a large wood that belonged to Eton College, but only the house's that surrounded it had permission to use it. On viewing this house "Woodside" I made a mental note of some of the improvements I would make that would require the use of this workshop. I made an offer and then met them half way. It was accepted; the price I got it for was forty thousand pounds less that it had been on the market for six months previously.

The very first improvement I made was to have a gas fired Aga cooker fitted, this made the kitchen the most popular room in the house. Since passing my City and Guilds in Cooking this was now another one of my hobbies. There was a walkway that passed the tool shed that doubled as Sheba's kennel, then the door to the workshop, then further on the green house. It was winter when I moved in and raining a lot so the next priority was to cover this walkway with corrugated translucent sheeting.

But this was not before I had moved my wood working machinery into the workshop. For many years I had always done my own electric wiring, this skill was largely gained by watching electricians and DIY books. I found it very satisfying making a neat job, running the cable, putting in the light fittings, the fuse boxes and the sockets and then switching on and seeing it all work. I put plenty of lighting everywhere, in the green house, the workshop, the garage, security lighting and garden flood lighting. All materials I bought from my local "trade supplier" on the Company account, one of the perks of having one's own business.

The next major job was to build a tank to hold one thousands gallons of water for the fish. I had studied the hobby and had seen many Koi Carp ponds. Fish need to be seen to the best advantage just like in an indoor aquarium where storks, cats, mink, even humans could not eat or steal them. Where bird droppings would not give diseases and where leaves and other rubbish could not blow on to the water. So my tank was four foot deep from the ground and four feet above ground. The top two feet on three sides facing the house was half an inch thick strong glass. Then over all this I built a sloping roof with lift up doors at the front, so that the whole thing was enclosed. An automatic feeder was installed that made a little noise that after a while the fish recognized and they would all come up to the top at feeding time. Flood lighting enabled the fish to be seen to their best advantage by daytime as well as at night. Koi do not grow and are not very active in very cold water, but the water never got as cold as a pond so they were active and grew all the year round. You can only have so many "fish inches" to a given amount of water. Eventually I had twenty fish from nine inches up to eighteen inches long; I would buy them from the annual Koi Carp exhibition and show at Aqua Billingdrome Northampton at a few inches long, then let them grow larger and become tame in a tank in the conservatory.

I learnt from my father that the best water to use on a garden is rainwater most people let it all go to waste down the drain. I placed water tanks under every down pipe. I put guttering on the covered walkway from the house to the green house. Then all the rainwater from the very large garage and workshop roof and from the green house was channelled into a brick built five hundred gallon water tank, into which I put a water-pump that pumped water into my water cans, or into a hosepipe and also into another tank inside the greenhouse. I remember several times there were hosepipe bans in place. I enjoyed using my own "rainwater hose pipe" and wished that some official would see me then I would have had the pleasure of showing him my "rain water conservation scheme".

Then I started the major woodworking projects. On viewing the house for the first time I was very nearly put off. There was this beautiful entrance hall and going up from it was what should have been a beautiful staircase. But some idiot had removed what I'm sure would have been an attractive banister with wooden rails and newel post and put in metal piping that looked just like scaffolding. I had in my timber shed at work a lot of Teak, part of a large amount that I had bought when fitting out Woody. I had bought a small Myford wood turning lathe and over a period of the next three months turned up thirty-eight identical spindles. I had always enjoyed woodturning but running my company I had not been able to do any for years. The maximum diameter was three inches, the top part being fluted. It took me another couple of months to make the banister rail and to erect it all. If I had employed someone to do this it would have cost me three thousand pounds. It cost me nothing except my time. I got a great deal of pleasure in doing it.

The southeast corner of the house was eminently suitable for a conservatory. Wicks the DIY store had the best selection so I bought two, one a lean-to-type and the other had five sides to fit around the corner of the house. I employed a builder to put in the foundations, the floor and a two-foot high wall. There were about twenty glazed units, one had to be fixed in the right position, rawpluged to the wall of the house, then it was just a matter of fixing other units on one by one. I found it one of the most enjoyable and satisfying jobs I have ever done. Whilst I found the sides the windows and the doors quite easy to do, the roof was quite another matter. What was supplied was all the timber not cut to size, this all had to be cut to shape and fixed to the wall of the house and to the top of the glazed units. I found that my workshop and the machinery was indispensable and fail to see how any one without such a facility could manage to do the job as I did.

All the timbers I painted with primer and it's first coat prior to fixing, this made the final job of decorating much simpler. Fixing the polycarbonate was also tricky, not the straight sections but the wedge shaped pieces on the half round section. I am pleased to say that when completed there were no leaks. But heavy rain on the roof made a great deal of noise. Fitting red quarry tiles on the floor was another satisfying job. A three speed large cooling fan in the roof and the whole project was finished except for one item. I had read many times where people planted a vine just outside a conservatory wall, then trained it through a hole so the it grew inside. I thought I would go one better. Before the contractors put in the floor I made a wooden box that I placed up against the inside wall, this they concreted around. Then all I had to do was to dig out this hole, put in some fertilizer and a large dead Koi carp fish that had conveniently died just then (it is supposed to be a dead cat or dog) and planted the vine. Three years later it was producing grapes. I don't remember them tasting fishy.

The doors into the lounge were large double ones with plain glass panels that rattled. I have always liked the narrower double doors that you see in big houses where the butler with white gloves on bends down and opens or closes both doors together. So I bought the oak through the company and built the doors and the fixed panels to match at each side. This job was too much for my small machinery, so I did most of the work at the Company workshop in the evenings and weekends. There was an archway into the kitchen from the hall that I framed in oak. When I bought the house the dinning room door had been removed. You don't need too many internal doors in a centrally heated house, but they had not even filled in the hinge recesses. So this doorway was also panelled with an archway in oak. The floor had an old carpet. When I pulled it up there was an oak block floor. So now on entering the house the hall was entirely in oak.

The frontage of the house was one hundred and fifty feet long, with an attractive soft wood white picket fence. Unfortunately being on the north side it went green and was rotting very quickly. I painted it twice, which took a very long time. So I decided to get rid of it and build a brick wall. That was when my troubles started. For some reason two of my neighbours objected. I knew I did not need planning permission for any thing up to one meter high. There was no pavement and I had intended to use the foundations of the kerbstones for the wall, which was where the fence had been, it was quite wide enough and deep enough. But the planning officer said. "No I could not do that, I would have to put the wall one meter in from the road'. I said. "And give up one hundred and fifty square meters of my property!" He explained that if at any time they had to dig up the kerb, it would affect my wall. I saw his point, but fought the matter, and it was agreed that two feet would be acceptable. I enjoy bricklaying, Winston Churchill was said to have enjoyed doing it.

Just in front of the workshop was an area about the half the size of a singles tennis court that was grass and seeing that there was quiet enough of that to mow as is was I dug it over making it into a small kitchen garden. It was amazing the amount of produce it grew. The green house was used to the full to "bring things" on in pots and trays, and enough tomatoes so that at times I had plenty to give to all my friends. Even though I was a gardeners son and grew up in one of the largest of gardens I was still amazed at how much can be grown in just a small plot of land. Very few fresh vegetables were bought, the surplus was frozen and friends always went away with something fresh.

I BUY 166a GLOUCESTER TERRACE.

On the day that I was sixty-five, the day that most people look forward to retiring I had no intention of doing so, but I did decide to draw my pension. So I found I had some disposable income. Property prices were at that time very low. I looked for something that would need renovation I found a basement flat in Bayswater. The estate agent showed me around and I felt that something was not quiet right. The occupants were squatters; at least that was what the owner and the agent's thought. I paid a return visit on my own, talked to one of the boys and found that they were not squatters at all, but were Polish students paying rent to some Irishman who had broken in, put in a minimum of bedding and furniture and then called on a Friday to collect the "rent". I returned to the house on my own. Talked to the one who spoke English best and was told that they would be leaving in about three weeks at nine o/c on a certain day. On that day I was there with a couple of other Irishmen who, as the students left boarded up the door and windows. Then I bought the property at a much-reduced price.

The whole flat needed extensive redesigning and renovation. I spent hours with a piece of graph paper and by the time I was satisfied with it I was up to issue eight. The Kitchen was very large, so that was divided into a small Kitchen and a dining room. The bathroom was also large next to which was a large passage, so a wall came down and that room and the passage became a bedroom with a shower and toilet. This left an alcove inside the door to the outside patio large enough for a small sink a fridge and a microwave. The other part of the divided kitchen became a small lounge. So I now had in effect two flats. I let the main flat; this paid the mortgage I had taken out. I would stay in the small flat at weekends so that I could drink and not drive. I also stayed there when I went to concerts and the theatre. It was my pied-a-terre in town.

When I had been at Woodside about eight years. I was not getting any younger. I was mowing the lawns that together with trimming all the edges took me over two hours to do properly. When I thought, why am I doing all this? Who am I doing it for now? For the first time in my life I found myself living on my own. Why don't I sell "Woodside and move into London"? I would have to have somewhere that suited Sheba that only left my Koi Carp. This would be a problem it may seem strange but I was very fond of each one of my fish. I decided to advertise and sell my Koi and auction all my many tools and pieces of machinery in the workshop. So I started to compile my catalogue. It was just prior to this that I bought my first home computer; I spent many hours giving all the items lot numbers and several weeks juggling items around for the best advantage.

My Auction

Over the years I had been to many actions both to buy machinery, tools and furniture but I had never been the auctioneer, the idea appealed to me. I had some time previously bought this computer. I told the sales man all I wanted was a word processor but he said I had to have all the many other programmes and facilities. I was later glad that this was so, for Asif turned out (as I suppose all young people do) to be able to grasp all the many complexities of this monster, very quickly. I have been using this computer now for many years and I am still only able to do as I am at this moment, using it as a word processor and even now I have to call for help many times.

Asif was able to use the graphics, and produced very professional posters to both advertise my Koi Carp and the auction. I enjoyed sorting out all my many tools, both garden and woodwork and pieces of machinery into "lots". Then I amused my self for several weeks typing the catalogue and placing the over one hundred and eighty six lots in the best order to keep the interest of the bidders. I enlisted the help of my friend Geoff as the "indicator", the one who points out or holds up each lot. Then Rob who is a "banker", agreed to be the "accountant" assisted by his partner Kim. Asif was the "recorder"; he records and writes down the bidders number and the amount bid. Another great friend who is a Lesbian named Elain took on the job of "runner" the one who takes what the recorder writes down to the accountant. Then finally Jason was the security man who stood by the only exit, the garage door and made sure all those who left with any lots had paid for them.

There was a viewing day prior to the day of sale and viewing for half an hour before the sale started. The big day arrived I had sent out posters and catalogues to all who I thought would be interested, only about twenty turned up but they were all bidders who had come for particular items. The couple that had bought Woodside were also there they bought most of the items needed to look after the house and garden, like the mower, ladders, water cans and garden tools. They also bought most of the garden furniture. It could not have gone better all the lots were sold in just under an two hours. I enjoyed describing the items and bringing down my "gavel" (A pin hammer that I did not want to sell). With in five minutes of the last bid being sold Rob presented me with a completed record of who had bought what, the price paid and the total came to approximately two thousand five hundred pounds. The sale of the Koi also went very well.

I had a tenant in the London flat with whom I had been quite friendly right up until I told him I wanted it for my self. He had been there for about four years and had settled himself in. It was quiet interesting how he came to be my tenant. I advertised in a Gay paper called 'the Pink', it was the only advertisement I placed. He was the second person I Interviewed. We had come to an agreement when he said. "You won't mind if I bring a big bosomed blond, which is the type I fancy, in now and then if I can find one?" I said. "You mean a woman?" He said. "Of course". But I said. "I thought you were Gay how did you see my advertisement?" Oh no he said. 'I'm not gay! But most of my friends are, I work in the film business one of them must have told me. I have read a book about being gay and I have thought about giving it a try. As far as I know he never did!

We became quite good friends, so much so that I invited him to one of my Bar-B-Qs at Woodside. There were about seventy people present, all gay including the person he came with a film producer. He amused me by saying that he was chatting up one of my female friends, telling me that he thought he was "in there". I told him. "You will get a punch on the nose she's gay!" Sheba my beloved little dog always enjoyed these events getting "tit bits" from people all the time. She had never to my knowledge bitten anyone. Eddy, (that was the name of my tenant) was the only "straight (heterosexual) person" there, Sheba bit him. I had a problem getting him to leave my flat. In the end it cost me most of the money I had made from my auction to get him out.

Having paid off most of the mortgage on the London flat the bulk of the money from the sale of Woodside was in the bank. My plan was to look around for something better than a basement flat. I was amazed, when shown several properties, that they were no better than the flat I already had, or could be if I did some DIY and spent some money on it. These properties that I was shown would have cost me more than all the money I had got from the sale of my house. I had not realized how property values had gone "through the roof" during the few years since I had bought the flat, it was now worth about four times what I had paid for it.

Once the auction and the sale of the fish was over it came to moving house. I was moving from a big house into a basement flat. I have found that in life if there is a space, it will be filled with something. So I had to have a very big clear out. I put every thing I didn't want in the double garage, the floor was completely covered

I wished I had extended the auction to include all the furniture and brick-a-brat I was throwing out. In the end I had a quote from someone who also ran auctions and it all went "for a song". Each time I went to London I took with me what I could get into my car, so that I saved the cost of a removal company. I hired a large "Transit van into which I was able to get all the large items". Several of my friends helped and I was in my London flat.

The benefit of owning two properties before you move from one to the other, is that you can improve and decorate, while the place is empty. A very good friend of mine is a professional decorator. I employed him for a week. I bought quite expensive wallpaper and a matching border. Then I was very extravagant. In the "pattern book" it showed curtains to match this wallpaper, I measured up and ordered a pair. I had a bit of a shock when I collected them and was presented with the bill. But I thought. "Well you've got to be a bit extravagant once in a while in life". The floorboard had been up and down several times, so that the floor was now a little uneven. The whole lot was covered in large sheets of hardboard. Then I designed and had wardrobes fitted on two sides of the master bedroom from floor to ceiling, giving plenty of space for clothes and storage.

The next item was the carpets. The same design was fitted right though from the lounge to the bedroom including the small hall in between. By having the wardrobes fitted first I saved several square yards. The firm that fitted the wardrobes spent several days doing the job and at the end there was quiet a lot of material left over. I gave the man a tip and he left it with me, otherwise he would have taken it all away. The bed room was quite large, but for two chests of draws I had there was no room against the walls, so I stood one on top of the other at the foot of the bed in the centre of the room, used some of the spare material to simulate a four poster bed, had some more curtains made, put a television on top of the chest-of-draws. Now I think we have about the cosiest bed we've ever had. This then gave quite a large area for use as a utility space, such as ironing and room for my "keep fit rowing machine".

If anyone has ever wondered what the small round cast iron "manhole" like covers, (which are far too small for a man) that you still see on many London pavements are for. They were used in the days when London still had coal fires, to put the coal down. These covers were round, so that it was impossible for them to drop down inside. Our London flat has three of these vaults. They are about ten feet by eight feet, with an attractive domed roof. One of them has an entrance door at the bottom of the steps leading to the front door. The flat had been the home of the "caretaker" of the whole row of houses and this vault had been used for many years by about ten other flats to put their rubbish in to be collected twice a week. When I was negotiating to buy, I complained about this together with several other faults I found and was given a "verbal" assurance (how silly of me) that other arrangements would be made, they never were and the verbal assurance was denied.

I had to put up with this for some time, in fact all the time Eddy my tenant was there. But when I moved in I was determined to change this practice. The council instructions were that rubbish should be put out on the pavement early on the morning of collection. The collectors had complained to me that it took four of them to empty the vaults throwing the bags one to the other up the stairs. I had noticed that further up the road bags were left on the pavement. At the annual meeting of Shareholders I complained again, but everyone was against me, they said, "the rubbish has been put into your vault for years you must accept it". I said the caretaker did not own the property I do. I told them I was worried about security and was going to put a lock on the gate with an entry phone. Those that were eligible to place rubbish in my vault, (which was only six, but several others did), would, half an hour before collection have to ring this entry phone, identify them selves, then I would tell them to leave the bag on the pavement. Not one person ever did. Rubbish was put into an unused doorway, the same practise used by most properties in the road.

The Landlord did not like this and claimed that I did not own the vaults. My solicitor did a search and to my dismay said, "He's right you don't, but neither does he". Apparently it was a bit of 'no-mans-land'. I took advice from council, made them a small offer expecting them to bargain for more telling them they had no access. This was to my surprise accepted. I then had all three vaults "Tanked", (that's a double coating of water proof cement). This work included filling up the holes where the coal had once been delivered. The vault that had been used as a rubbish store I turned into a cosy little workshop. The middle one of the three had once had a door, but his had been bricked up. I knocked out enough bricks to make a half round window at the top, then the contractors broke a door though between this middle one and the one that had it's entrance inside, so now as well as the small workshop we have two quite nice sized studies, one of which contains our "London" computer on which the bulk of these memoirs has been written over many hundreds of hours.

There were three steps up to the front door from the lowest point of the front patio, then seventeen steps up to the street. As the whole street is "listed" permission has to be obtained for any work done. I got planning permission to raise the floor of this patio, thus eliminating six steps three down and three up. The whole area has been tiled in "non slip" tiles. The "entry phone on the top Iron Gate was not only to get around" the rubbish problem, I was genuinely concerned about security. This was the point I put to the meeting of the shareholders. I pointed out that most of the occupants of the other basements used a padlock and chain. If someone comes down to the front door, unlike most other properties they are completely out of sight. I had many callers trying to sell me some thing, including a regular call from the "Jehovah's Witness's trying to sell me religion". A padlock and chain was too much of a problem. I contacted three companies for a quote to fit an entry phone with a "key pad". The job was done by one of them for a few hundred pounds. Walking around the streets of London there are thousands of basement flats with an iron gates at the top, just the same as mine, but I have never seen another with an entry phone and keypad. There are three handsets in the flat, when some one rings the bell they have to identify themselves, then we release the lock or not depending who it is. If we are in the lounge then we can see who it is thought the window.

Even though I told myself I had had enough of gardening I could not resist putting some pots and boxes that I had saved around the patio filling them with flowers. Now during the spring and summer people stop and look at my little garden.

CHAPTER 14

THE SADNESS'S OF MY LIFE

Considering my age there are happily very few. I suppose the first was the death of Grandmother Montague who must have looked after me for most of the first three years of my life and then lived with us until she died, at the age of 76, when I was 14. I can remember the last moments I spent with her. It was a beautiful spring evening. I was standing at her bedroom window looking out onto the garden where there was no other buildings to be seen, but a large expanse of beautifully keep flower borders all just bursting into bloom, with neatly clipped yew hedges and beyond that the park. I told her to get well soon and enjoy it all; she did so much love the garden. I'm sure the years she spent at "old Garden Cottage" were some of the happiest of her life. Nowhere nowadays would you find such a small, humble and amenity less cottage with such views. She died the next day while I was at work.

That evening when my brother and sister had been put to bed, mum and dad said that they had to go out and were leaving me in charge. I think they must have gone to arrange the funeral. I kept thinking of Gran upstairs, I thought about it and thought about it again. Then I crept up before it got dark, Gran's bed looked as if it was empty, (she was very tiny) there was a sheet pulled tight from top to bottom. I carefully pulled back the sheet; her head was not on a pillow, this puzzled me, she looked so small, pale but peaceful, I walked over to the window, lookout out on to the still beautiful garden and the pond that she had rescued me from and said my good bye to her, ending with the words so often used in our house when anyone was going anywhere. "See you later Gran".

My next sadness was the only really tragic one. It was one of the days between Christmas and New Year 1949; I was working at my workshop, (we did in those days). I had early that year started my own business. I had a phone call. My Bother had been involved in an accident; I rushed home to find mother in a flood of tears. A policeman was there. He told me that Edward had been returning from the pub, riding pillion on his friend Peter's motorbike and they had collided with a lorry. My Bother was dead. The policeman had come up from his station on a bicycle and asked me if we could both go up to the hospital on my motorbike and there, I was to identify my bothers body.

Apparently, they had both been to the "Oak and Saw" Public House for a lunchtime drink, but there was no suggestion that they had had too much to drink. There was neither breathalyser nor unfortunately were there crash helmets in those days. Had he been wearing one, I'm sure he would have survived. On the way back from the hospital we stopped at the crash scene; this was on a T-junction. They were almost home. On the last left hand bend they must have taken it a bit too fast and too wide. A lorry going the other way and turning left swung out to take the tight corner and they met head on. My bother was thrown though the air and his head struck the tall garden wall of the house, that years later my parent were to move into, to spend the rest of their days. I found a small tuft of Edward's hair on the wall. It took a very long time for my mother to get over this, I think partly because he was always a little on the delicate side and because she had fought so long and hard to keep him alive when he was so ill as a baby. She said, ' to lose him like this, after all we went though". He was 23 years old.

After the war the Hanbury estate never got back to what it was, many of the servants who had been young enough to join the forces did not return. Those, who like my parents that were older and lived on the estate in tied cottage's were able to stay on for the rest of their days until they died. For about the last ten years of their lives, father and mother were able to move into a smaller bungalow that had been converted from an apple store. The entire windows faced south looking on to a pleasant garden that kept dad busy maintaining and improving. They certainly were the happiest years of their hard working life.

They had a large black Labrador bitch that every day mother would take for long walks she and Bess were devoted. But one-day mum phoned me and said that Bess (who was now 17 years old) was unwell. I took her to the vet knowing what the out come would be. I made a coffin and buried her in a corner of dads garden. Mother was then in her eighth year and from that day she gradually changed. She stopped going for long walks, saying there was now no need now Then one-day dad said to me. "There's something wrong with your mother son, she has become very forgetful, she gives me egg and bacon for every meal" My wife and I had a look around Mum's kitchen and found there was nothing in the larder but eggs, bacon and marmalade.

With the help of my sister in-law who lives with my Bother John just a hundred yards away, my wife and I managed to humour mother and with out upsetting her saw that they both had proper meals. If we said anything to her, or questioned her she would smile and say something that often did not make sense. Doctor Summer's was consulted. He quickly arranged for her to have a brain scan; the diagnosis was that her brain at the front of her head had shrunk. 'Alzheimer's". It was the first time any of us had ever heard or read of it, including the doctor I think. She spent some time in hospital never questioning us, or getting upset. I visited her every day some times twice a day. Once she said. "You've just missed Margaret my dear", my sister had last visited her two days before.

She was sent home, but it was too much of a worry for dad. She would turn on the gas stove then forget to light it, she also started going for walks again and we would find her half a mile away when it was getting dark, sitting on a seat by the roadside. She would go to bed at six o/clock in the evening saying she was tried and then get up again at ten, just as father was getting ready to go to bed. We had a family conference where we decided we would do all we could, not to put her into a "home". I would sleep there and the others would do shifts during the day. One night when I had gently guided her back to bed in the middle of the night, she put her hand on my knee and said. "Oh! I didn't think it would be like this my dear".

Inevitably the shift arrangement did not work for very long, every body had there own family commitments and mother was getting increasingly more difficult to look after, but never aggressive and rarely upset. She was in a world of her own for most of the time, we had lost the mother we all knew and loved. Very occasionally there was a brief moment of sanity and recognition. Doctor Summers was wonderful; he managed to get her into hospital several times which was a great relief. But of course she could not stay there.

For some years before all this mother had been in the habit of giving me money, fifty pounds, then a hundred pounds at a time every few months or so, saying 'put this away dear you will need it for us one day. They both drew a full pension, mother having worked all her life. They still paid no rent, rates, heating or lighting bills. Having given a life time's service to the "estate", the "estate" would looked after them to the end of their lives no matter how long that might be, That was the custom. When I said "why don't you spend it on some new clothes, furniture or a holiday" she said, "We don't need anything now, when we needed it we didn't have it", now we don't need it we've got it.

The time came when we had no alternative but to put mother into a private nursing home, using the money mother had saved. I was very distressed about this, she was very unhappy and cried asking me to take her home every time I visited her which was at least once a day. She had been reasonably happy in the hospitals she had been in all the nurses were so kind and she was in bed most of the time. But in this "home" (which was extremely expensive) I think they bullied her a little. Some of the other inmates were loud and aggressive. It was there during one of the moments when she was almost her old self and I had discovered (going though her private papers) that she and father had not married until I was three years old. I asked her about it, was dad my father? I said "I didn't mind in the least and that if he was not. Having taken me on and treated me just the same as the others, then he was just as much a father to me and more than the real one". She cried and just said. "You must ask your father my dear".

Dr. Summers visited her at this home, he was not happy and 'bless him' managed to get her back into hospital not long before her 82nd birthday. On this day I collected her and took her home, sat her in the sitting room then all the family one by one greeted her including ten Grandchildren, she named each one as they wished her happy birthday. My wife and I took her back to the hospital where she had been given a small room all to her self. We tucked her up in bed with all the cards around her. The nurse's came in and sang happy birthday she was very popular with them saying that unlike so many of the other old patients she was no trouble at all. At seven o'clock the next morning the telephone rang; it was the sister to tell me that mother had died during the night. She was 82, she was like the queen mother as old as the year 1982.

We were of course all very sad, but also very thankful that she had died, we had already lost most of the mother we knew and loved. We had found out a lot about Altzheimer's and seen some of the worst cases where they had lived for a long time becoming a mere shadow of their former selves, incontinent and aggressive, totally unable to recognize anyone. It is a very distressing thing for all concerned.

The one who suffered most during all these difficult days was "dear old dad" torn between wanting to look after her and feeling guilty that he was totally unable to do so. She had always managed every thing, made all the decisions, done every-thing except the garden. We were so lucky in having parents that were devoted to each other. At the time she became ill he was at the age of 88 still very fit, spending most of all the daylight hours looking after quite a large flower garden, lawn and kitchen garden, In the winter spending many hours cutting logs for the fire. He went down hill very quickly. He stopped doing the garden, saying "There's no one to do it for now". I visited him at some time every day, often sitting with him for many hours in the evening going over happier times. It was constantly in my mind to ask him if he was my real father. He had no idea I knew about the marriage certificate I had seen. He was so unhappy; I was never able to bring myself to ask him.

Some five years or so before mother became ill, father was suffering from the usual prostate problem that most men get before or during their' eighties. He was, the doctors said at risk if he had the operation because of his high blood pressure. The whole family was consulted, dad did not seem to know what to do, they all looked to me for the decision. The alternative was a catheter bag. I was familiar with this as many of the boys on my camp had this solution and seemed to cope very well. So this was the decision. But dad hated it from the moment it was fitted; it was very difficult to get him to go anywhere. He was a very shy and private man. Then unfortunately, some thing I had never experienced with my boys, the bag would become blocked every two or three months or so. Then a male nurse had to be summoned urgently. Some times this would happen during the night. He was very reluctant to trouble anyone and so would end up suffering acute discomfort.

During mothers illness and after her death, my wife would several times a week walk over two miles to take him his dinner, I would drive over to bring her home. On this particular day I was unable to do so, neither was I able to visit him that night. The next day she took his dinner she found him sitting in his chair, his head on his chest with the empty dinner plate placed on the floor at his side. She phoned me and said I think daddy is dead. He had died of a heart attack, (we called it a broken heart) less than a year after mother. He must have died shortly after eating his dinner the day before and had been there for twenty-four hours. He was 89.

Mother had requested to be cremated and so there was room in the family grave for dad on top of my brother and Grandmother. Mother's ashes had been placed in the grave in a little casket; this was placed on top of dads coffin. The little churchyard and church at Hitcham is about as beautiful spot as you could find, overlooking the park, with which we were all so familiar. Standing at the graveside that is up against the wall one can see no building of any kind for 180 degrees.

Dad had for some years looked after the boiler for heating the church and the very difficult job of cutting the grass around the graves. I used to help him sometimes, then as well as being in the choir, both man and boy, a bell ringer and server. I was very familiar with every detail and almost every grave. We would see if we could find the oldest gravestone and found that many of them had eroded away and were no longer legible. I decide that the family gravestone would always be readable. I had the names of Grandmother, Brother Edward, Mother and Father engraved in bronze, mounted on a piece of Italian marble. It just gives the dates of birth and death, my Christian name and that of my brother and two sisters and the words "See you later"

What I am writing now is an insert. At the time of writing these memoirs were virtually finished. There has been a most unexpected, and distressing addition to my sadness's. At the age of 68 my wife has died of a severe stoke. We were married and living together for over twenty years almost as long as we have been living apart, it has come as a great shock. There was some bitterness on her part when I first left her, but I have always fully supported her and would have continued supporting her no matter what her circumstances, or however long she might have lived. Since she met Harold a few years after we parted we had become good friends and I visited her often. The very last time was with my partner Somchai just before we left for two months in Thailand. She greeted him warmly and thanked him for looking after me while I was so ill. It is a regret that we were unable to visit her as planned just three days before she had the stoke, we were about to go down to see her when we got the telephone call from my son. Somchai and I still went down, but instead of seeing her at her home, we saw her on her deathbed, she died three days later with out regaining consciousness.

I quite naturally agonized for a long time, and felt terribly guilt when I finally left her all those years ago, but I have, over time, been able to see very clearly that what I did was right for her. She loved me so much that she would never have told me to leave, she knew and accepted the fact that I was gay, that our sex life together was over and that I had male lovers. I was quite comfortable with her looking after me as a housewife (although she would be the first to admit that she was terrible at house keeping) but I could no longer give her the attention and the fun in life that she deserved. I hoped that she would meet someone who could give her these things that I could no longer do. In just a few years she met Harold.

Harold was a widower with his own house and car they went dancing and touring. They also went on holiday together. They were together as a pair for fifteen years, but she never moved in with him. I'm sure she never would have asked him to move in with her, for she knew she was a jackdaw, she kept everything, she never threw anything away. Old clothes magazines even daily newspapers they just piled up. She was a very good Mother totally devoted to the children's well being every minute of the day and at night when it was necessary. Every so often whilst she was out, I would have a clear-up overloading the company van with a trip to the local tip. Oddly enough she didn't seem to mind for she never said anything. Apparently the same thing has been happening since she moved into a smaller bungalow a few years after I left. My son Martin who has never left home has been doing just that.

In all those years I had never met Harold until I visited my wife's bedside at the hospital shortly before she died. There was just him, sitting besides her holding her hand, I said. "You must be Harold". He said. "Yes and you must be George". Talking to him I gathered that he did not know how serious my wife's condition was. Hospitals that are supposed to be places of kindness, attention and healing, have rules that are so downright thoughtless and cruel, regarding to whom they give out information. Harold who had been her constant companion for fifteen years was not a blood relative and so was not entitled to be given any information what so ever. If Harold (who I gathered from our short talk was a retiring type not one to push him self forward) had told them that he was her common law husband they would have told him what they later repeated to me and what they had told my son Martin, that my wife has suffered a very severe stroke. That if she regained consciousness she would be severely disabled.

Harold had told me that he had known several people who had had strokes who had been unconscious for many days but had only had slight disabilities. He was hoping that would be the case with Vera my wife, but that even if her disabilities were severe, he would have her living with him and would look after her. Martin was too distraught and up-set to convey to Harold the seriousness of my wife's condition.

While writing this I am angry, because the same situation occurs with gays who can have spent decades living together, loving each other and caring for each other through good times and bad. And yet only close blood relatives are allowed to visit if the situation is critical. Blood relatives who may not have seen or contacted the person concerned for many years. Blood relatives who may well have disowned their son or daughter because of their gayness. Blood relatives who will grab every thing and even turn a partner out of the residence if the deceased name was the only one on the deeds and there is no will, despite the fact that the surviving partner may have shared all expenses including mortgage payments. I don't particu-larly blame the blood relatives, many people these days will grab what ever they can whenever they can. I blame the system. No court of law will help, how can this be right, or just. I have personally known two people to whom this has happened.

Whilst a very sad occasion, at the funeral and the wake afterwards I was pleased to meet so many of my wife's family again most of whom I had not seen since my wife and I parted. I was also pleased to see several from my side of the family. I was proud to be there with Somchai and to introduce him to every one as my partner. But whilst I have always led the singing at all the many funerals I have been to. I was unable to sing a single note at my wife's funeral.

THE OTHER GEMINI.

When I started writing these memoirs there was never any thought in my mind about publishing them. It was to keep my mind active, give me something to do if ever I became senile (like my poor mother did) then maybe these would help me. If there were no computers like this one with "Word 2000" (particularly the spell checker) then I would have had to use a typewriter, or write them long hand, then this would never have been written. I have found it very therapeutic. It has kept me busy and the hours just fly by even when I was so ill and could not sleep. At three or four in the morning I would come down to my study and tap away. I highly recommend it to all, once they retire. I am very slow constantly adding and revising. To date I have been many years and many hundreds of hours to get this far, during which time I have thought I would perhaps print off a few copies just for my very close friends, ex lovers and family.

During our trips to Thailand I have continued. We bought an identical computer for less than half the price of the first one. When I bought my first PC I wanted just a word processor to enable me to do just what I am doing now. But I was told it was just as cheap to buy one that had all the many facilities such as e. mail and the Internet. What a good job I did for it has enabled us to keep in touch with family and friends all over the world and so easily. A friend of ours working in Thailand as a professional writer saw what I was doing. I asked him if he would read some of what I had written and give me an opinion. His comment changed my outlook, he said "George you have a very attractive way of writing, you must publish it?"

I have thought very long and hard over several years about whether I should put down everything about my life, my sexuality, my relationships and my sex life into these memoirs. Why do I hesitate? The great majority of my present friends and acquaintances who might read this will not be shocked or disgusted in the slightest. I have never worried about what complete strangers think, like so many people go through life doing. I toyed with the idea of writing two separate books entitled, Gemini One & Gemini Two. Who is it that I am concerned about? And would not want them to see Gemini Two. It's JUST MY FAMILY and family additions yet to be. All I can say is, that this is the WHOLE story of my life and how I have lived it. This is who I am. (I am what I am the song says).I just hope they will understand.

I have up to now put down every thing that I can remember that I have done in my busy life, except about my gay relationships. Those that I have very much loved and been very much loved by. What is wrong with LOVE? Is it wrong for people to love each other? I've never done any thing with anyone I shouldn't have, or with out their consent. I hope people will try to understand. That sex is a small part of one's life. What you can do for your country, for other people and especially for your family is much more important. I could not have done much of what I have done if

I had not had an almost constant loving companionship and a very happy and fulfilled love life.

Since the age of twenty-five, long before I got married I had set up a home with someone to come home to, someone to hold to hug and yes make love with and kiss when I needed to. Why do so many people say it is wrong and immoral if it happens to be two adults of the same sex? Two people who feel totally at ease relaxed and comfortable in each other's company? Where there is no harm done to anyone except perhaps in the minds of those who say. (Misguidedly I think) "that it is a threat to the institution of marriage". I wish someone would explain to me how that can be. So I feel I must continue with this story of my life as I have done up to now, "warts and all". I ask those who feel that they should not read any more to continue and try to understand.

My wife knew about my life style and some of my gay friends before we got married. She knew I had lived with my boy friend in the flat (The Pentagon) into which we moved once we were married. But we did not discuss it, as we should have done. Nobody did and people still do not today. We both wanted to get married, we both wanted children. My wife was twenty-nine, I was thirty-seven. I cannot regret what I did, for if I did it would be to deny our children and our Grandchildren. They were my wife's life. She was a wonderful mother and had every right to be very proud of them, as I still am.

When we were young, unlike almost every adult today we knew very little about homosexuality, it was still against the law. After all I had been attracted to women before and was determined to give up the gay life style. I now know that although I loved her, I was not "in love" with my wife when I married her. But I loved her and continued to support her until she died. I miss her not being there as the mother of our now grown up children. I feel so sorry for them having lost their mother so many years sooner than they should have done. We were together for twenty-one years. How many marriages last that long today?

I hope those who, reading this and finding it difficult to continue, realising that they may have deep-seated prejudice's and traditional beliefs, viewing same-sex relationships as morally and ethically wrong, will carry on reading this memoir. They have read so far and they should by now have an idea of the kind of chap they though I was up until now. I say to them even if you have strong views you should know all you can about things you have strong views about, so please read on.

As I have got older, a political factor has become more and more important to me. Of my family only my eldest son and my wife knew about my conviction for "Gross Indecency" that caused my resignation from the Scout Movement. This is something that I feel strongly about. I'm sure many people do not realise that only a gay men can be charged with this offence. Two heterosexuals having sex in daylight in public, or two lesbians cannot be charged with this offence. I agree that there should be a law to cover something like this. But it should be a law that does not discriminate between heterosexuals and homosexuals. Over the last few years since the election of the "new Labour" government with Tony Blair as prime minister there have been many welcome steps eliminating much of the unfair discrimination. I just hope to live to see the removal of the several others pieces of homophobic legislation that still remain. The attitude of the general public has changed for the better in these last few years, due partly to more favourable publicity and famous people "coming out". or "being outed" At one point not too long ago we had four openly gay cabinet ministers in the government.

The Discrimination.

If your partner of many years is killed in a road accident, where the driver is jailed for dangerous driving there is no compensation claim allowed for same sex partners.

Same sex Partners are not recognised by hospitals as next of kin. You may have shared most of your adult life together, but they will tell you nothing. It will be blood relatives who are given all the information and maybe asked to decide how you are treated and to decide if a life support machine shall be switched off.

We don't even have the right to register a partner's death a partner must vacate the home he or she has contributed to the cost of, if their name is not on the deeds and or in the will despite very many years together they have no claim on the estate. Even if there is a will, you get clobbered for inheritance tax much more than a wife would. Having to sell the home you have built up together None of the major public pension schemes in local government, health or teaching provide benefits for the survivor of same sex couples.

Gay couples are not allowed to adopt, when there are thousands of kids who need love, affection and a home they can call their own. Not a council home where they are at a greater risk of being abused and ill-treated as we have read in the news many times. Single people can adopt. A large percentage of children these days are brought up by a single parent. These children are more likely to be those who are disturbed and would benefit, and would need more than one adult to cope with them. Opponent's and homophobes like dear old Lord Tebbit and his fellow peers and peeress's say, "ask the general public if homosexuals should be allowed to adopt and (he says) they will say no. The public should be asked "do you approve of discrimination?"

The number of male gays who want to adopt would I think be very small, and those who do, would have to go through even more searching interviews and be more suitable than anyone else. But those who qualify should be allowed to adopt. It is a matter of principle and a gross denial of human rights otherwise.

Note made on the 5th Nov 02

Today is a red letter day, The House of commons have voted overwhelmingly by 199 majority that gays should be allowed to adopt and the Tories are in turmoil.

"Homosexuality is not something you decide to be, it is not an illness or something that can be cured, it is just something that you are". That quote was made some years ago by a then almost unknown Tony Blair.

Why is it so wrong to love people of the same sex? The usual answer is that it is "not natural" but most people want to love and be loved.

Conventionally, society says there are two sexes, male and female, and natural relationships only happen between these two categories.

Men and women are expected to play roles as physically dictated. Procreation and the creation of families comprising a father, a mother and children are held up as the ultimate ideal, one that calls for universal heterosexuality. Pressure to achieve this ideal is behind many couples remaining in unhappy marriages and often results in those that remain unmarried into middle age being teased as undesirables, bachelors and spinsters.

Such ideas legitimise heterosexuality as the only viable choice in society.

Heterosexuality is thus not just a preference, it's an ideology that people are supposed to uphold and live by. As something that challenges the dominant social ideology, homosexuality becomes something that's fiercely resisted.

A measure of that resistance is that homosexuality is still widely regarded as a social illness-even though since 1970 the World Health Organisation and leading psychiatrists world- wide have stressed that it is not a mental disorder but a matter of individual "preference" (this last word "preference" is a word I very strongly disagree with). It is not a preference. We have no choice, only that of being celibate.

Human beings should first and foremost be seen as just that, rather than stereotyped in terms of their sexuality.

Sexuality is rather a fluid matter that alters and changes at different times and in different environments.

Take same-sex schools or prisons, both male and female, every one knows that sex goes on, but that then most go on to, or back to, a heterosexual life style.

A young good looking Thai man happily married with two children who had sex with other men but not other women, when asked by me who did he prefer said. "I just like sex".

What does this tell us about what is natural? It suggests that we should understand that love is about more than just sex or sexuality, rather, it is about friendship, companionship and connection.

Although gays have a place in the main steam media they are often portrayed in a negative or absurd fashion.

Male gays with flamboyant outrageous demeanour are taken on as comics to spice up dramas and other shows.

Many think that if a person is not "camp and effeminate" they are not gay.

Scriptwriters and producers involved with news and educational programmes, as well as prime time television dramas should be given more information about homosexuality.

If only seven per cent of the population (male and female) are living a gay life style, that comes to three and a half million people. Then in all fairness seven percent of films and plays should be about gay love, gay romance and gay relationships.

Most of the soaps have included gays from time to time and when we hear about it we watch them. But the vast majority of television songs and films are totally heterosexual, so also are almost all advertisements.

Sexual orientation is a human rights issue. The right to love and to develop a relationship with another human being, regardless of their sexuality is a basic human right.

Education on sexual issues helps only to a certain extent and only among those who are open-minded and willing to listen and understand.

The best way for gay people to change things is for individuals to just "come out" be them-selves, be what they are. The song says "I am what I am".

Already these days the growing and stronger communities of sexual dissidents are paving the way to social acceptance, though full acceptance may be a long way off.

Human relations and human behaviour are infinitely varied. It's not possible to dictate what exactly is right or natural.

We should have the flexibility and openness to accept the rich variety of human possibility and lifestyles. We label people by their sexuality. This with a vast section of the public is incorrect at any particular point in time.

There is a certain amount of homosexuality in most men, Alfred Kinsey in his book Sexual Behaviour in the human male, said that two out of every five men have had a homosexual experience.

Years ago the royal navy was much larger than it is now and the ships were at sea for longer, with no women on board. Being a merchant seaman was very attractive to anyone who preferred all male company, he could visit exotic ports where sexual oppression was much less, or ignored. Many is the stories I have listen to, of the "goings on" of retired "Matloes" and ex merchant seamen now replaced by foreigners. Most of these would not be "gay" as most people perceive gays. They would have a wife and family at home. As well as a "woman" in ports here and there. But also a "boy friend or male mate while at sea". This would all be done very discretely. If it was risky then the flow of adrenaline would heighten the pleasure of the moment. A very close bond of secrecy existed. What they did at sea was put entirely out of their minds when ashore.

Living a largely heterosexual lifestyle does not preclude a man from having sex with a man, if the circumstances are favourable, any more than a man living a gay lifestyle cannot get married and father children. I know from personal experience and have been told by others, that although most woman would prefer their man to be totally faithful., when it come to it, if she is unable to prevent him from "have a little on the side", then she would rather it was with a man than another woman.

For a highly sexed young man whether homosexual or not, quick, anonymous, uncomplicated sex in parks, toilets and cruising places can be a very great relief. If you think a socalled respectable married man would not take the very considerable risk involved you would be wrong. Sex and adrenaline go well together! It is addictive.

We are condemned because they say we are promiscuous. But so are so many heterosexual people, where unlike gays there are a great many more reasons and pressures to stay married. We know many male couples that have been together all their adult lives. But people change and it is "better to have loved and lost than never to have to loved at all".

If it were possible to have a record of every homosexual act of men born in the first half of the twentieth century between 1900 & 1950 including those who have already died, starting from when they were ten years old. (My reason for this is that boys seem to be having sex three or four years earlier than we did and they all know about "gays" these days)

Then we make up a diagram at one end of which we plot all those who never did, or have ever done anything or thought of any thing of a sexual nature during their lifetime with another male. (Usually referred to as straight).

I have been directly involved in the "so called gay scene" for almost sixty years and have always wondered why I was gay and I still do. I have also been blessed or cursed with a very inquisitive nature. My parents used to call me "nosy parker" for I have always asked lots of questions. Based on this my estimate of the percentage of "straights" on the diagram would be only fifty percent. For example, every other male in my survey will have, at some point in their lives had sexual contact with another male to the point of having an erection or a climax, (although many would never admit it, not even to themselves). In my class at my school out of 15 boys the same age, only one would not join in when we frequently had "wanking sessions". Two of us to my certain knowledge lived much of their lives in the gay life style.

Then at the other end of the diagram we plot all those who have found (some as young as ten years old) that they were sexually attracted to other males, a few to their contemporaries, but most to men much older, a father or grand father figure. (Many have told me that they knew for certain that they were gay at that age and some much earlier), those who throughout their lives found it physically impossible to have sex with a female. My estimation of the percentage of this group is three to five percent. These we now call gay.

So now we have over forty percent, some of whom would claim to be bisexual, some transsexual and some transvestites but the majority of this group would have led a seemingly heterosexual life style, with a loving wife and family. They would never admit to anyone that they had ever done anything "gay". A great friend of mine had a partner for some time that told him he was not gay, but that he liked having sex with men.

I have found very much to my surprise how many of those to whom I have spoken have been fifty, sixty, seventy years old and more, when they had their first experience of gay sex. For the most part I am not talking about penetration. (See my section on Sauna's, Cottages, gay pubs, Club's and Cruising areas). There is my reason for my diagram also containing those who lives have ended.

Almost every part of the human body is connected to and controlled by the brain, the genitals very much so. It is quite possible for a lesbian to have sex with a man, to marry have children and suppress her sexuality. But this is where men and women are so different. For a totally gay man at the extreme end of my diagram it is physically impossible.

I read once where a woman managed to tie up a man and had sex with him against his will. She was accused of Rape. I can't remember the outcome, but what I do know is, that the man would have been heterosexual, or bisexual for if he had been totally gay, rape would have been impossible.

On the subject of rape we hear very little about male rape.

Understandably so for often the victim is gay, he would quite likely have been assaulted in a gay cruising area. The police and the general public would be unsympathetic. It's only human nature for it to be even more of a humiliation for a man to be raped than a woman. Some will say "so what" it was only what he was looking for. Sexual   attraction between two people is just as important what ever their sexuality. Others will say well it can't affect him as much as it would a woman, I know from accounts I have read in the gay press and from several that I have spoken to that the   permanent damage and the trauma is, if anything worst. How many of those who have committed suicide in prison were raped?

Here's an example that is just about as "unjust" as the "system" can get.

We have two boys in their early teens. We call one boy Gay and the other Het. Then we have two adults who could be any thing from 18 to 80 and we call one of them F standing for foolish and the other we call P for pervert or paedophile. Gay will have had no doubts that he is gay from an early age. He quite likely has a "crush" on a male adult. Lets say it turns out to be F. Gay will most likely be the one who does the seducing. They have sex. Gay might even be penetrated but he will have come to no harm unlike girls apparently do if they have sex too early. He will be exhilarated, fulfilled (excuse the pun). He will consider he has become a man. He will have lost his virginity and will feel just like other boys do when they lose theirs, (and why shouldn't he?) Because he is young he may feel there is nothing to be secretive about. It was all perfectly natural to him, what he had many times dreamt about. He may tell people about it, or write it up in his diary. Then if the affair comes to light F will be in very serious trouble. No notice what ever will be taken of what Gay might say. "They will throw the book at him". and his life will be ruined.

Now we come to Het, a boy who is or will be heterosexual, often from a children's home, who is seduced and regularly abused suffering anal rape by P, a person whom he respected in a position of authority often a Roman Catholic Priest or member of his own family. Het will go thought unbelievable torment, humiliation, shame and self-disgust that will increase as he gets older, to the point where it ruins his life, a life that he might and sometimes does take, committing suicide still telling no one. F is far more likely to be caught than P.

Hear are the names of just a few famous gays now deceased.

Alexander the great (read "the Persian Boy by" Mary Renault) Michelangelo, Leonardo da Vinci, King Edward the III, Prince Albert, (Eddy heir to the throne.) Lord Byron,Oscar Wild, Cecil Rhodes, Ivor Novello, Sir Michael Tippett, Evelyn Waugh, Noel Coward, Mongomery Cliff, Benjamin Britten & his lover Peter Pears, W.H.Auden, Tennessee Williams, Angus Wilson, Anthony Blunt, Quentin Crisp, Gilbert Harding, James Dean, Tom Driberg MP. Terrance Higgins, T.E. Lawrence, Christopher Isherwood, Derek Jarman, Freddie Mercurty, Gianni Versarsace, Paulo Pasolini, Andy Warhol, Sir John Gielgud, Nigel Hawthorn, Rudolf Nureyev, Diaghilev and Najinisky, Ralph Reader, Frankie Howard, Dirk Bogarde, Rock Hudson, Kenneth Williams, George Michael, Alun Turin and very many more. Very strong rumours and some evidence exist about Lord Kitchener, Lord Louie Mountbatten, Lord Montgomery and Lord Baden Powell. Two others that I have mentioned, not famous but who have been a great influence in my life Dr. Sydney Watson and my singing tutor Harold Mead.

Gilbert Harding was for many years "on the box" in the early years of television more than any other person, his face was universally known. He was a very brilliant man. He was a very famous man. He was a very popular man. But he was also a very very unhappy man. Interviewed by Alan Freeman he said. "He wished he were dead". He said, "His doctor had told him if he did not cut down his drinking by half he would be dead within a year". He then said, "do you know what I did?" I doubled it!

Gilbert was gay, in the days when it was illegal to be so. With in one month of that interview he was dead. The "man in the street" could find a companion in certain places, so long as he was discrete. Gilbert could not. The whole country was, through ignorance, very homophobic. The BBC was more Homophobic than most.

Alun Turin many will not have heard of, which is typical of the discrimination that is dealt out to those who do not conform. He was, during the war personally responsible for the successful out come of many of the major operations that took place, more so than Churchill himself. He alone with his brilliant brain broke the secrets of the German Enigma code machine thus considerably shortening the war and saving countless lives. But he was gay and did not see why he should make a secret of it. He was recommended for the highest honour at the end of the war, but was only given the OBE by Churchill who was known to be homophobic. He entertained a rent boy, who rob him, he reported it, was interviewed by a single policeman to whom he admitted the facts. He was then charged with Gross Indecency and convicted. He then later committed suicide at a reasonably young age by eating a poisoned apple, thus the name Apple, given to the well-known computer company. He was the inventor of the first computer. Many people have tried to get him posthumously recognised for what he did. All that exists is a small street named after him.

(Authors recent note;- I was pleased to see that Alun was very favourably placed in the list of 100 Great Britons)

They gave me a medal for killing some men "Said the soldier"
But when I loved one they gave me a dishonourable discharge!

MY VERY FIRST EXPERIENCE OF SEX

Was at the age of eleven, I was in my Cub Scout uniform for the last time. I was with a boy who was a little older than I. We had just left the Scout meeting where I had been accepted into the troop and were walking though the woods. He jumped up onto a fallen tree and started masturbating (I didn't know that word then of course). I saw this white stuff come shooting out of his penis, "how did you do that? I asked". It was some months (rubbing my self sore many times) before I experienced my "first time". I have talked to many very much younger friends and I realise that things are very different today. We until we left school at the age of fourteen had nothing to do with girls. The word gay meant colourful, happy and outgoing. We had never heard of the word homosexual or queer, if we had we would not have known what it meant. All boys in those days had to wear shorts, until the day they left the village school, at the age of fourteen.

There was a great deal of "group masturbation" we thought nothing of it but made sure no girl or adult saw us, the risk was part of the thrill. It would happen in the school classroom occasionally during class time. There were fifteen boys and fifteen girls, all the boys sat together. In the scouts, particularly when camping a whole patrol of eight would sleep in one ex army bell tent. The scoutmaster and his wife slept in a ridge tent and at night after "lights out" for the troop, if the younger members of the patrol had gone to sleep, we would watch the silhouette of the scoutmasters wife getting undressed and we would have a competition to see who could climax first. It was always with those of the same age group. Nothing ever happened other than what we called "Bashing the Bishop", (masturbating). One day when walking home from school, some older boys strangers to me shouted. "Whip it in, whip it out and wipe it!" I recall very clearly thinking about this, surely they must have meant, "Whip it out, wipe it, then whip it in". It was a long time, even after consulting with my friends that we worked out what it meant.

There were dire warnings, a couple I understand still persists to day, such as "you will grow hairs in the middle of your hand" and "You will go blind". These we did worry about, often closely examining the palms of our hands. There was no sex education at all, no books or pamphlets of any kind mentioning the subject. If there had been I'm sure someone would have discovered them and they would have been eagerly sort after and passed around. No adult, schoolteacher, scout leader, parent or priest, ever mentioned the subject. Baden Powell's book "Scouting for boys" (which meant much more to me than the bible) was the only one, it said quite clearly not to do it. He called it "self abuse", he stated, "it was unclean, unmanly" illustrating that only a cigarette-smoking weakling would do such a thing, telling us to have a cold shower if we were tempted. Well I'm sure there may be some, if they had a low sex drive, who could refrain and would manage with what I believe is called "nocturnal emissions". " Wet dreams". I had those too. But for me and many of my contemporaries you might as well have told us to stop going for a pee.

My next experience was very soon after leaving school on my working visit to Scotland. Living in the cottages on the 'shooting lodge' estate were several boys of my own age. We quickly became friends and when I was not working we would play about together. Being a strange speaking Sassenach (English) I was bound to get a "Ragging"; this took place in a hayloft. They held me down on the floor and one of them said. "Lets get is wee winkle oot". They got my small penis out and then to my surprise and disgust at the time one of them sucked it. It was very many years, some years after I had become involved in gay sex with adults, that I experienced oral sex again. These boys had also recently just left school and like myself were now wearing long trousers, there were girls about, but at the age of 14 we had no interest in them but went about together most of the time.

Practically all the boys who left the village school at the same time as myself were either in the scouts, the choir or both, so we continued to see a great deal of each other. Quite a number of these I would get together with for mutual sexual relief, but usually only two of us at a time. Very little was said about what we were doing and nothing at all to any one else. We talked a lot about girls and now and again one would boast that he had, "done it". I felt very envious but did not know whether to believe him or not. The village of Burnham was a mile away in one direction. The layout of Hitcham Village was very long and narrow with the Church, the old School House (the Scout Headquarters) and our house at one end and the nearest houses where all my friends lived was over a mile away in the other direction. So whilst I saw all my friends at school, scouts and choir meetings I rarely saw them at other times or in the street. Compared to today, we were all several years behind today's kids in sexual experience, very naive and I, a little more naive than most.

I must have been about sixteen when I came into possession of a magazine called "Health and Efficiency". It was about naturism. It showed full frontal pictures of nudists. I would keep this carefully hidden only getting it out at bedtime and looking at it during my regular "going to sleep masturbation". I was puzzled that I got more of a "turn on" from looking at the penis's of the men, than at the virginas of the ladies. It was also about this time; I found that most of my friends no longer wanted to "play around", I wanted to, but they, without saying any thing tactfully avoided my advances. There was one time when a number us both boys and girls this time were larking around together and it was suggested that there be a kiss chase. This involved the girls chasing the boy of their choice and kissing him. A girl named Joy, a big girl caught me, not fat but big. I ended up sitting on her knee being kissed. That was the first time I had been kissed on the lips by anyone. I got an erection.

The next two years were the busiest of my life up until then. The war started and there was no social life for me to meet up with girls. The scouts, work, night school and the church took up all my time. I still masturbated two, three, sometimes four times a day. I would try not to and would avoid going to the toilet as long as I could, for I would when there, sometimes do it again. I had been in the RAF several months when I first heard the expression "brown hatters". On listening further to the conversation I gathered it meant men who had sex with men, Homo's (homosexuals) it was the first time I'had ever heard the word. On further tactful questioning and learning exactly what these "Homo's" did, I was genuinely just as disgusted and shocked as they were. Nothing was further from my mind at that time that I could ever be like that.

I LOSE MY VIRGINITY

As I have already mentioned, at 17 there were three things uppermost in my mind. To go aboard, fly in an airplane and lose my virginity, with a girl of course. The first two I achieved very soon after becoming a corporal and ending up in Southern Rhodesia. It took a little while for me to realise that, with sixty thousand RAF (men only no WAAF). In a country with a population of sixty thousand white people, I was not going to get a white girl. At weekends we would go in the liberty wagon (as it was called) to the capital Harare (then called Salisbury) a journey taking about an hour.

There one weekend I met a girl whose father had been a Scotsman, but her mother had been black. Her name was Ann; she was about the same age as my self. I lost my virginity that evening but I felt that she must have lost hers some time before. She was very experienced. Most of the men on the camp went with girls like Ann, but with a different one each time. I don't think I fell in love with her, but I think she did with me. I was very fond of her. She was very poor, living in just one small room. She did have a job but I gave her some money each time I saw her and

I don't think she went with any others during the year that I was with her before I was posted to another camp many miles away. There was one occasion; we were training for a weight lifting competition. Oscar, my sports officer had trained us and said "Now I know some of you have girl friends in the town, don't get into bed with them before the show". Now I rarely had sex with her less than three times if I only spent the evening with her and twice that if I spent the night. I made love to her twice that afternoon and then did my personal best at the Competition that evening. Some time later I was then posted to the other end of the country.

It was about year later that I was able to get a "flip" (we called it) a flight with one of the instructor pilots back to Salisbury. We only had about a couple of hours on the ground, just time enough for me to go and see Ann. When I got there she was out but her room was open. I went in and waited hoping she would return before I would have to get back to the airfield. While waiting I noticed there was evidence of a baby in the room. Just before I thought I would have to leave she returned and she had a baby with her. The first words I said to her were "Whose baby?" She said "Mine". The baby, a boy was whiter than her but still recognizable as coloured "He's nine months old" she said, She guessed my next question and answered it before I could ask it. "Yes it's yours," she said.

My immediate feeling was one of guilt. But during the next few minutes she convinced me that she was quite happy. She now had a coloured boy friend, he was in the army and supporting her. He accepted the baby. She accepted my situation and that there was nothing I could do. They were both happy that her son was whiter than if her new boy friend had been the father. I found that difficult to understand, but talking to colleagues the fact was confirmed, that that was the case with many of these girls. Naturally I have though about them many times. I wondered if she is still alive and the thought that he would be coming up to sixty now. I can't remember if she told me his name, if she did then I can't remember it. My one slight regret, I have no photograph of them both, I had a little camera but I didn't have it with me that day.

During my last months in the RAF my thoughts were increasingly, about getting home, getting a job, finding a girl friend and getting married. I bought several presents that I promised my self I would give to my future wife. At last I was "on the boat, on the way home". Our first stop was Mombassa. We were given several hours shore leave to spend touring the town.

MY FIRST GAY THOUGHT

A very good looking native boy, about nineteen or twenty came up to me and said, "would you like to have my sister boss?, my sister very pretty". So I went with him, we did the deal and I "had" his "sister". When I came out he was waiting for me, I thought he's going to ask me for some more money but no, he asked if I had enjoyed his "sister", I said it was OK. It seemed he wanted to talk to me; we sat down on a seat overlooking the docks and we chatted. His English was broken but quite extensive. He asked me all about England. "Had I got a girl friend?". I told him no not yet.

He sat quite close to me his hand was on my knee and he was looking straight into my eyes and I somehow knew he wanted sex with me. I had just had sex with his "so called sister", but I had an erection and I realised I also wanted him. I was totally confused. I said I had to get back to the boat this I did in a bit of a daze. We sailed soon after, if we had not I am sure I would have gone back to look for him. For some days I worried over this. I'm sure somehow he must have known I also wanted him. How did he know? What was the matter with me? Something happened that helped to take my mind off him. I had a terrible itching in my pubic hairs. I told a close friend who said, "let me have a look, yes" he said "You've got crabs" (pubic hair lice) I was horrified, 'don't worry" he said, "All you have to do is shave all the hairs off". That was in the days before Quenella (an ointment that does the trick). The problem is once the hairs started to grow again it was like walking with a man's stubble haired chin between your legs.

MY FIRST HEART BREAK.

It was some time after getting home, settling down, going back to work and taking up singing lessons that I met another girl named Ann, she was still in the land army. She was from Wales and she sang and played the piano. I would practise my singing while she accompanied me. I saw her as often as I could which was not a great deal, we worked long hours, I was having singing lessons and I went back to night school for a while. However I took her home, introduced her to mother and went all the way down to Wales to meet her family. We talked about getting engaged. I thought I was in love for the first time. Looking back, I could see that she, like my self was not a virgin and I believe many times she must have wanted sex. It was not that I was "old fashioned". She was a white girl, not like the others, the one who was going to be my wife. You didn't have sex with your fiance ? before marriage in those days. We had no date on which we planned to marry. I had no money and we would have had nowhere to live.

I then discovered that she was seeing friends of mine on some of the days I was unable to see her, going to dances and pubs. I was then told; by a very close friend that she had had sex with one of my friends. I confronted her, we had a row, she admitted it and that was it, we broke up. She tried very hard to get me to forgive her, even going to see my mother to enlist her help. Mother did try, but for me that was it, I was very bitter and hurt. It would be many years before I touched another girl and that was my wife on our wedding night and she was a virgin. That was when

I was twenty-five, I did not get married until I was thirty-seven. I have often wondered if any of what happened in those years between would have happened, if I had married the second Ann.

For almost five years after that, I just concentrated on work; singing and scouting, that's when I produced a scout play, took it to the hospital at Cliveden and as a result started the scout group there. I started my own business and I learnt the meaning of the word sublimation.

MY FIRST VISIT TO A GAY "COTTAGE"

(A Cottage is a public toilet, where men "cruise" other men for sex. So-called) because many of them had a pitched, tiled or thatched roof.

One day I was in a toilet in Slough, standing at the urinals urinating, when a man next to me put his hand over and was about to catch hold of my penis. I was instinctively furious, he saw this and run out otherwise I would have hit him. This incident played on my mind for some time. As a result I found myself back in this same toilet and hoping that it would happen again and if it had I would not have hit him. It was in this same toilet where I met and started talking to my very first gay friend, his name was Steven.

I don't think any thing actually happened not even when, after speaking to Steven for some time we went back to his sister's house. We just sat and talked. He subsequently became a very great friend and still is to this day. I was very naive, whilst talking to him I remembered the young man in Mombassa and realised that I might be bisexual or even homosexual. Strange as it might seem I was not greatly worried about this at that time, but wanted to meet someone.

MY FIRST TIME WITH A MALE PROSTITUTE.

Soon after this, late one Saturday evening I went to Piccadilly Circus, as I had heard that this was the place to go. Most of my sexual experiences up until then had been with females of that profession. I thought the thing to do was to find a male equivalent. I was very soon solicited; by a young good looking man. He took me to a cheap hotel where we spent the night. I must have enjoyed what happened for in the morning whilst we were both still in bed I told him I wanted to see him again. He agreed but he said he needed cigarettes, would I settle up with him, he would pop out to get some and then come back to bed with me (it was still early Sunday morning). As he got to the door he look back at me and said. "Do you trust me?" I said. "Yes". Then he said. "Would I mind if he wore my coat as it was cold out side". I said. "OK". The minute that door closed I knew I had made the first of many similar mistakes in my life. But I was naked and in bed what could I do?

Despite what he had done I still wanted to see him again, it was not difficult to find him, he was still wearing the coat a not very expensive one, he made some excuse, I said. "OK you can keep the coat but can we go some where for a short time". This time I did not pay him until we were about to leave the small hotel to which he had taken me. Then I said, "that session will cover the cost of the coat" and "Can I still see you again?" He was somewhat disgruntled and did not seem too keen and then he said. "Yes, if you give me a fiver now". I took out a five-pound note then started to tear it in half. He protested strongly, but I gave him half and said. "See you" and walked off. The next time I saw him I bought him a coffee then he said. "Shall we go to" (he mention the small hotel) I said. No I "don't think so". I gave him the other half of the note and left him. That was the day I realised that except for the ones I fell in love with. The second time with anyone was never as good.

During this time I fought a great deal with my conscience, resolving to stop what I was doing, change the way I was thinking and what I was thinking about. There was no help what so ever, nothing in print, never anything on the media and no telephone help lines. Only my one friend Steven and a few others like him that I had now met. But they were no help at all towards my resolution for they had not only accepted "the way they were" but seemed very happy about it. I decided to go and see the "family doctor" Dr. Summers. I went to his surgery. There were only a couple of patience's in the waiting room, the first one was in and out in a short time, the next had been in for twenty minutes when I suddenly got up and rushed out. It would have been a big mistake; he was the epitome of a typical "red blooded British army colonel" a very large man with a loud voice and an Eton college accent, about as heterosexual as they come I would think. He was close to and fond of my mother and family. And he would probably have said. Pull your self-together my boy and grow up".

I tried very hard to bury myself in my work, scouting and singing. I would be "on the go" from seven in the morning till midnight seven days a week. But then, in some of us the sex drive is very strong. Looking back I realise that I have always been addicted to sex. Those addicted to tobacco, drink, drugs or gambling (which unlike the above is self inflicted and can be cured) will know what I mean. I started to mix more and more with those that I reluctantly admitted to my self I was like, but only on a Saturday evening. There was a pub in Windsor called The Ship, that was where "men who went with men" would go, together with men who went with other men for money, such as some of the local Guardsmen stationed locally and in the Castle. I told my father, a former guardsman who had been stationed there I was going to Windsor for a drink; he said, "Steer clear of the Ship son, that's where the queers go". I wondered had he guessed?

Occasionally I would go to London, there were very few if any "gay bars" as such, only a few clubs tucked away in small side streets usually on the first floor, or in a basement with just a plain unmarked entrance door known only to those who knew where to go. You had to be a member and sign in each time you went. To become a member you had to be introduced by an existing member. Homosexual acts of any kind, even in private were against the law. A law that was rigorously enforced if one was caught. Almost every week the papers would contain reports of those that had been caught, convicted and sent to prison. So perhaps you can imagine the atmosphere, one of very relaxed gaiety, (I've just this second realised that's why we evenually called ourselves gay) a few of the very "Camp" ones (whom I vowed not to become like) would "let their hair down". Almost every one there, even the effeminate ones would be what are termed as "in the closet". Leading double lives, having secrets from their families, unable to set up home with a partner. They could only get relief from their pent up sexual energy by taking huge risks, going to certain toilets and cruising areas, where many would be caught by the police, or beaten up by "Queer bashers". So you can see that once inside one of these clubs, which only existed in the large cities, where many had had to travel long distances and could only go occasionally, it was a totally relaxed and happy place, unlike anything that exists today. It was electric!

These clubs were only open until eleven o/clock, so people would arrange bottle parties. There were always several being arranged, all you had to do was decide which one to go to. I would invariably meet someone about my own age, go home with him, arrange to meet again, think about him all week, then meet him again on the following Saturday, but "second time" was never the same.

STANLEY.

I met Stanley in a gay bar in Brighton and we got on well together and mainly from his part to start with we started to see a lot of each other. He was very good looking a few years younger than I. He was very popular with a large circle of friends. I was very flattered that he wanted me. He had a very comfortable flat in London and never seemed short of money. I asked him what he did for a living but never seemed to get a straight answer. I enjoyed his company very much and started to see him and sleep with him as often as I could, but many times he was unable to see me in the evenings.

After a month or so I pressed him to tell me where he worked and if I could ring him there if the need arose. Then he gave me one of the first big shocks of my gay life. He told me he was a high-class male prostitute with just a few regular rich and famous clients, most of who he did not know or had ever seen. There was a "Pimp" a well spoken well dressed one who would pick him up in a large car with "smoked windows". He would be blind folded and driven around for some time so that he could not tell where he was. It would always be late at night, and before getting out of the car he would have to wear a pair of dark glasses that were impossible to see though.

The place he was taken to would be usually the same he thought. He was led to a dark bedroom where the clients were mostly fat and old. Sometimes the room would be lit, then the client would be naked and wearing a hood or a mask. On these occasions he would be asked to use a whip. He said he had to do anything and let them do any thing to him with-in reason. He was told that if he were to try to see or recognise the client, his life might be in danger. 50 pounds was his fee for each visit. Three or four times what he could have made in those days if he had a good job. He usually did two or three "jobs" a week.

I of course was horrified, but being the "do gooder" that I have always been, instead of walking out on him, I tried to get him to give up his "way of lif" and get a ordinary job. He was I believe in love with me. I was apparently what is called in the "trade", "his bit of mess" and when I said you either give up what you are doing or give me up, he promised to give it a try. I got him a job at Selfridges in Oxford Street. It lasted one week. We lasted another month or so together then we split up. I saw him again about five years later he looked 10 years older. He told me. "If you sell your self for sex you lose the joy of sex" I felt sorry for him.

ERNIE

I first saw Ernie when he was a rent boy in one of the gay pubs in Earls Court. I noticed him because he was only about 16 at the time he was always in the same pub and was I was told, the boy friend of the landlord. I next saw him about ten years later in Brighton. He was no longer a rent boy but was working. I took him out sailing and unlike so many others over the years he really liked it and he sailed with me often. He fell in love with me and we had a short relationship. I particularly remember friends of his saying. "What have you done to Ernie, we have never seen him look so happy his eyes are shining when he looks at you" At the time the song at the top of the charts was. "Bright Eyes Burning Like Fire". But I was, at the time in love with Michael. My children were too young to sail far in one go. I was going to sail to Ramsgate. It was Ernie's hometown. He crewed for me. The family came on board. Ernie came back to the boat late that night very drunk.

RODNEY

RODNEY My FIRST MALE LOVER (Seven years)

Through Steven I met Rodney, he was only just eighteen at the time. He was bright and very intelligent having been to grammar school and what he did not know about gays and the gay life, "was not worth knowing", he was just naturally homosexual and told me he had known that he was since being a small boy. He used to "baby sit" for my friend Steven's sister. So I saw him from time to time and always enjoyed talking to him. He was not obviously gay in any way, but all his family and friends knew and accepted the fact, I envied him that. Some time later he told me that he had fallen in love with me almost the first day that he saw me, that was 7-7-52, (seven was always my lucky number) I was thirty years old.

We would go up to London on a Saturday evening in my car, where he would show me gay clubs that I did not know about. Then he would sit in the car while I went in. He was under twenty-one and looked it. He was too young to be admitted. There was not a great deal of Homophobia as such, people just did not know very much about us, or just how many of us there were. There was no Gay press, there was never any thing written about us in the Media, only reports of arrests and convictions, quite briefly and never in the headlines, unless it was someone well know like a vicar or magistrate. Most people did not yet have televisions and if they did, it would never have been mentioned on "the box". We were underground. Then the Kinsey Report was published which stated, following a great deal of research, that thirty per cent of men at some point in their lives had had sexual relations with another male, to the point of climax.

Then there were the court cases involving my namesake Lord Montagu of Beaulieu the premiere peer of England. On the first case he was found not guilty, but on the second together with Pitt Rivers and Michael Wildeblood, were found guilty and sent to prison. They were convicted on the evidence of two gay, consenting airmen, both of whom were adults. It was a totally victimless "crime" and a deliberate persecution of Lord Edward by the police, who "browbeat" the two airmen into giving evidence for the prosecution, giving them immunity from prosecution.

This case was a turning point for gays and directly resulted in the disapproval of the public and the eventual change in the law. A significant factor being that Peter Wildeblood admitted his sexuality and was the first to "come out" as a gay man. I identified with and admired Peter. Born the same year as myself. I enjoyed very much reading his book. "Against the Law" (The classic Account of a Homosexual in 1950s Britain)

During the summer I would drive to Brighton for the day on a Sunday, or sometimes for the weekend, Brighton being one of the most "gay" places outside London. There were several Gay pubs and clubs. On the beach just where Brighton ends and Hove begins there was, in those days and had been for many years apparently, a "men only" part just between two breakwaters. Seeing that most heterosexual men would go to Brighton with a girl friend or would be looking for one, this beach was, on a good day very full and every one was "gay". Strange as it may seem in those days the authorities were totally unaware of this, we would hold hands and cuddle (but no more than that) it was wonderful. Then in the town were guest house's owned by "gays", all the rooms had double beds, where of course no questions were asked. I always looked forward to going to Brighton.

Rodney had a problem with his big toe. He had to go into hospital where they had to break it and reset it. It surprised me that he had to be there for over a month. I visited him regularly to find him sitting on the bed or chair with a spike down through the middle of his toe and a cork on the end of it. He was very bored. One day I saw someone doing tapestry, they showed me how easy it was and told me it was a very therapeutic and time passing hobby. I thought just the very thing for Rodney. I bought four small sample pieces about six Inches Square. He finished them all before he was discharged and said he enjoyed doing them. Sometime later I thought I must find a use for these. Then I had an idea. I made two more the same size with my crest that I had carved onto the backs of my dining room chairs. I had twelve pieces of glass made, six of them an eighth of an inch larger all round. Then had them laminated together. The next step was to make six frames in oak, mount the six tapestries and there I had six very permanent tablemats, where the glass was level with the top of the frames. That was over fifty year ago and they have been used almost every day since.

Rodney being in hospital for that length of time was a problem for me, I was unfaithful. The result was that I caught a sexually transmitted disease. Gonorrhoea was very common in those pre "Aids" days among both straight and gay people. Most people that were unfortunate to catch it went quietly to a special clinic, where they received (very anonymously) an injection of penicillin and all was well. Once infected with this problem, it takes about six to nine days before you find out about it. In men this takes the form of a small yellow discharge from the penis. On one of my visits to see Rodney we had a kiss and a cuddle in the linen cupboard. He also gave me oral sex. That evening I was horrified to find that I had caught my first "dose" of s.t.d. My first thought was, Bloody hell! Rod will have VD in his stomach.

Dr. Osmond Frank (Four times Mayor of Maidenhead & Stanley Spencer

Rushing for advice to my "friend' Steven I was told to go and see a Dr. Osmond Frank in Maidenhead. My friend telephoned him and explained the situation. He was told to tell me to go to his clinic and to wait until after the last patient had been seen. I saw the Doctor several times while I was waiting, he saw me and smiled reassuringly, I think he must have seen that I was very nervous. He was about fifty, still quite handsome with red hair. At last my turn came, I went in and sat down in front of his desk. I told him of my problem and my fears, he laughed. Then he told me something that I should have known if I had stopped to think about it having done some study on Anatomy and Physiology. The acid juices in the mouth, such as Saliva, Pancreas and Bile, are very potent and kill most germs. So we chatted and he asked me all about myself in such a way that I knew that He was gay. Then he got up and said. "Follow me" and took me to the other side of the room where there were medical instruments etc., He said. "Drop your trousers and let's have a look". He gave me an injection of penicillin, he then became affection-ate, dropped his own trousers and we had sex.

Soon after Rodney was discharged from Hospital he was called up to do his National Service. So I saw very little of him for some time. Meanwhile Doctor Frank had ("taken a shine to me") as the saying goes. He invited me to dinner at his house. I was very flattered, he was a very well educated man and I was even more flattered when he picked me up as arranged in a Rolls Royce! I expected to be taken to the large house part of which was his surgery, but no, we drove to about half way between Maidenhead and Bray, then into the driveway of an old beautiful large house on the banks of the Thames with a well-kept garden where the lawn swept down to the river. He took me all over the house, that was full of antiques and oil paintings. We had a drink in the "drawing room", which to add to my surprises, was served by a butler.

When we were called into the dinning room, (the only room I had not yet seen) by the butler, there was the dinning room table, about twelve feet long in heavy oak in the "Cromwellian' style". The table was "laid" for two only, one at each end with real silver cutlery and candelabra. The table was very old the top had been scrubbed throughout its life so that it was an unusual white colour. This table was to be the inspiration for my own oak dining room table, for which I had the oak and was about to build. We talked a great deal, I told him about my singing, he said. "I should love to hear you sing and with your permission, I should like to accompany you". I had seen the grand piano. He was also a pianist.

It was very plain to me that he was a very rich man and no ordinary Doctor. I made enquiries and found that he was very well known, almost famous. He was the only man in the very long history of Maidenhead who had been Mayor of the town for four years running, 1946 to 1950. He was married and had grown up children; his wife was a senior Psychiatric Consultant at Windsor hospital and he had fallen in love with me!

I must admit, I allowed myself to be seduced by this man; he took me around to places I could never have gone to and have never been to since. To the Ritz and the Junior Carlton Club of which he was a member. He also took me to several art galleries (which I have been to since). He taught me to improve my speech, my table manners, which piece of cutlery to use and when, the correct way to use a soupspoon. This was the time when I was asked by Dr. Sydney Watson to sing the solos at a coral concert with a large choir and orchestra. I needed a dinner jacket; he bought it for me at Simpson's in Piccadilly London.

I had designed my own crest that I intended to carve onto the backs of my dinning room chairs. He said he wanted to buy me a ring and got me to have the size taken at a jeweller's. Then a few days later he presented me with a gold signet ring containing a large bloodstone with my crest engraved, so that it could be used as a seal. Some years later I was cleaning and freeing with oil a wood vice in my workshop, closing and opening it when I felt and heard a slight bump. I thought nothing of it until later in the day I noticed the bloodstone was completely shattered. I intended to have it repaired, left it in a drawer in my house, where it was, together with several other valuables, stolen by a guest during a house party.

This was a period following the trials of Lord Edward Montagu, Pitt-Rivers, and Peter Wildeblood. The police were very active in hunting down gays. A regular (cruising) meeting place would be the local "cottage". The police made very good use of this by hiding in the loft, making a small hole at just the right spot, then spying on those down below. Then they would arrest any one they recognised as gay even if they were not doing anything other than just standing there and not peeing. They would be charged with soliciting and convicted of "Gross indecency". This would be fully reported in the local, press and sometimes the national press so that the man's family would be devastated, often destroying a marriage and costing him his job. There would be several cases each week in just the Slough area; sometime we heard that the man had committed suicide, if this was reported in the press, then often there was no mention of the court case, which would have been the reason for him taking his own life.

One of the most underhanded things the police would do, would be to use a good looking young policeman in civilian clothes, who would act as a provocateur. Tempting those in the toilets, or sometimes in the other cruising places such as the parks and the riverside watched by two other policemen also in plain clothes. These two would then make an arrest, when the young one was successful. Fortunately all this is now not allowed.

My relationship with Osmond Frank lasted about six months during which time he took me to Brighton where we stayed at the Metropole Hotel. Another time we had planed to go to Brighton again to meet some friends, when at the last minute he was unable to go. He pleased me a great deal by telling me to go alone and take the "Rolls". He was very much "in love with me". I was very fond of him but I did not love him, I was in love with Rodney. I felt very guilty, letting myself be "spoilt" by him. I still feel guilty about that period as I write, but I have promised myself that I will put it all down, and not be "economical with the truth". I don't know how I would have got out of this situation, if something tragic had not happened.

STANLEY SPENCER

One day I went to see Osmond and was shown by the butter on to the lawn to wait for him. There I saw a small man with glasses, oil painting at an easel. He did not see me, or if he did he took no notice. I watched him and could tell that he was a very good artist. When Osmond came out of the house he introduced me telling me this was Stanley Spencer. I had never heard of him then but I was told he will be very famous one day and his pictures including this one will be very valuable. The picture he was painting was that of a woman's hand, a rather fat hand with several expensive looking rings on. There was a large red flower right in the foreground. Osmond told me that it was a picture of his wife's hand. Some time later he took me to Cookham where we went into a tiny cottage and were taken straight upstairs. There, stretched around two of the walls was what I now know was the not yet finished "Christ Preaching at Cookham Regatta" (1953) I remember Stanley saying. "If they ever clean this picture they will ruin it I have been cooking in here".

There in the corner was a gas ring and cooking utensils. I have seen this picture again since the artist died, at the Cookham gallery. It was never finished. Spencer died a few years after I met him. Despite seeing several illustrated books of his paintings and going to an exhibition of his work at the Tate gallery, I have never seen "the painting of the hand of Osmonds wife" nor do I know what became of it

The local chief inspector of police for Maidenhead must have been informed that Osmond was gay. Yes there were those that were gay that were also police informers. It was, as I say a very dangerous time for us. We knew that this inspector was out to "get him". He was charged with sexual assault on a boy of seventeen. I knew Osmond well by this time and that there was no possibility that he was guilty. Yes the boy was a patient of his and yes he did, wearing a surgical glove put a finger up the boy's rectum but that is what doctors often have to do; they massage the prostate gland, which gives them a small sample of fluid from the penis for analysis.

It was an agonising time before the case came to court. I was glad I had not broken off our relationship as I had seriously thought about doing. We had to be very careful where we met now, but we did and I was glad to be able to give him some comfort and relief from his torment. The prosecutions case was, that what he did was not required and therefore was an indecent assault. Sir Peter Rawlinson (the top QC. In the country at the time) was the defence council. The case lasted several days and it was plastered all over the national papers. The jury after an agonizing time failed to agree. The case was put forward to another date, for it to be all gone though again. This time the result was exactly the same the jury were split. Then the prosecution withdrew its case.

Poor Osmond was a broken man in spirit and financially, he had aged ten years, the case cost so much he had to sell his beautiful Thames side house. He moved into the house where his surgery was and carried on for a while, but he had lost most of his patients. I felt so sorry for him. I telephoned him but he did not seem to want to see me, saying it was best in case suspicion fell on me. I tried again several time's but got the clear impression he had told his secretary to tell me he was not in. I was hurt but I understood. My hatred of the police at that time was like fire.

Some years later, I wanted some memories of him, so I took my camera along to the main road bridge over the river Thames, there on the "Cookham" corner is a bronze plaque with a mark commemorating and showing the height of the record flood during the winter of 1946-1947, signed by The Mayor. Osmond Frank. Then I went to the new Maidenhead town hall and there, in the very impressive entrance hall in gold letters on many large boards are the names of all the previous Mayors of the town over the last hundred years or so. Dr. Osmond Frank is the only one that appears four times consecutively. There was a commissionaire in uniform who looked if he had been doing the job for many years, so I told him "I knew Dr. Frank" and asked him. "Did he know him and where he was now?" "Yes" he said. "I knew him very well, a fine gentleman he went to Jamaica and he died there a few years ago".

CHRIST PREACHING AT COOKHAM REGATTA -STANLEY SPENCER (1891-1959)

Rod and I move into a bedsit in London

When Rodney was half way though his national service he moved from Catterick to Woolwich in London so we were able to see each other more often. Then he found that he could now "live out" from the barracks. We looked around and found a cheap furnished room in Colherne Road Earls Court. We bought bits and pieces and made it into the first "home of our own" that either of us had ever had. I would drive to Slough Railway Station and leave my car parked in the road right out side. There were no yellow lines or parking signs in those days. Catching a fast train to Paddington, then the underground, I would be home in just an hour. We were both very happy together. We would get up at six in the morning, him to the army, me to work.

On Sunday morning if Rod was not on duty we would have a lie-in (first time in my life) until nearly lunchtime. Then we would go for a drink to the pub at the end of the road. A typical London pub called the Colherne. Although this was a "straight" pub in the week in those days, we discovered that only on a Sunday morning there were quiet a number of "guys" there in pairs just like us, or singles who would be "cruising", we felt really at home. We told all our friends and during the year that we there the Collherne became almost totally gay on a Sunday morning and now, it has been a totally gay pub for many years.

My Great Grand father Joseph Montague made a tapestry of Windsor Castle looking from the "long walk" that had been given to me years before. On it is woven his name and the date 1855. Following my giving Rod the small pieces to make while he was in the hospital, we decided we would like to do some together. We found a canvas with the conventional view of the Castle painted on it. It took us most of the year we spent living in our little nest to complete it. When finished I wove my name and the date 1955 in the corner

One evening Rod was very "down", he hated every minute being in the army. I said. "What's the matter luv?" apparently some of the guys had suspected that he was gay and were giving him a hard time saying things such as, "come on Rod lets have your bum". So I told him to stand up to them, call their bluff, drop your trousers and say, "come on then". I didn't hear any more about it so perhaps it worked. Then the day came when he was discharged. A day of mixed blessings for it meant that although he would be getting out of the army, he would be going back to live with his parents and we would have lost our little home. We were determined to stay living together. That year in London had been the happiest of both our lives

One of our gay friends was Bernard Frost; he was the owner of a very large chain of building societies. We approached him and to our delight he offered us a beautiful flat. It was a detached building with a large car park at the front, a road on either side, a large spare piece of ground at the back and two shops underneath. It was a very unique shape; it had five equal sides, so we called it "the Pentagon". Rodney was working for Slough Town Council, he was not very settled there and the pay was very poor. So I managed to get him a job at a customer of mine called Chambon Foundry as the accountant. These were the days of pounds shillings and pence and no calculators, Rodney could add up a long row of figures quicker than any one I ever knew. He stayed at this foundry for many years until it closed, as did most of all the foundries in Slough. The manager, who was an alcoholic, relied on Rod totally and at one time he was running the office and managing the works all on his own with a little help from me.

I was never totally faithful to Rod, he accepted this and years later I found that he could remember the names of every one of my "one night stands" as we called them, although I rarely slept all night with any of them. There were no secrets we had what we call an "open relationship" he said he was never jealous.

JOHN MY SECOND LOVER (together with Rodney four years)

Then we met and became friends with John. He was an only child and did not get on to well with his father who was quite old to have an eighteen-year-old son. John spent a great deal of time with us, often spending the night and the weekend. As we only had one bedroom and one bed he slept with us. Rod was just as fond of him as I was; we were a "threesome". Then one day someone used the name Tuptim when referring to John. That is the name of the second wife of the king of Siam. That name stuck, John didn't seem to mind. Many years later I was to meet and entertain in my London flat a Thai Princess (a friend of Somchai my lover) who turned out to be a direct descendant of the real Princess Tuptim.

During this time I was producing the Burnham District Scout Gang Show. John had been a scout and he now rejoined as an assistant scout leader. He helped me at the Hospital with my group and he enjoyed very much taking part in the Gang Shows. One particular sketch we did was the Floral Dance. I sang and John dress up as a girl as did most of the straight men in the show at some time, they all enjoyed it immensely. John looked every inch a pretty girl and we danced the Floral Dance together on stage in front of a packed audience where on the Saturday evening performance, were a great many of our gay friends, some from London.

Inevitably after some years we started to grow apart and go our own ways. John and I both wanted to get married and "go straight". There was still no advice to be had from anywhere. Rod was a hundred per cent gay and was in the process of buying a house in Slough. John had a girl friend and I encouraged him. I was now thirty-six, putting up with a great deal of subtle pressure from several quarters to get married. Mother kept dropping little hints, she was very wise and she had an idea of the kind of life I was leading. During the very sad moments of Osmonds trail she knew he had been an influence in my life, she had met him and she liked him. I was upset and started to talk to her about it and she guessed that I was going to tell her that I was gay, she said. "If one of my sons were like that, I would rather that he did not tell me". Since then I have always advised many that have asked me. "Shall I tell my Mother?" I have said, "don't tell her unless she asks you". My reasoning for that is, if you tell her you "put her on the spot". She has to say something and may not want to. Mothers are usually very wise where their offspring are concerned. She probably knows anyway.

I would not be telling the truth if I did not admit that I enjoyed the events leading up to and getting married, the "getting engaged". Mother was so happy. There were so many invitations, both being older we knew so many people, they would not let us have a simple wedding. From the time I got engaged I cut my self off completely from all my gay friends except Rodney he told me that most of them did not approve of what I was doing. But he supported me totally as he always did with every thing, his love for me was so complete that all he wanted was my happiness. I would take the children around to his house and he, knowing that he would never marry, or have children, enjoyed seeing mine grow up.

For over four years, from the day I got married I led a totally Heterosexual life style. I very much enjoyed it and was proud to introduce people to "my wife". I looked forward to seeing the children each evening, helping with bath times and bed times. I got a great feeling of "belonging again" especially at family gatherings with the children of my brother and two sisters. The total happiness of my Mother was so plain to see. We all gathered at our house at Christmas, as it was the largest. I was, next to my father the "head of the family". All my time was totally taken up with my work, the family and scouting. When we were married I made a promise to Vera that what ever happened; as far as I was concerned I would not leave her until the children were adults. But as time went by. Despite the sublimation, I could not control my thoughts.

This was the time that I was doing a lot of travelling on business, two or three times a week, one hundred miles in all directions, my sex drive was as high as ever. At all the toilets, without exception that I had to pass on these journeys there was temptation. There were no motorways or service stations in those days. But there were toilets specially built for travellers, miles from anywhere in dual carriageway lay-bys. There were always at least half a dozen lorries, vans and cars. At least half of the drivers of these would be loitering either inside or out side looking for sex. Most of these buildings were made of wood, including the cubicles, which always had holes two or three inches in diameter between them. That is where it went on. I'm positive that most would be married men with a wife and children at home, those who would not consider them selves to be homosexual or bisexual. And would more likely be homophobic at their works or in the pub.

I did for some time resist the temptation that was there. A friend who was just like me, married but gay once said to me. "That bloody thing between my legs". I knew exactly what he meant. I would try not to stop at these places but go for a pee in a lay-bye where there was no toilet. But eventually my resolve was not strong enough. You do it quickly, hate your self for a short while, then forget about it and pretend it did not happen. One thing that always "put me off" was very normal, good looking guys who, when they took down their overalls had black silk stockings and suspenders on and asked you if you had any pictures of naked women.

With John singing the floral dance at one of my Gang Shows

MICHEAL (My third lover thirteen years)

 Then I met some one who told me that he was not gay (he had just had sex with me), but that his brother was. Some time later I had an occasion to visit him at his home, where he introduced me to his two brothers. David and Michael, I asked him which was the gay one and he told me David. I later met Michael in circumstances where I knew that he was the gay one; his first words were "You wont tell my brothers will you".

Michael became my lover. By this time the law had changed, it was no longer an offence for two men to have sex so long as it was in private and there was no other person present. Michael worked as a milkman starting very early in the morning and would finish work by lunchtime. I gave him a part time job at my company driving the van and other jobs in the works. He worked very hard, I admired him; I fell in love with him. He told me all about his life and his family, his mother was mentally ill, and his father was dying of lung cancer. He told me that he and his brothers had all been sexually abused from about the age of eleven or twelve by an "Uncle" Ted. His father knew what was happening but said nothing, accepting bottles of whisky from "Uncle" Ted, who by now had disappeared since the boys had grown up. I told my wife all about this some time after she had met him, she took to him and liked him.

Michael would come around to the house frequently and became friends with the children. We went by coach on a family outing to the miniature Blue Railway. Michael was invited. During the journey something happened that made my wife suspicious, perhaps she saw the way he looked at me, or heard something we might have said to each other. She asked me if he was my lover. I admitted that he was and had been for some time. There were tears from both of them; it was a very difficult time. Later I talked at length with her and told her I had done my best to go straight and what had been happening on my business trips explaining the risks I was taking in doing that and that since I had met him I was no longer doing it. Instead of telling me to get out of the house as she had every right to do, she reluctantly agreed that I should carry on seeing him. She said it was better that I should have Michael than every "Tom Dick and Harry".

Michael continued to come around to the house. He was very unhappy at his home; his father who was by now bed ridden was permanently on a couch in the one room downstairs demanding Michael buy him a bottle of whisky a day. If he did not get it he would try to hit him with the fireside poker. His brothers had left and Michael felt he just had to stay to look after his mother. Michael needed someone to talk to and he found he could talk to Vera about his troubles; she helped him and felt sorry for him. I managed to help by getting his mother into a home for a while. Then his father died, and instead of being relieved Michael was completely distraught for some time.

In talking to my wife about Michael she asked me exactly what we did together, so I told her in some detail. She did not seem too shocked. Once a week he would baby-sit for us while I took her out to a restaurant for dinner. Michael would stay the night sleeping on a put-u-up in the study. One night on returning home, I was missing for a few minutes she said. "Where have you been?" I said, "I've just been to kiss Michael goodnight". She said. "Oh you "don't kiss him as well do you" She didn't like that.

Michael was not naturally gay. He had been sexually abused as a small child and had been in a very unhappy home. He needed love and affection and was looking for it in public toilets when I meet him. He remained good friends with my wife and the children. His Mother was back at home and since the death of his father she was a lot better. Then I discovered that he was meeting a girl. This I encouraged. He wanted to do what I had done, get married settle down and have a family. The first girl he had I approved of but then that broke up. His next one I had serious doubts about which eventually proved to be well founded. She was older than him with two small children; I thought she needed a "bread-winner". But he married her, had a son by her. Then a few years later he was lucky and won 2,000 pounds on the pools, (a lot of money in those days) I was happy for him.

Then I lost touch with him until a friend told me he had left his wife. She had spent all the money then kicked him out and he was living rough in a squat and "doing drugs". I found him and helped him on to his feet again. The reason I am writing all this about Michael is because we became lovers again, during which time he went to see a Psychiatrist or Councillor of some kind who told him that his problem stemmed from his being abused as a child. He told me all this and I felt guilty and said. "What about me and what he and I had been doing?" But he was adamant saying; "You have never ever done anything wrong as far as I am concerned". You are the only one that has ever helped me. You have loved me and were always there when I needed you.

I think that is what a relationship is all about, who ever the relationship is with. "Man and Woman". "Man and Man". "Woman and Woman", It's a matter of "need", needing each other. "What can be wrong with that?" Michael is now living happily with another woman. We are still great friends. Michael came to Vera's funeral and to the Wake afterwards. (At his request) we managed to find a quite spot for a kiss before he left. He told me he still loves me.

STEVE Lover No. Four Seven years

I saw Steve in a bar in Brighton. He was extremely good looking. He was with some one that I knew so I asked him to introduce me. I asked Steve if that was his partner? He said. "No just a friend". We sat and talked for a long time, he told me that he was twenty years old. His English was a little strange, he said he had recently come over from Germany where his parents were. His mother was German and his father English, formerly a British soldier. Then I asked him where he was staying, he surprised me by saying nowhere, "I slept under the pier last night". This put me on my guard I was thinking he may be a "rent boy'. Continuing to talk to him I found him very cheerful and out going, he didn't seem to have a care in the world.

I spent the rest of the afternoon with him weighing him up and finding out more about him. He said he didn't know whether he was gay or straight. He had had a boy friend in Germany, he had a row with his parents and left. He was looking for a job and somewhere to stay, he didn't seem to know much about the British system of social security. I invited him to stay on the boat for the night and said I would help him sort him self out in the morning. That night I took him to a Gay club but when we got to the door the doorman, who knew me said. "You can come George in but not him". Apparently Steve had hit some one who had "tried it on" with him. We retired for the night to the boat where I put him in the fore cabin and I slept in the saloon. In the morning he said, "You are the first bloke I've been back with who didn't try anything".

In the morning I helped him as I promised. I had the use of a small room by arrangement with a sailing friend; he had no boat so sailed with me in the summer. I left, telling Steve I would see him the following weekend. When we met up again as arranged he said that jobs were very difficult to find in Brighton. This was during the winter and as I was working on "Woody" I asked him if he wanted to help me with the work and I would pay him. He worked very well and the more I got to know about him the more I liked him. I was also attracted to him, but did nothing about that.

Then I met some one where there was mutual attraction and took him to the room telling Steve about it and asking him to clean the car while we were in the room for half an hour or so. When I came down Steve and the car had gone. I though "what a fool I am" and I thought I was a good judge of character! While at the police station giving details of the car telling them that there was a possibility he would make for Dover and then back to Germany the telephone on the desk rang. It was my friend to tell me that Steve was back. My relief was short lived. Oh dear! I thought what do we do now? Steve had no licence or insurance. I looked at the policeman. He said. 'Tell him to come down here but not in the car". I sat down with my head in my hands, wishing I had waited longer before reporting it. Steve came in with a large grin on his face. I said. "What are you grinning for"? You are in trouble now. The policeman asked Steve about it all and then told him he has been very foolish and what would have happened to him if he had been involved in an accident or had been stopped by the police and never to do it again. Then I said. "Are you not going to charge him?" "No". He said. "Fortunately for him we didn't see him". (My estimation of the police improved just a little). On the way back to the room I asked him why? He just said he was Jealous. From then on we became lovers and we were together for almost exactly seven years.

Steve came up to Slough where I told him there was a much better chance of getting a job. He stayed in a social security hostel and very quickly found jobs. I think employers were very impressed to find that he spoke fluent German. He passed his driving test (never try to teach a lover to drive!) most of the jobs he got were driving vans and small lorries. We spent most weekends at Brighton sailing or working on "Woody".

We were in a gay bar on Brighton front called. "The Heart in Hand", many members of the public, not gay, would call in and probably not notice that it was gay. Steve was chatting to two good-looking girls, the "chatting up" was being done more by them than Steve. Then he told them that he was gay and that I was his boy friend. Their comment was. "What a waste!" I said. "What a cheek!". Then they said "Are all these chaps in here gay!" We said "Yes, most of them". "But they "don't look gay" they said. This was the case with the general public. They all thought that gays were very obvious and camp, like Quentin Crisp, John Inman from, "Are you being served" Dick Emery and Larry Grayson were another two and like lots of others on the television in those days, they were always "Camp". They thought all those that were gay were just like that.

It was during my time with Steve that my Mother became ill. So I of course saw a great deal less of him. I was very busy and upset and worried about Mother at the time, so perhaps I did not communicate with him enough. I got a telephone call to say that he was in Hospital. He had taken an over dose, had been on a stomach pump, was very ill and had nearly died. It was more than an attention-seeking attempt; he was having great problems with his parents who had come over to England to live at the time. He had a love-hate relationship with his mother. They were both very much alike and they both had a problem with nerves. But the "last straw" for him was, apparently he though I didn't want him any more.

Soon after this, as is the case I understand, he was referred to a Psychiatrist at the Windsor Hospital. By this time I knew Steve better than anyone alive including his parents. I knew that at this point in time he needed me, we needed each other. I was prepared to do any thing that was best for him. We were briefly seen together and then I was told to leave the room. Soon after Steve came storming out leaving the door open and shouted out "that idiot wants me to leave you"

I decided to get Steve out of the hostel. I saw an advert for a room in Windsor. Mother was frequently in and out of the hospital there, so I rented it. It was at the very top of a large old Victorian house, it had a beautiful view of the castle from the window. The landlady told me that the house used to belong to Queen Victoria's Physician. Steve smoked very heavily I hated it, he promised me he would try to give it up, I said we had to plan it and only do it when the time was right and he was ready.

With a magic marker I wrote out on one of those yellow sticky strip pads all the "bad" words I could think of like, unhealthy, dirty, smelly, expensive and very many more and stuck them all over the walls. Then the big day came. He had his last cigarette after breakfast and then I took down all the cards and put up dozens more such as, healthy, clean, sweet smelling. He lasted until lunchtime then he started to sweat, I found if I could talk him out of having one for one minute, then he was OK for another hour or so. We went for long runs in Windsor Great Park that was just close by. He lasted for four days then his nerves got the better of him he swore at his manager and walked out to the nearest tobacconist. He is still a heavy smoker.

Steve and I arrived at a Bar-B-Q given by one of the members of our gay sailing club at his beautiful house near Beaulieu. We arrived and were greeted by our host who said. "Hello George your namesake is here, his lord ship". Later on in the evening I went up to Lord Edward saying would like to introduce my self for we have several things in common". I said. "We are both about the same age. We are both married. Both had the same number of children. We are both Yacht owners and Sailors. Were both gay and are both named Montague only that I had an (e) on the end of my name. He was friendly we chatted for some time him telling me that we would be related going back some distance in time originating from Normandy.

Then Steve joined us and I introduced him, where upon we were invited to Palace House Beaulieu (I wondered at the time if I would have been had it not been for Steve). We kindly accepted and duly made our visit. His Lordship personally showed us around including parts of his "Palace" not normally seen by the public. Then Lord Edward said. "George why don't you go and fetch your car? Drive it around the block to the front door while I show Steve some more of the house". (I thought to my self I know what part that will be, the bedroom). About half an-hour later I arrived after walking a long way to the car, then driving right around his huge estate. I must say I enjoyed driving through his impressive entrance gates and up to the stately front door. I sat in the car and waited, then they appeared, Lord Edwards arm protectively around Steve's shoulder. I took a photograph. We said our thank you then set of for home. As I have said I am not the jealous or possessive type, but even if I were I need not have worried for I am positive Steve never let any other man touch him from the day I met him and I am sure that would still be the case today.

During the time that Steve was going out regularly with his girl friend he stopped coming down to the boat with me. I would go down every weekend. It's not many people who take to sailing. I would say about one in twenty. Those who have never been are all very keen to start with. I have taken dozens of them out. Every thing is fine if the sea is very calm but if it's a little rough they get queasy or bored and they don't come again. I enjoyed sailing on my own, but it is difficult going thought the lock and when casting off from, or coming back on to the mooring. It is so much easier with two, especially if the crewmember takes and interest and enjoys learning to sail.

So Steve like John and Michael had a girl friend. I encouraged him, (I loved him that much). He started to go out regularly with her. I remember her name was Melanie. He brought her around to the house and then said. "Could she stay on the week-ends that I went down to the boat"? Often I would come home and she was still there. Then one Sunday evening I put my hand into my dressing gown pocket and there was a pair of Camay knickers (I think they call them). Melanie knew all about our relationship, but I think she thought that Steve would leave me for her. I told Steve that she deserved him more than I did and that he would be so much better off with her than me. She could give him acceptance and children. But he wanted us both. We all three went out to dinner where I told Steve that we must finish. There were tears all round I think, but he reluctantly agreed.

MY WIFE AND I PART

A few months after the death of my mother, I managed to persuade my wife that we should live apart. We had a little family meeting, where I said. "Sorry Guys but your dad is Gay". Paula said, "Oh Dad we've known for years". It was a very sad day. Some years earlier I had decided that where my sexuality was concerned I should try not to shock my children if it could be avoided. Some years previously Martin had found a copy of The Gay News while he was earning his pocket money cleaning my car. He took it straight to his mother who told him to ask me about it. I told him no lies; I said some of my best friends were gay and that I wanted to know more about them and that if people in general were to know more about them there would not be so much anti gay prejudice. There were also about that time programmes on the television about gays and some times play's with gays in them. I always wanted to watch them. When they asked me why I was watching programmes like that (they probably wanted to watch something else at the time) I told them the same thing.

I moved into a small three bed roomed house in Slough. I got it very cheaply as it needed a great deal of work done on it. The first thing I did was to put in central heating with the help of a friend. Then I rewired the house, followed by complete decoration of the whole house, both inside and out Next I built a large conservatory that included a cupboard for the washing machine and another toilet. The house doubled in value in two years. I then persuaded my wife to move into a Bungalow and we sold the big house. Steve and I and then my fifth lover Asif lived in No 24 for eight years and were very happy there, we regularly held Bar-B-Que's and parties there, then we moved to "Woodside" Farnham Common.

I TEACH WOODWORK

Once I had finished all the renovations on No 24 I found I had time on my hands especially in the winter evenings. Not being one to sit down and watch tele. I looked around for something to keep me occupied. I was chatting to someone who was also a professional woodworker, when he said. "Would I be interested in earning some extra money by teaching woodcraft at a local adult evening class?" He was doing that but was going to have to give it up. I did not really need extra money, but said. "Yes I was interested". I went along to the school and was taken on as the woodwork tutor. I enjoyed it, there were usually about 10 in the class all age's and sex's. I would take along scrap wood from my works some of which was Jelutong, a soft wood with no knots that was very easy to carve. The woodwork master of the school saw this and asked me to bring in as much as I could. I did this for two winters, when one evening I happened to mention to the supervisor how old I was, she said. Oh my goodness! You look 10 years younger than that, you are over the age limit. You can finish this term but I'm sorry I can't let you continue next year.

RODNEY DIES

I had always kept in touch with my first lover Rodney. One day he came to see me and brought with him several pieces of furniture that we had made together, some with the tapestry on it that we had spent so many happy hours doing. These we had divided between us when I got married and he had bought a house. But I said. "You can't, we made all these together they are our memories of that time", he insisted, telling me that he now had a boy friend in America and was going to see him for a month and that he might be going to live out there. I said goodbye to him and wished him well not realising that that was the last time I should see him.

I was at home when I got a telephone call from Ken, who lived with his partner Richard in part of Rodney's house. He had received a phone call from America to say that Rodney had died of a heart attack he was only forty-eight. It took six weeks to get his ashes back from the states. There were about two hundred at the funeral. My wife came with me she had know him and was fond of him, He was a very popular person, he had served behind the bar of the "Noah's Ark" the local gay pub in Windsor for several years. Rodney's brother Ralph told me that Rodney had told him that he was very ill and that the doctors had told him to stop working, stop having sex and live the life of an invalid. But he told his brother that he would rather die than do that. He told no one else but his brother and no one else knew or suspected any thing was wrong. It was then that I knew why he had given me back those things that he must have treasured. He left only one letter with his will it was addressed to me.

LETTER FROM ROD

My dearest Monty,
You will only read this letter when I am no longer here. You may ask your self "Why?" I can only say I wanted you to know. It would be wrong to say I loved you from the moment I first saw you, But certainly soon after knowing you I realised I loved you and have continued loving you ever since. No one else ever really came into my life because no one could fill adequately the ideal you had created.

Knowing you intimately for so many years, years that were important because they were formative ones, gave me a standard to live up to, and an ability to calmly accept compromise in life that was at least not easy. The years spent with you were unquestionably the happiest I have ever know, certainly enough to sustain me for the years I didn't have you, yet you had become so much a part of me that I was never truly without you. The joy of your children pleased me and the happiness you had from your "friend" made me happy To close is difficult, all I can say is "thank you for being who you are, and for knowing me.

God bless you
Roddy

Roddy 1936 1984

Why so young so many of us say.
"Those whom the gods love" they would not let him stay.
His heart was big and oh so full of love,
It could no longer take the strain, an order from above.
There is a love that dare not speak its name.
Knowing him, Oh no, love is love and just the same.
An understanding family to whom he was so good.
A beloved Mother gone before, things seem to be as they should.
His family, "and one much larger", thinking of him today.
All blow him a kiss together, perhaps we will meet again one day.
By the one he loved the most, (Written before I lost my religion)

I take up watercolour painting

Having had to give up teaching at an adult evening class's I thought I would become a pupil again, having previously done two years on a Yacht Masters course I signed up for a beginners course at the local school. I bought all the materials, paper, paints and brushes. I made a box to hold it all and an easel I stayed for two winters enjoying it all very much. Of all the many things I have done in my life I have never found the time go so quickly. It is all-absorbing and after a while quite easy to do something which is self pleasing. When I have finished this memoir then that will become my main hobby.

TREVOR (JUST A SHORT TIME)

It was early spring, I was working on the boat that in those days was moored just below a gangway, when a young voice from above called out "Can I'help yer mister?" I looked up and there was a young lad, he told me later that he was 16 and would be leaving school in the summer. There is always a lot of work that needs to be done on a boat at the end of a winter especially on Woody, with all the wood that I had put on her. So I told him yes come and help me with the varnishing and rubbing down. We got on well together. Over the next few weeks he would sometimes already be there doing some of the work when I arrived.

Over the years I have had others who have helped in return for a sail but they usually wanted to bring several others along, they didn't work very well and always started to, what I call "Muck about" Trevor never asked if any of his mates could come and when I asked him if he would not rather be out playing with friends he said "No, I would rather be with you" After a while he asked if he could stay the night on the boat, I said no. For one thing I said I would need his parents permission and the other thing was I always went out for the evening on the town.

The weekend before the Easter holiday I told him I was going out for the first sail of the season. Down to Newhaven for the weekend with another friend. He pleaded with me to let him come saying his parents would not mind and that they knew he had been helping me. I gave in and said OK. I told him that I could not get down until the Sat. as I had a singing engagement on the Good Friday. But that he could come down on that day and finish off the work on the boat and showed him where I had a spare key hidden. I would be down early on the Saturday as we would not be sailing until the afternoon we would have time for me to pop back to his home to get the permission of his parents.

On the Saturday I arrived on my own my friend being not able to come at the last minute. Trevor was sitting in the cockpit with a big smile on his face and said, "I've finished all the work" I could see right away that it did look as if he had done a lot. When I got inside I sort of half noticed the waste bin was full and made the remark that he must have eaten a lot during that day (I always kept a lot of tinned food on board). As often happened the sea was too rough to think about going out, but as the forecast was better for the next day I told him we could go tomorrow. Then two men came alongside who I thought straight away were policemen, they said to Trevor, are you (his surname?) Trevor who by now looked very guilty said. Yes. Then one of them said get off the boat and come with me and he took him off. The other one with out an invitation stepped onto the boat and went down into the cabin and started poking around. I said what has Trevor done and what do you think you are doing. He asked me to confirm my name and then said I am arresting you on suspicion of child abduction and abuse.

Apparently Trevor had been on the boat all of the previous week without telling his parents who had reported him missing. One of the Marina staff had been given a report about a missing boy. He had seen Trevor on the boat a day or two before. On the Saturday morning he told the police who had asked him details of the owner. On checking they discovered that I had a conviction for gross indecency, then they then put what they thought was two and two together. I was taken to the Brighton Police Station.

There I was told to strip. Swabs were taken from my penis, anus and mouth. Trevor told me later that exactly the same thing happened to him. Then I was put into a cell and left there and for over four hours no one came near me. Then two detectives came in, one of them "brow beat" me, by accusing me in a very loud voice of sexually abusing Trevor. They said they had all the evidence, that they had examined my waste bin and the boat and found what they wanted. (I said a silent prayer that Trevor had not had a "wank" and put the tissue in the bin). They told me that they had examined Trevor and that he was in tears in another room and had confessed every thing. All this time I was angrily denying it all. They kept me locked up for another four hours, then without charging me they released me. I was to report back in one week. I was in my working clothes without a penny on me, when I told them this they said hard luck. I had to walk the mile back to my boat.

On the Easter Sunday Trevor came down to the boat. When I had finished telling him the trouble he had caused, I put him in the car and told him to direct me to his home. On the way he told me how sorry he was, that he had been away from home before and no one had cared or reported it. He told me that the police had done to him the same that they did to me, telling him that I had confessed and told them everything. He told me he said. "You are bloody liars you bring him here and let me hear him say that". On arriving at his house his parents didn't seem to mind that he had come to see me that I thought they would do, they didn't seem to want to listen to anything I had to say, so I left.

I was due to appear back at the police station a week later, so I asked around and was given the name of a lady Solicitor who was a Lesbian. On the way down to the station she asked me about Trevor and what he had said. When I told her he had said nothing, for we has done nothing, she said "You are very lucky, you have a good lad there they usually bully the kids into admitting something happened even when it didn't". On arriving they told me no charges would be made, they gave me back items that they had taken from the boat and my camera but with out the film on which I had taken several exposures.

I tried to get Trevor to stay away from the boat, but he continued to come down to the Marina I would find him waiting for me, not on the boat but in the car park. So we sat down and had a heart to heart talk. He told me that he had been going with men since he was fourteen. That he was told I was gay by some one that I knew, when he had asked me if he could help me. Then he told me that he was in love with me. Although by this time he had left school and was seventeen I told him that the age of consent was 21, and that I would go to prison if they found proof of a sexual relationship between us. I reminded him of the "examinations" that we had both been put though at the police station and that his consent would make no difference I told him that I was still in love with Steve. I also told him that he might not be gay, that I had known and heard of quite a number who had started having sex with men some as young as 12 but who had turned out to be straight in the end. These were often boys from unhappy homes, or who were in council homes and that it was to do with being wanted and affection. We remained close friends for many years, the last time he rang me was to tell me that he was to get married.

Whilst driving back from South Wales this poem kept going through my head. I composed the following without writing down a word until I got home. It's about Trevor.

A voice said "Can I'elp yer Mister".
I looked up at a fresh - faced youngster.
Lonely - old enough to be his father.
I of course replied "rather".
Sailing fishing happy weekends.
Sometimes worried about gay friends.
Admiring eyes on pickup bent.
Lay off I cried he's innocent.
Trevor dear, I am a queer.
The boat is gay please say away.
But would he listen no not he.
His eyes would glisten as he looked at me.
Unhappy home, he graves affection.
Send him away! I have no intention.
It's girls he fancies, but he fears.
He has no chance for several years.
Highly sexed and full of fun.
Now my frustrations have begun.
Then one day there came another.
Who took him off for a "bit of the other".
Why was that? "I said" do tell us?
I only did it to make you jealous.
And then it was that we could see.
That at least for a while we were meant to be.
In love.
One day he'll marry, T'wont be the end.
After secret love he'll still be my friend.

ASIF (Lover No five seven years)

When I got home on the night I parted with Steve, I thought. "What have I done"? It was one of the several most miserable moments of my life. The next day I went to Harrods, spent a lot of money and then walked into a gay pub in Soho. I sat facing the door still feeling and I'm sure looking fed-up, when suddenly filling the doorway, standing there with a smile that only Asians have, I saw Asif looking straight at me. He was nineteen, very slim and good-looking. This pub was, at that time known as a pick-up-pub for male prostitutes. He told me that he was from

Birmingham, I believed him his accent bore that out. He told me some of his life story he said he had known he was gay since his early teens, that he had had several lovers since leaving school. When his father said to him. "That it was time for him to think about getting married" he told his father that he was gay, the reply was. "So what!" What's that got to do with it? That doesn't have to stop you getting married. He had left home and had been living for some time with an older man named Bob. Asif had come down to London with another friend.

He told me that he had found this friend waiting for him near Bobs flat when he arrived home who told him that his father had found out where he was living and whom he was living with That the police had been informed and were waiting in Bobs flat for him to come home. If he went in they would both been arrested. So both he and his friend had come down to London. I think Asif believed this story, but I was a little sceptical and told him that the police could not arrest either of them unless there was evidence of them "sleeping" together. I told him that since he was over eighteen, there was nothing to stop him living at Bobs flat. He then told me that his "friend had introduced him to several men, telling him to go off with them, do as little as possible, but get some money from them. He said he hated doing this, but he had to get some money. I asked him where he was living; he said. "Nowhere I have slept rough for several nights now".

I talked to him for a while longer. I didn't entirely believe all that he told me, but there was something about him. Had I met him some time before; while I was still with Steve, I would probably have given him some money, some good advice and wished him luck. But for about the first in my life I was going to go home to an empty house. I told Asif he could come home with me and the same as I told Steve, that there were lots of jobs going in Slough he could sleep in the spare bed room, look after me and the house until he found a job.

On the way home he asked me to stop, saying he had to pick up some things he said, he would be only a few minutes. He went off down an alleyway. I waited for fifteen minuets and then I thought. "Oh well that's that" and I was just about to drive off, when he came running to the car, carrying some clothes and a pair of shoes, I thought, so much for him saying he was sleeping rough. But I didn't question him on that but told him if he was straight with me, he would be OK, but if not he would be out.

When we got home, I showed him into the spare room and then went to bed. I was just dropping off to sleep, when he came and got into bed with me. Nothing was said and nothing happened, just a cuddle. That night we both, for very different reasons, "needed each other". The following day was a Sunday, so we spent the day talking and getting to know more about each other. It was plain to me that he was quite fond of Bob, (the man he had been living with in Birmingham) and was worried about him. I asked him how old Bob was, I was relived at what he told me, for it meant that Asif was one of those quite rare younger men who liked older men. I wanted him to ring Bob, but he said he was scared to do that and that Bob would be angry with him.

His family were from Kashmir; the part that is under Pakistani rule. His father had been in England for many years before his family joined him. Asif had been eight years old, at the time. His father was a councillor and quite an important man in his community, who worked quite closely with Roy Hattersley then deputy leader of the opposition and now Lord Hattersley. He told me that there would eventually be a great deal of pressure on him to get married, he was obviously scared of his father and of his very extended family finding out where he lived, or about his life style. He said I would be in danger if they found out about us. He did not want to go back to Birmingham.

Eventually I persuaded him to let me ring Bob. I had put my self "in the man's shoes" and I was sure I knew how he felt. The minute I spoke to him and started to talk to him about Asif I knew I had done the right thing, the relief in his voice was plain to hear. Young people are so thoughtless, they just do not realise the deep mental agony they cause those that care about them, when they just suddenly and unexpectedly disappear.

By arrangement Bob came down the next day to Windsor by coach. We all three met up at a restaurant. Then the true facts came out about what had happened. Asif's "so called friend" had managed to gain the trust of both of them and to get a key to Bob's flat. He then, when Bob was at work robbed it of all valuables. He then told Asif the "story" about the police. Then on top of all that, he took him to London and tried to be his "Pimp" and put him "on the game" (be a male prostitute). Poor Bob was not only very hurt having helped Asif a great deal and been very fond of him, he quite naturally thought it was possible Asif had robbed him as well. Then it came to the decision, what do we all do now? Asif made the comment that, "he was uncertain what to do". My heart sank a little. I had by now become very fond of As (as I always called him).

Then Bob said the words that made me admire him very much, since when he has always been my close friend. He said to Asif. "You had better stay with George, it will be a lot better for you with him than with me and also safer for you to be down here in Slough". Bob was similar to a supply teacher he was a supply Landlord to many of the very large pubs in Birmingham, where he would often have to "live-in" for two weeks at a time. I often had to go to Birmingham on business and when ever possible I would call in and see him. Sometimes As. would come with me and we would stay the weekend. Then Bob would come and stay with us during his holidays.

Several months later As. said he would like to go to Kashmir to see his relatives, especially his Grandfather. I was warned that if he did they might keep him there and marry him off. I told him to go into Islamabad to the British Consol, where I had been several times on business and to give his passport and ticket to someone that I knew there and who would understand the situation. He didn't listen to me, for he must have told them he was coming. His relatives met him at the airport and took him straight to his old home. They took away his passport and ticket and then he became very ill. We had not thought of giving him immunisation injections, after all he was going home, but of course he was just like any other British person having lived here for twelve years.

We had booked up to go on holiday and in the event I had to go alone. I didn't enjoy it very much. When I got back there was a pitiful letter from him asking me to help him to get back to England, I had no idea what to do, I even thought of going out there. He told me not to write to his address but gave me the name and address of a contact that he could trust. I wrote back telling him to do all he could to find his passport and ticket if possible. After about three months he managed to do that. I had a letter giving me the flight No. He was coming home. I went to the airport where I waited and waited. Then I rang the immigration dept to see if they were detaining him for any reason, I couldn't see why, he had a British passport. Eventually I drove home very despondent. As I turned into Westfield Road I thought I saw something white suddenly disappear into our gateway. When I got to the front door I felt a pair of arms around me from behind, it was him; he was wearing an all white Salvar. (Asian dress). We had somehow missed each other at the airport. When we got indoors and I held him in front of me, I could see the "Love light; in his eyes. I had been in love with him for some time, now I could see with out any shadow of doubt he was with in love with me. As with Steve, we were to be together for almost exactly seven years (The seven year itch!)

He got a job at "Kentucky fried chicken"; he did very well and soon became an assistant manager. I taught him to drive (with great difficulty). (Never try to teach a lover to drive). He saved his money, bought a brand new car and kept up all the payments until it was paid for. He moved with me to "Woodside" where he took great interest in the large garden and especially in the rearing and keeping of the Koi Carp. We would both go to all the different aquaria buying new fish.

One day he smiled at, met, and then fell in love with a man on holiday from Lebanon. He was about forty-five years old, the "affair" was doomed from the start, they wrote to each other. Then he scared us all by going over there, where the hostilities had barely come to an end. The man came back to England on his second holiday, that's when it fizzled out. Not long after that Asif told me he did not love me any more, but he did not want to leave the house.

When we moved to the big house at Farnham Common, "Woodside" I put Asif in my will leaving the house in Westfield Rd to him. With the money I got from the sale of my works I was able to keep the cottage, which I rented out. I had thought at that time that As. would be with me for the rest of my days. But I had forgotten about the "seven years itch". So we then came to the agreement that he would take out a Mortgage and pay me half the value of the house. This we did and I used the money to pay off most of the mortgage I had on the London flat.

Asif stayed with me, sleeping with me for almost another year, which some might think strange, but it helped me to get him 'out of my system", it spared me the hurt of seeing him pack his bags and move out. We had no sex during that time, but we still cuddled each other in bed and often gave each other a hug during the day. This is what happens with many gay relationships, the important thing is the companionship, the helping and looking after each other, sharing the housework, the cooking and shopping. Having someone to talk to at the end of the day and yes, even exchanging details of any casual sex we each might have. I didn't blame him for falling out of love with me, how can you 'blame" some one for something like that. It is something that can happen at any time. That is why I have always said if you love some one you should tell them at least once every day.

Asif's wife now lives with his parents back in Birmingham, he is in a long term relationship with Kevin, we are still great friends, we all meet up for an Indian meal now and then.

Note added 14 3 02

While we were in Thailand Asif emailed us telling me he wanted to pay off the balance that he owed me on 24 Westfield Rd and clear his mortgage with me. Coincidently Somchai was in the process of buying another house for his Mother and family, which would have entailed selling part of an investment that we had. But his offer came in just right almost to the pound. So together with funds we already had in the bank we did not need to raise any more.

With David

David (lover No. six eighteen months)

Then I met David in the Quebec pub at Marble arch. When Asif did not come back from his visit to Kashmir I was very "down". A friend said to me. "You can't" go on like this he might never come back, why "don't you go to the Quebec"? I said. "Where is that"? He told me. "It is where all the older gays go and younger men who are only attracted to older men". The great majority of gay men go for men their own age or younger. The average age of those that crowd the many gay pubs that there are in London now would be about thirty. If a much older man like my self goes to these pubs, which we do sometimes we feel a little out of place and are usually completely ignored by those in there and the music in these places is always so loud you can't have a comfortable conversation with anyone.

The Quebec "upstairs" is very different, it is quite large, very nicely decorated and the music is never too loud. On a busy evening there would at least a hundred and fifty men aged from nineteen to ninety and another hundred down stairs where it can be very noisy as there is a small disco there. There are men from all walks of life and all income brackets, men whom not one, except for a very small handful, would be recognised as gay. All "birds of a feather" wanting to be at ease, in a friendly relaxed atmosphere, most not particularly looking for a "pick-up". It is Famous all over the gay world, for there is not another anything like it, not even in what is supposed to be the gayest city in the world, in America, San Francesco.

It was about a year after Asif and I ceased to be lovers that David smiled at me in the Quebec. I was dressed in a dark suit, having been that afternoon to the funeral of a dear friend of mine who had died of Aids. David was about twenty-five with an attractive oriental look. He told me that his father who was from Malaysia was dead and that his English mother was a nurse living in south Wales. He was living with an "Uncle" in Woking. He travelled to Southwark London each day where he was doing a degree. He spent several weekends at "Woodside" and others on "Woody" When he first arrived at "Woodside" I told him I had a lodger, which was the truth. Asif was no longer my lover, we had stopped sleeping together and he paid for his board and lodging. But David was suspicious; he annoyed me by not believing me, was unpleasant towards Asif, and wanted me to tell him to leave. This caused some friction between us. I spoke to some of my friends about it and they surprised me by saying that they understood how David felt. I had told him that Asif and I were no longer lovers and that I had always remained friends with my ex lovers. I have never believed in jealousy and possessiveness in the gay life. If there is an arrangement to have an "open" relationship then so long as there is complete trust and openness between you both, then where is the problem?

Asif and I had a talk and we decided he would move out. I felt so sorry for I knew how he loved the house and the garden, which he still worked on a lot and the Koi Carp that we had chosen and reared together. So I had to be practical. He could not move into the Westfield Rd. house, for at that time we had a tenant in there we could not get out, So he moved into a tiny room in Slough about twice the size of the single bed in there.

To be "in love" with your lover and your lover to be "in love" with you is to be in the best of all possible worlds. I was not "in love" with David, but he was very much "in love" with me, obsessively so. Here was I, two and a half times his age. I was flattered. David was still trying to find his way in life and I was no "loner". He was still a student existing on a ten thousand pound grant from Barclays Bank. One day he came home with a new Hi Fi. I said. "How can you afford that?" He said. "I've still got some of the loan left! I wondered how the bank could possibly loan that much money to a student with no collateral. I had a large freehold property but had never found getting an overdraft easy. He enjoyed sailing but took no interest in the house, the garden or the fish. After a turbulent eighteen months together his love for me had burnt it self out at about the time I started to fall in love with him. He met an American (in the Quebec of course). His new love went back to the states, so he courted him on my telephone. He left me with a large phone bill.

I visited Asif several times in his "box room", he was not very happy there, so when David left he moved back in. We made an arrangement, whereby he would buy all the food and I would pay all the other bills. He loved working in the garden, looking after the fish, cooking on the Aga and of course he was just as fond of Sheba as I was and as neither of us were "loners" it worked very well. Some time later the pressure on him to get married became unbearable for him. It is the custom for the eldest son to marry first. His younger brother wanted to marry but could not do so until he did. Asif was (as more gays than straights are I think) very close to his mother, she, apparently had to hold her head down in shame as she walked down her street because her eldest son was not yet married. Her husband, Asif's father, treated her badly and blamed her. So Asif gave in. I was invited to the wedding and seeing that I would be the only European there Geoff our mutual friend was invited to keep me company.

The wedding took place in two large halls each holding about two hundred people and they were both full. All the males including the groom in one hall and all the females including the bride in the other. No one except the groom went into the other hall and then he went in only for a short while. There did not seem to be any ceremony, except that which took place very briefly during Asif's visit to the other hall. During the three hours that we were there Asif sat together with his "best man" and about a dozen other, I suppose important people at the "top table" Geoff and I were conducted to this table and there we sat. Later I asked Asif if they wanted to know who we were. "Oh yes" he said, "I told them you were my landlord and Geoff was your Chauffer". Nothing at all happened, except that they all milled around talking to each other, but I did notice that occasionally one would press some money into Asif's hand a bit secretively this would be as much as forty or fifty pounds. Apparently the whole affair was an excuse for a huge get together to chat and to give some money to the groom. Only Asif told me that his father collected most of it, which could have amounted to a couple of thousand pounds. Asif did not see a penny of that, no wonder they wanted him to get married!

Eigg (lover for two weeks)

When I went to Australia in 1986 they asked me which two of the three cities I would like to stop at, I chose Hong Kong and Singapore. Bangkok was the one I missed out. So I decided to go to there to get David "out of my system". When I arrived I went straight to the most famous and the largest gay sauna in the world called Babylon. It has one thousand lockers and at times they are all full and one has to wait. It has a large balcony where you can have food and drink, which overlooks beautiful gardens that belong to the Austrian Embassy. There I met Eigg (pronounced egg) who was thirty years old and as most Thais do looked ten years younger. He had the most wonderful "come to bed smile". We talked for some time over a cold drink and then he said he would like to come back to my hotel, so I invited him back for dinner.

Although my hotel was only about a mile away, it took over an hour to get there, though the traffic that was at that time about as bad as you will find any where in the world. After dinner we walked out for a drink. I told him that I would be leaving in the morning on the hotel bus for Pattaya. Then it was decided that he could come with me, he said he could get some time off. But he had to go to his home to get some clothes, but that it would not be worth going now as it would take him three hours. So at four in the morning he was up, dressed and off to his home and back again with some belongings in just over half an hour and back into bed with me.

At the hotel at Pattaya they only charged me a small amount extra for him to stay with me for the two weeks; there was a large double bed in the room anyway. He was a great help, he knew the town and all the best restaurants. There are no taxi's only converted pick-up-trucks that do "just that". They have two bench seats in the back that seat ten or twelve at a crush. It costs 10 Baht to any-where in the town, that's about twenty pence. Every day we would go to the beach in a Baht bus, have breakfast in a cafe there and then go to the section that was gay. Most Thais speak very little English. Eigg's English was very good. At the beach you rent a deck chair and can then have all sorts of food and drink brought to you during the day. At the end of the day when the sun is well down, we settle up the bill and then get another Baht bus back to the hotel. In the evening after a rest and maybe a swim in the hotel pool we would go out for an evening meal. Every day I would give Eigg a certain amount of money, then he would pay for every thing and give a tip where needed.

Whilst on the beach I found myself on my own most of the time, Eigg was off chatting to friends. I started talking to another Englishman, it turned out he was born the same year as myself but we did not get around to asking each other where we lived in England. He said he was an English teacher who subsidized his visits to Thailand by teaching the Thais English. We saw each other for several days before I said, "by the way where do you live back home?" The surprising answer was Burnham. I said. "Burnham Bucks". He said "yes". We both lived in the same village! Almost always when you meet and become friends with someone while on holiday you find that their home is nowhere near yours. So we began to see each other quite a bit he came to dinner at "Woodside" and was very complimentary about the house garden and especially the dinning room with my furniture.

Eric told me that he was a friend of a colonel in the Nepalese army who was chaperon to Prince Nirajan the second son of the king of Nepal who was seventeen years old and at Eton College. Eric told me that his colonel friend had on more that one occasion taken him to his home for dinner and that he felt guilty that his house was small and not at all suitable to entertain the Colonel and His Royal Highness. Would I allow him to entertain them in my dinning room at my house? He said he would do all the cooking and cover all expenses. I have always loved entertaining and for that matter cooking as well, I said I would be pleased help him out and that I would do the cooking. They duly arrived and I enjoyed preparing a special four-course meal where Eric had paid for all the ingredients and the wine. HRH turned out to be a very ordinary quite likable lad. I had invited (with Eric's approval) another friend to make up a table of six. So at the table we had Chris Chinese, Asif from Kashmir, the Colonel and HRH. from Nepal, Eric and I British. The conversation was most interesting all throughout the meal and afterwards in the lounge for another couple of hours until the Colonel said. "He must get the Prince back to Eton". Before he left the Prince told us that if ever we got to Kathmandu Nepal we must call at the palace to see him.

I probably would not have remembered to put this little story in, if it had not been for the tragic news five years later, that the Nepal Crown prince had shot his bother Prince Nirajan and most of the Royal family before shooting himself.

During my time with Asif I bought him a gold necklace probably for one of his birthdays. Gold looks so good on the darker Asian skin. When he told me he no longer loved me he gave it back to me. So I took this necklace to Thailand with me, I "don't know why, I wore it just the once I think, it's not really me. Then I said to Eigg you wear it; it looks so good on you. We had a wonderful two weeks together and I became very fond of him. Despite there being literally thousand of good-looking Thai's "available" I stuck solely with him. Occasionally I would say, I think I will have an evening in tonight, but you go out and enjoy yourself and I would give him some money. He would come back never very late, put some money on the side and say I didn't spend it all.

I made enquiries about getting him to England. But the more I looked into it the more impossible it seemed it would be. However I told him I would be back. We went back to Bangkok for the last night and he took me to another hotel this time. We had our last evening meal together and then he said he wanted me to meet some of his friends in the hotel lounge. There were about six of us sitting having a drink when Eigg excused him self to go to the toilet. After about twenty minutes and he had not returned I went to look for him, then went to the room where we were to have spent the last night together. His small suitcase had gone, on the side was my expensive camera and my suitcase, but nothing was missing except Eigg and the necklace. It was one of the unhappiest nights of my life.

184

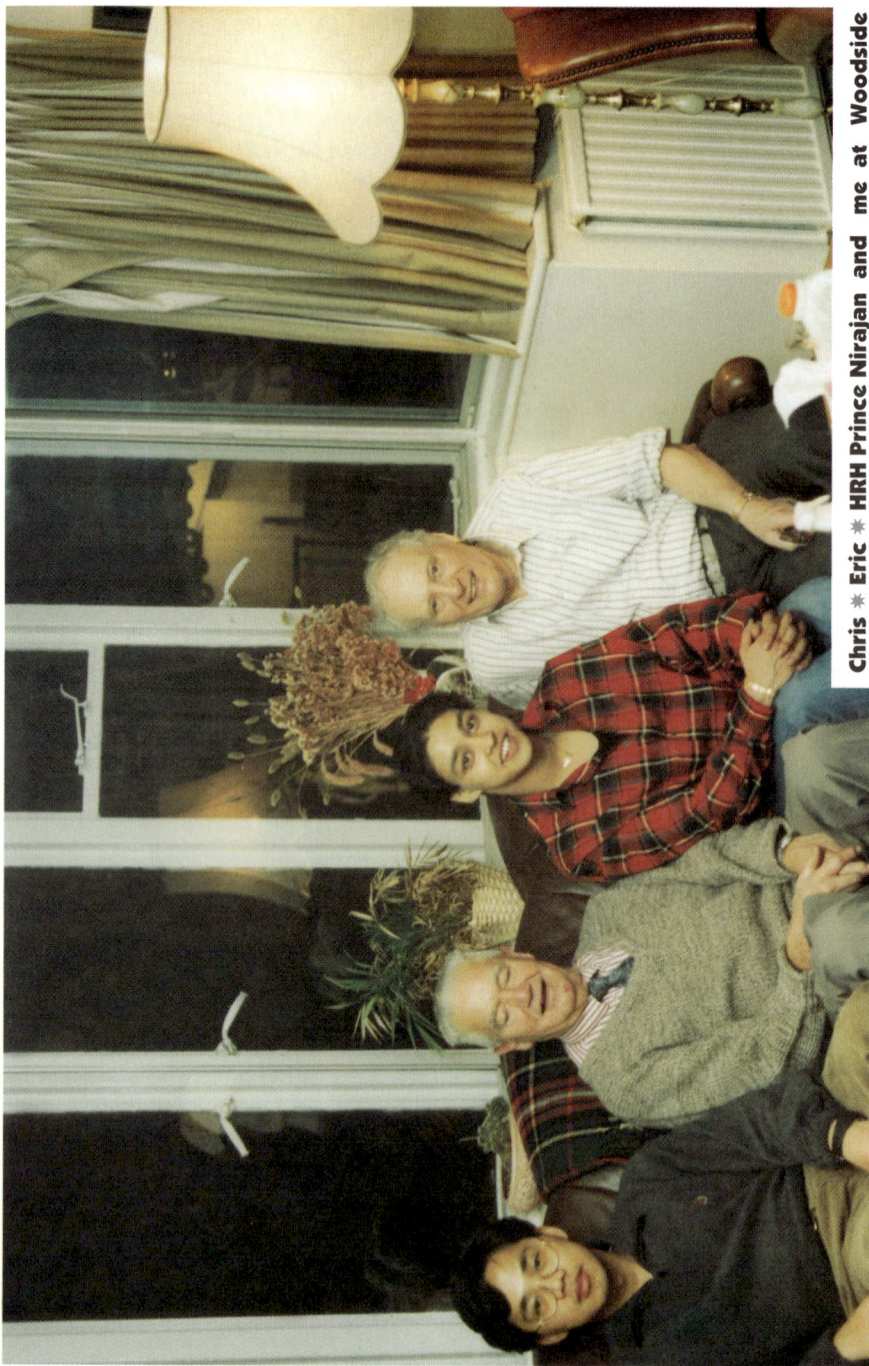

Chris * Eric * HRH Prince Nirajan and me at Woodside

The next morning I was taken to the airport by the hotel bus that fortunately, as it turned out got me there nearly three hours before the flight instead of two. I presented my ticket folder that I had not touched since checking in at Heathrow. I was then asked for my return ticket, I said. "It should be there". "No" she said. "It was not there". I was convinced that if it was not where I thought it should have been then it must have been removed at London together with the out-going half. The Thai check-in female became very official; she refused to accept my suggestion demanding that I search my entire luggage. My suitcase had been though the "scan tunnel" and had been bound with a metal strap. An official took the case back to the check-in, the strap was cut and then I was told to search the case while he stood over me.

As you can imagine I was not feeling in the best of moods, as it was I became very angry telling them that at no time did I, nor would I put my ticket in my suitcase. I stormed back to the checking desk demanding that they fax London for confirmation that I had paid the return fare and to check at that end. I could not see the problem for all the details were on the computer screen. Eventually some one did Fax London. All this time I was stood on one side whilst the rest of the passengers were checked in. Then back came the reply. No, it was not possible for my ticket to have been removed at Heathrow. I was informed in a very "official" manner I would have to pay again. I presented my gold card and was told that will be Nine Hundred and Fifty Pounds. I said. "I "don't want a return ticket I'm never coming back". "No" she said. "That is the single rate".

Now I had bought a "package" that had included a return flight, all hotels for two weeks, plus transport to and from Pattaya and the airport for just over one thousand pounds. But I was told that was the price. By this time two hours had gone by. I was feeling like a sit down and a drink, so I paid up thinking I would sort this out in London. Then I was told I must go to the police station on the airport and make out a report as to why I had lost my ticket. I protested, saying I have bought another return ticket why do I have to do that? At first I refused to go but I had no option, she would not give me my boarding card. I was then "escorted" to the police station about a quarter of a mile away, where I was sat down in front of an officer who did not even look up for some time, then he said what did I want, I told him what I had been made to do, trying not to show my anger too him to much. He then looked around not seeming to know what to do, he then put a piece of paper in front of me and I wrote down what I knew must have happened. He took a long time looking at this and by this time it was getting near to takeoff time. I told him this but it did not seem to register. Eventually he gave my "escort" a piece of paper and I was escorted again back to the check-in.

At last feeling weak from exhaustion and thirst I started off to the boarding gate that was another quarter of a mile away, before I was half way there it was

"Take off time". If I missed the plane there was not another for two days and they were all booked up any way. Fortunately there was a fifteen-minute delay. I arrived at the gate soaked in sweat sagging at the knees. I was "told off" for being late and that they were about to unload my baggage. On falling into to my seat I asked a stewardess for a drink. I was told to "belt up" we are about to take off. Half an hour later I was given a drink.

On arrival at Heathrow twelve hours later the aircraft came to a halt, but before the doors were opened there was an announcement over the speaker system. "Would a Mr George Montague please contact a senior official of Eva Air as he leaves the aircraft". As I did so I was I was asked by a man in a suit (not a uniform) was I Mr Montague? (They must have faxed a description) "Yes I said". I was taken gently by the arm and led to a small lounge. I was aware that this person was apologising all the time saying how sorry he was. We sat down and he explained that this was the first time this had ever happened the check-in girl had inadvertently taken out my return ticket together with my out going one. He refunded my gold card and handed me a letter of apology together with instructions to claim VIP treatment the next time I travelled by Eva Air. I said. "I shall never be going to Thailand again, you will hear from my solicitors". I sued them; I rejected their first two offers and then on advice accepted four hundred pounds plus costs in compensation.

I had no intention of going back to Thailand but then I met Somchai and have been back every year since. The first time I visited the beach with Somchai I saw Eigg. He looked very shocked when our eyes met. He could not avoid me as I signalled him to come to where I was sitting. I proceeded to tell him all about the meeting with my latest boyfriend and how I was a little in love with him right up until the night he stole the necklace and deserted me leaving me to one of the unhappiest nights of my life. I told him it was not the part about the necklace that hurt so much but that he did what he did when I was looking forward so much to our last night together. I told him I would certainly have come to see him again within six months and have done my best to get him to England, which was what he had told me he wanted to do. (I now know that would have been very difficult). I also told him I had every intention of giving him the necklace once I had returned to England and had a word with Asif about it. For after all it was Asif's even thought he had given it back to me when he told me he no longer loved me, but I had told him I would not accept it. Eigg was very crestfallen and asked me to forgive him, this I had already done before he asked me.

Jason (Just less than one year)

I visited a new gay pub in Maidenhead, new to me anyway. In there I met an old friend I had not seen for some time. We sat and talked over a drink. Then he said. "There is some one in here who only likes older men". I was at least thirty years older than all the other customers in there. He said. "Shall I introduce you"? I of course said, "yes" he called over a young, fairly short chap with a beard, without the beard he would have looked even younger, my friend said. "This is Jason, Jason this is George". We exchanged a few words and then he said. "Nice to meet you" and then walked back to join the friends he had been talking to. I thought. Oh well that's that.

A few day later, when I had forgotten all about him, after all we had not exchanged phone numbers, the phone rang and a voice said this is Jason remember me? He had to explain where we had met before I remembered. "Can I come and see you"? He said, "how did you get my Number"? "I asked" "Walter (that was the name of my friend) told me" he said. Jason came around and that was the start of a very intermittent relationship. He would come around to see me some times three times in a week, sometimes staying the night, then I would not see him again for a month. He was twenty-five years old and a mathematics teacher at a local comprehensive school. One day he came around and I hardly recognized him, he had shaved off his beard, he looked about eighteen. It was just at the start of the school summer holidays. He explained that if he did not wear a beard, some of the other teachers and pupils thought he was a pupil. He said he would grow it back again before the end of the holidays. The "affair" lasted for just under a year, nether of us fell in love with the other, but he just came to satisfy a need, I of course was flattered that someone like him, as young as he was and a mathematics teacher should fancy me. As we were together for less than one year we mutually agreed that he was not one of the seven loves of my life. He knew I was writing these memoirs; he helped me with it at times. He asked me not to put him in it. But the last time I saw him he said. OK yes you can.

Through me, Jason met my great sailing friend Richard who had only recently lost his lover Ken to a smoking related decease; they had been together for almost 40 years. For some reason that seemed strange to me at the time they both formed a great friendship together. Jason even moved in and lived with Richard. When I suggested that there was more than friendship between them they both laughed very loudly. Some time later I saw Richard becoming more and more ill, with frequent periods in hospital. I then learnt that Richard had full blown Aids he died not long after that. I had known for years that Richard would not "make old bone's" Both he and his lover Ken had been heavy smokers for most of their lives and it showed in their health. They were both many years younger than I, they both died from smoking, yes, even Richard the combination drugs available by then would have saved him, but it was too late. It was smoking that killed them both.

After I learnt that Richard had Aids I asked Jason if he had known. "Yes he said a few days after we met". I had known Richard since he was 16 years old he had always been one of my closest friends. I was not offended I understood. Richard had needed a "buddy" a companion Jason filled the bill. Human nature is a funny thing we will often tell a complete stranger intimate details about ourselves. But do not confide in someone close to us.

Another thing that I have found in life is that familiarity breed's contempt. Some will get upset, row and argue with a loved one. But in an identical situation, where another person is concerned, nothing will be said. A typical example often happens in a driver and passenger setting, where if one of them say's anything about the others driving or about the directions being given all hell breaks loose. This has happened to me on so many occasions with at least four of my lovers. And this has been apart from the time's I was teaching some of them to drive. Of the four Jason was the worst. On one occasion we were both in evening dress on our way to an annual sailing club dinner. Jason was driving and I gave directions. In Parliament Square where there are about five lanes of traffic we needed to turn left, so I told him to get into the left hand lane, but when we got near to the turning it was blocked off. We didn't want to go over Westminster bridge so we had to do a right turn across all the heavy traffic and go around the square again. Jason was fuming at me. He stopped the car, got out and walked off. I just sat in the car and a few minutes later he came back. We then had a very pleasant evening. We are still great friends.

SAUNA'S

I went to my first sauna while I was waiting for the boat to come home from Durban South Africa, since then I doubt if I have been as long as a month, without going to one. You have never been so clean no matter how many baths or shower you have than when you leave a good sauna. Before I went to my first I would have blackheads in the corner of my nose and in other places. If you bare the heat as long as you can for three sessions the sweat just rolls off you. All your pours open up and all the dirt comes out. We shed our skin all the time if you rub your self over in the shower after the steam room or sauna all the dead skin comes off. The reason you just have to get out of the heat after maybe fifteen minutes is because your heart beats so fast. This is good for your heart which should beat at the highest speed you can bare once or twice a week. That is of course unless you have a heart problem. We all eat too much salt, when you lose four or five pounds in weight through sweating you lose a lot of salt. So I have been going to saunas now for well over fifty years, I'm positive they are good for you. Everybody tells me I look 10 or 15 years younger than I am and that my skin is so smooth so few wrinkles.

I've always liked saunas for the three 's', the Sauna, the social side and the sex. You can't do anything in a sauna or steam room except sweat, talk, or play about. There is a great deal of "putting the world to rights" you meet a great many people all of whom have some thing in common with each other. I have met many of my greatest friends in one particular sauna at "Uxbridge now sadly closed. Those in "male only" (so called straight heterosexual saunas) are either totally, or thirty to forty per cent gay or bi-sexual. But not all of those in there would admit it, not even to them selves.

It is well known that many if not most women lose much of their sexual appetite increasingly after the "change of life", "the Menopause" around fifty. Whereas men only lose it very gradually right up to the age of ninety and some not even then. So what is a respectable, or not quite so respectable man to do? Many of them as we know go off with younger women. Men of fifty plus make up the largest part of prostitutes clients. The majority of rent boy's clients are married men struggling with their sexuality and may not be happy to confess their bent. But I can tell you that very many who may never have done anything gay except maybe a "wank" with another boy like I did all those years ago, go to these saunas for their sexual relief. I have talked with and listened to the conversations of many hundreds who fit this bill, in the Uxbridge sauna alone. Their wives would have no idea where they were, or if they did would never guess what they were up to. They were married men with families who genuinely still loved their wives. But who find themselves doing what they do rather than going with another or younger woman.

Unlike at an outright gay sauna nothing very "disgraceful" usually happens like penetration. Nothing more really than we boys used to do "Group Masturbation". Often a couple will massage each other ending up in the steam room working on the bit that gives the most relief. Every one seems to know instinctively who is OK and who is not. No harm is done to any one and no one is offended. Many years ago the police used to raid these places but they have learnt their lesson. If you disturb a swarm of bees, they will cause a lot of problems to other members of the public, then they get together again and swarm somewhere else.

There were about five ladies who ran this sauna. One of them held the franchise from Hillingdon council. Admittedly they would be out of a job and lose their "pin money" if it was closed. But they all knew that it was an "unofficial" gay sauna and if a stranger turned up they would tell him and ask him if he still wanted to go in. If it was one man on his own he almost always did. There was no advertising there used to be a board but it disappeared years ago. There was not even a sign on the door everybody got to know about it by "Word of mouth". In all the years that I went there, that must have been about twenty I have never seen anyone there younger than his mid twenties. Occasionally you would "bump into someone" usually in a Gay establishment who's face you would know quite well but were unable to "place him" or where you had seen him. Then one of us would remember and say. "I didn't recognize you with your clothes on".

THE INTERNET.

Is a Godsend for gays or anyone looking for a partner, but unfortunately a paradise for Paedophiles looking for their prey. So many people of all sexual persuasions are too shy to go to bars or cruising places, even if they live near where these might be.

Caffmos is a society that was formed in Brighton specifically for men over fifty. Just like many heterosexuals, gays, before they are forty tend to think that sex finishes soon after that. But I can tell you that there are thousands of men who are partners with other men of round a bout the same age. They are not often seen on the gay scene. But are at home, or out and about enjoying each other's company and companionship, living together just like other people. It is a myth that gays whatever age they are, only like young men.

There is however a note in brackets after the tile that states (and their younger men admirers). I was sixty-four at the time Steve and I parted and I needed to find another lover, but I never dreamt that there would be so many young good looking men who only want a man who is at least twice or three time their age. I didn't know about the Quebec at Marble Arch, so I was lucky once again to find Asif. As far as I am concerned I shall stay with Somchai till the day I die if he will put up with me till then. So hopefully I will not need the Internet. But I still look.

HOLIDAY PLACES FOR GAYS.

Gran Canairia is probably the most popular. There are at least two enclosed complexes with fifty or so self-catering double chalets, with a large swimming pool and pool bar in the centre. There is a restaurant, social room and many other amenities. The whole area is totally enclosed and not over looked, so that no clothes need be worn at any time if you wish. At Maspalomas (about a half hour walk away) is a perfect sandy beach that must be about a mile long, one large section of which is recognized as gay, nude sunbathing is the norm. Behind this beach is "the dunes", an area of about a mile in all directions with hills and hollows and nothing but sand except right in the centre where there are a lot of bushes and small trees. Any paths or tracks that there are don't lead to anywhere. What goes on there, is nothing more than that which anyone can see in any public park on a hot day between two heterosexuals, a bit of kissing, cuddling and petting. But many of these "Hets" would object if they were to see two gays doing the same thing.

Walking home from the beach and the dunes before the sun goes down you have to pass near to a shopping complex called the Cita Centre. There are several levels on one of which there is a cafe called Marlines. This is where many of "the boys" will stop for a coffee before making for "home" and dinner after which they will have at least an hour or so sleep. In the town is another very large shopping complex on three levels called The Yumbo Centre. During the day and up until about nine o/clock this will be full of the "general public" and family's spending their holiday money. At ten o/clock all the shops will have closed, but other "units" that were built as shops will begin to open their doors, these are gays bars, at least twenty of them.

These will cater for all tastes, leather, disco, porno, or just ordinary gay bars. A few will be where the older men go and there you will find a fair number of younger men who will only be attracted to those of twice or three times their own age. I am constantly surprised when talking to young gay men who are "butterflies" (those who are always on the lookout for a new "one nighstand" and fly from flower to flower, usually good looking young one's) that say. "When I can no longer 'pull' (pick-up) I shall retire from the gay scene". Thinking, that will be when they are thirty something and certainly long before they are fifty. They have no idea that in certain bars unless they have grey hair and wrinkles they will have no chance to pick up any young men in there. They often know about these bars but think that it is only old men that go in them. Young men who are attracted to those twice or three times their own age are called Gerontophiles. (Not a lot of folk know that). They are those that are about as far removed from a Paedophile as you can get.

I have been to Gran Canairia on three occasions with three different lover's, Asif, David, and my present partner Somchai. I wandered into one of these bars, (sometimes referred to as "the Elephants Graveyards") with David. Now David was one of those who liked to "be admired" and he was "very presentable I was proud to be seen with him". We went into what to me, was a new pub (each year new one's open and old ones change hands). This one was now called "so What!" it was full of old men from sixty to ninety years old. We sat down and ordered a drink and then David said. "No one is looking at me?" We discovered on talking to one of them that they were all Partners, all old men who only liked old men. Some of them had been together most of their adult lives. Others were "butterflies" who still liked older men even though they were now old themselves. Every one felt completely "at home" at this complex and walked around arm-in-arm For every single person you would see, either in the bars, walking the different levels, or sitting near the gardens, would be "Family" all gay, thousands of them (and no queer bashers). The younger one's would be there till five or six o/clock in the morning before going home with their lover or "the evenings pick up".

Brighton is the "San Francisco" of England, where it is estimated that between twenty to twenty five per cent of the resident population is gay. There has been a Gay beach there since I can remember. It is at Telscombe Cliffs. A very long walk east of the town at a part of the beach that is a cul-de-sac and it gets cut off at high tide. No families or "straight" people ever seem to walk that far. Gay couples have always been completely free to do exactly what all other couples do, when lying on the beach in the sun together, nobody takes any notice of kissing and cuddling between two men There are no police, no disapproving glances and again no Queer bashers.

Then there is the nudist beach just a few hundred yards west of the marina. One will notice that there are a great many more men than women. The cruising that goes on is very subtle, just a "meeting of eyes" between those that are walking around and those lying down. It is interesting to watch the gangs of youths (still fully dressed) that come down and walk around for a "look". If you watch carefully you will see that most of them look at the women, but there is nearly always one who will only look at the men. I have many time's motored my boat Woody out of the Marina, when there was not enough wind to sail, then anchored her just off the marker buoys which are to stop powered craft of all types going near to the beach. Then I would strip off completely, get into the dinghy and row ashore in the nude. I would be observed doing this and having reached the shore and pulled the dinghy up onto the beach, it would not be long before I would be chatting to someone telling him, that is my yacht out there, would you like to go out to her with me for a drink?

Then there is Studland an area on Brownsea Island belonging to the National Trust that is designated as a nature reserve, part of which is marked by boards that say, "Beyond this point clothes need not be worn". If you get there by walking along the beach you obviously have to wear some clothes. It is interesting to see some one walking along with a small rucksack on their back then when they get to this notice board they stop, take off all their clothes, put them in the rucksack, then walk on. Now we, (that is me in Woody and others from our Gay Sailing Club) would sail there, anchor off and then go ashore in our dinghies, in the nude of course.

Another place that must still be popular, although I have not been there for years now is Parsons Pleasure. This is a stretch of the river Isis (The Thames really only they renamed this bit) at Oxford. The story goes that many years ago the professors from the university would go to this stretch, sun bathe in the nude and won the right to do so in perpetuity. So for all those years before they approved places like Brighton, it was the only place in England where you could legally sunbathe in the nude in a place that was also open to the general public.

Sitges in Spain is about an hours drive south of Madrid. This is an average sized town similar in some way to Playa d la Englise and to the Yumbo centre in Gran Canairia. A typical family seaside holiday town except that a careful observer would notice an above average number of adult males with out female companions. Every day during the long summer the streets; shops and the beach are crowded with holidaymakers. If you swim out from the beach and look back you will notice that while as far as you can see, the beach to the left and to the right of you will be busy, a section in the centre is packed solid. That is the part that will be exclusively male and gay. By eleven o/clock in the evening it looks as if the place is closing down for the night but that is when the Gay bars of which there are dozens are getting busy. From then on until daylight you will find only men on the streets walking from one bar or club to another They are all gay except for a few standing in pairs on the corners in uniform, they are the police who are perfectly well aware of the situation. It is tourists gay and straight who bring prosperity to the town.

PAKISTAN

Ian Bothham the famous cricketer said. Pakistan was the place where you would send your Mother-in-law (but he is not gay). Next to Thailand I would say that here is a place where Homosexual acts, not Homosexuality as such are most common. Next the on the list would be India then many Muslim countries.

But it is secretive and unacknowledged. The prevalence should not be surprising. In a strict Islamic society, interaction between male and female is severely restricted due to the medieval system of purdah (A Persian word meaning curtain). However human nature being what it is, relief is sort after and the oldest profession flourishes. A man I saw regularly and with whom I became friendly on my several business trips to Karachi (a married man with six children told me, "There is nothing to do in this country except work and making love to your wife and I can't afford any more kids". Contraceptives of any kind are forbidden.

Lahore is the most famous; a loose network of male prostitution pervades the entire city, unconfined by red-light boundaries the rent-boy trade is mind boggling both in its scale and extent. Male prostitutes can be found plying their trade in every alley, bus stop, shopping centre, cinema hall, hotel lobby, park, railway station or college campus in all the major towns of Pakistan.

In a country where the genders seldom mix socially, particularly in public, male bonding is obviously very prominent. Even where sex is not engaged in commercially, it often becomes a factor in intergenerational relationships between men and boys, taboo in the west, but not uncommon in the Islamic world although kept hushed up.

Another factor is that Pakistan is one of the few countries in the world where the male population significantly outnumbers the female in every age group. So in the scarcity of the vagina, it seems any orifice will do, or where There's a Willy There's a way.

Although no law specifically prohibits homosexuality, "unnatural offences", (presumably including sodomy and bestiality) are covered by a Penal Code that punishes sex outside marriage, but it is rarely enforced. Despite creeping westernisation marriage remains a duty not a pleasure. Those that are homosexual, even hijras or so called "eunuchs" (they are really transvestites, or katoeys as they are called in Thailand) are obliged to marry due to family pressure of strict social conformity. (See the chapter on Asif.)

Paradoxically while there is homosexuality or apparent 'gayness" there are no Gays as such, unlike India where urban gays are now "coming out". In Pakistan homosexuality is still deeply ensconced within the almairah (closet) and never admitted to in public.

"In Pakistan there is no gay subculture to speak of in this land of the pure". That said, however interest in boys as objects of pleasure has a long history on the subcontinent going back to Afghan and Persian influence made famous by Alexander the Great. Turks and Greeks, who all squeezed though the Khyber Pass. Mogul emperors such as Babur and later Persian conqueror Nadir Shar who sacked Deli in 1739 were known to have kept harems of beautiful boys.

Despite its common practise, pederasty is considered immoral and officially frowned upon in Islam. (Not only in Islam!). Although alcohol is also taboo and hence illegal in strict Muslim countries, bootlegging and boozing are nevertheless also widespread. The two-faced attitude of illicit sex and intoxication being officially condemned but widely practiced and winked at, smacks of hypocrisy to outsiders. But Pakistanis "don't see it that way. As the popular cricketer-turned politician Imran Khan puts it" it's the public show of immorality that Islam condemns. What people do behind closed doors is entirely up to them. This seems to confirm one of the sayings of the Prophet that Part of someone's being a good Muslim is his leaving alone that which does not concern him.

THAILAND

I would say that Thailand was "the' most tolerant country where Gay sex is concerned in the world. Throughout this section I shall refer to all young Thai men as "boys". All those I shall be referring to will be less than forty years old. All those working in the sex trade are called "Boys", Beach "Boys", Bar "Boys", Massage Boys", Boys that work as waiters, Boys that work in hotels and guesthouses. The main reason for this is that. Thais are on average three to four inches shorter than Caucasians. They all look five, ten fifteen years younger than they are. They are nearly always very good looking. Most of the time they look very happy and always greet you with an ear-to-ear smile.

In recent years Thailand was a haven for paedophiles, but thanks to reports in the western press and the international pressure that followed this it has now been severely curtailed. It has not stopped altogether, it never will of course, but people are now reporting their suspicions and the police are taking action. All Thais have to carry an identity card that has their date of birth on and the police regularly check these days.

Although many Paedophiles have been caught, few have been imprisoned I understand. Corruption is endemic, the police are paid off, the parents of the boy are paid off not to prosecute, but "good news". Now a days details of the culprit are sent to his own country and if he returns he would be prosecuted there. So he is stuck, very much poorer than when he arrived and not permitted to work. His name will be on the child sex offender's computer file and he gets no sympathy or protection from the gay community. So now all the "working boys" (those in the sex) trade that you see are over eighteen although many of them do not look it.

I read in the Bangkok Post that there are 5,000 bars, nightclubs, massage and sauna venues across the country. These are all male and female brothels, "although they are never referred to as such". All in the large towns and cites. It says there are very many freelances, as many as a million, some of them working only when they need the money.

Maybe some of the girls are, but none of the boys are ever forced to do it physically. They are forced to do it by hardship and poverty and by the sheer size of the financial temptation.

In Pattaya, where I have spent most of the last six English winters there must be 5,000 girls and yes! 5,000 "boys"! all working part time or full time in the "sex-industry". As you walk thought the town a great many of all those you see will be OAPs or middle-aged mostly Caucasian men, twice or three time's as old as the boy or girl that they are walking arm in arm or holding hands with. There are as many men walking with boys as there are men walking with girls, nobody takes any notice.

One whole street is called Boyz Town. There it is all gay bars, a gay sauna, gay restaurants where most of the boys are "available" and boy bars. The biggest of these is called Boys Boys Boys; they say they have 100 boys. Inside in the centre is a large "all round" stage on which will be about 40 boys, all doing a simple dance to pop music, moving very slowly around so that every one gets a good look at each boy   They all wear a very brief pair of underpants and a number on a pin disc. The punters (customers) mostly men, but sometime there is a woman (wanting a "toy boy") all sit around the out side at small tables and chairs where they "pay through the nose" for drinks.

When a customer takes a fancy to a particular boy he will signal him to sit next to him. Then if all is well and they decide to leave he will signal a waiter who will come and make up his bill adding 250 baht (£4), this goes to the management. If they go upstairs where there are rooms for the purpose, he will pay extra to the management and 500 baht (£8) to the boy for what is called "short time". If the boy is taken back to the hotel it is 500 baht for short time and a minimum of 1000 baht (£16) for "all night".

Jomtiem, which is part of and just next to Pattaya has over two miles of perfect sandy beach. This is all divided up into sections of about 50 deck chairs and sun umbrellas, all run by different owners helped of course by many boys. They will bring you almost any kind of food or drink that you might want. Here is where the "free lance" boys will "ply their trade". One is constantly pestered by hoards of Hawkers who will try to sell you almost anything that can be carried. If you want a massage then there are dozens of boys in white coats with a number who are registered masseurs. These tend to be boys who are older and no longer suitable for the boy bars. They put out a large sheet on the sand and will give you a very good Thai pummelling for 200 baht.

The initial introduction into the world of sex for hire for many male prostitutes is from their friends. They go back to their village with a lot of money in their pocket, much of which they give to their very poor parents telling them they have worked hard in restaurants and hotels. They talk to some of their friends who work long hours for a week to get the same as he gets for one night. Then they tell them about the sort of money they can get if they go to bed with gay people Thais or foreigners.

There is a code of conduct among the boys, they are very careful who they tell what they are doing or what goes on. None under the age of eighteen are told and none who might inform on them. They are very careful that the parents should not find out.

I heard about one mother who was suspicious about the money her son gave her and when questioned as to why she did not try to stop him she said. "We need the money, what else can we do" at least he will not lose his virginity and get pregnant like his sisters.

Many people reading this will say. "This is outrageous it should be stopped". I must say when I first went I was saddened by what I found. Unlike the thousands of men who come here from all over the world, almost always on their own, most for a short holiday. But very many to settle, work, live or retire here. I don't come for the Thai boys; I come because Thailand is my partner's home country and where his family is. He is Somchai, a Thai. I met him in England. He is my seventh long term lover and he lives with me in England, his sisters, brother and Mother, of whom I am very fond and where I am now consider as part of the family.

As always I have asked lots of questions and spoken to many "boys" in broken English of course and I have come to the conclusion that unlike a pre puberty or very young teenage boy who is seduced, very little harm if any is done. They know exactly what they are getting into. They genuinely seem to enjoy what they do and certainly what they get out of it. Almost all those they go with are twice or three times their age. They do nothing they don't want to do. They give as little as they can get away with. They get as much out of the Farangs (foreigners) as they can. They often get the "punters to fall in love with them, this they are very good at. Many of those they go with are already very old, when they die the boy ends up a Bart millionaire. The "Farangs" can't seem to mind for they regularly come back year after year for more. And until there is a very great improvement in the economic situation nothing will change.

The sensible ones (except those that are genuinely gay and there are many of those) when they have a nice little "nest egg" in the bank and they are getting too old to "pull" easily, get married and do something else. Some will say "they" should close all these venues and put a stop to these men coming here just for sex. What would the poor boys do then, the smiling faces would smile a lot less and they and their families would go hungry. One way to look at it would be to call it "International Aid". It has grown to such a size, that if they clamp down on it, (this they are constantly talking about doing), it would decimate most of the tourists "play spots". After all it is a thriving industry. And as such must be very good for the economy.

Before people condemn what goes on they must come to Thailand and see for them selves the poverty that exists here. Not so much in the cities and towns. (Thanks partly to the sex industry!) But where the bulk of the population live, in the country where the parents of these boys live. Poverty here has become a great deal worst since my first visit in 1996. The next year saw the Asian economic slump, with the Thai currency losing one third of its value. These boys have three choices. One, to stay with their families where although they wont starve they will all be extremely poor,two, get a job in the towns and cities where most of them will only earn barely enough to survive, which many of them to their credit do, but unable to make enough money to help their families. Or three, take up part time or full time as a "Bar Boy" or "Money Boy" "the word prostitute" is never used. They say "Love makes the world go round" Sex also makes the world go around. What is so wrong with "paying for sex", when so many more men than we know (and some women) prefer it that way. There has always been and there always will be a very big demand.

Whilst I don't know about the girls (I wouldn't would I?) The boys (unlike in some other parts of the world) are not recruited or persuaded by anything other poverty to do what they do. The two Ps Poverty and Prostitution go together. As it says in the bible "the poor are always with us" I am reminded of a remark made by Mahatma Ghand". "There is enough in the world for every ones need, but not enough for every ones greed" Thailand is very much a land of the "haves" and the "have-nots" very many very rich people and far too much corruption.

People look down on and disapprove of prostitutes very few counties in the world have legal brothels. Yet it is called the oldest profession in the world. It goes on and has been going on and will go on for all time. What is so wrong with one person who has the money paying another for sex where there is no coercion?

I think that registered brothels would be a great practical improvement on that which happens now. There would be control and regular inspection, regular health checks, less soliciting in the street, less kerb crawling, less offensive advertising, less assaults and they could pay income tax. Why is it that promiscuity and prostitution are such dirty words? Immorality Adultery. Is not against the law, only church law. What if one does not belong to any church? Less than 50% of people in the UK say they believe in a God and less than 10% ever go to church now.

AFGANISTAN.

Something that I would think most people will find surprising is, that given the Afghanistan's, especially the warlords who are known for their toughness and fighting abilities are, now that the Taliban regime is gone, reverting to their traditions of Homosexuality. In Kandahar this medieval city that apparently has long been known as a bastion of man-boy love in Central Asia. The Pushtun men have started to become visable again with their teenaged catamites, or pleasure boys called "ashna".

Before the Taliban took over in 1994 Pashtun men could be seen everywhere showing off their handsome "ashna" upon whom they showered expensive gifts, as a sign of prestige. As in the Northwest Frontier of Pakistan once the boy is taken in, the beloved "ashna" become part of the family as most Pushtun men are married, with children out of a sense of duty.

The Pushtan tradition is even reflected in their poetry with odes written to the beauty and complexion of beardless youth, just as in ancient Greece. It is said that when a boy starts growing a beard- the shaving of which was forbidden under the Taliban - it is like a cloud covering the radiance of the moon-.

RELIGION.

As you will see from what I have already written a large part of my life has been taken up with singing, more so with sacred music than secular. I believed and "felt" the words I was using, just as I did for years when I read the lessons from the bible to the congregation at church. I found many of the stories from the bible hard to swallow and I thought how can something go on for "ever and ever Amen". But I was "brain washed" "indoctrinated" from a small child. Then quite late in life I realised that according to the church I am a "sinner". Most religions condemn homosexuality out right some even execute gays. Religion says that sex between man and man is an abomination.

There has never been any thing like the recognition of the gays that were put through the gas chambers, during the war, like there has been of the Jews. At least the Church of England now, only condemns the sin and not the sinner.

How can we in this day and age treat people, condemn people based on something like the Bible, Koran or the Torah? (Pentateuch) Written so many years ago, written by people who just like many today do not understand or want to, do not even want to discuss it. How can a healthy young male go without sex, even with him self? don't tell me the priests do, look how many of them have been caught eventually, often protected for years by "their own" to continue abusing children and that's just the ones who get caught. We all know how reluctant children are to complain, partly because they know they will not be believed and partly for the publicity that will hurt the one's they love.

How can the "church" condemn those that want to "love" another person? Most humans are not loners like some animals. If "God" made us why did he make about ten percent of males and seven percent of females, (Yes I'm sure it's that many), during all or part if their lives attracted to some one of the same sex. The priest will say we should resist temptation. What have "we" done that we should have such "temptation" put in our way? I can't believe Jesus Christ had no sex for all of his thirty three years, after all there was John "Whom he loved" it says so in the bible. Yes I believe there was such a person and if ever there was a saint it was probably him.

I don't know believe in a God or the book of Genesis or miracles. I don't believe in the virgin birth and I don't believe in the resurrection or an afterlife. Yes, I believe he was crucified, but he didn't die on the cross, that's where "the resurrection comes in. Every thing has grown up around the story of him, it has all been exaggerated and grossly coloured by humans who just have to believe and worship. And who desperately want to believe in an "after life" and that they will one day see again their loved ones who have died. This I now no longer do, I believe its ashes to ashes dust to dust and that is it, until someone can prove to me otherwise.

The Bible and the Koran contain a great deal of good advice for people to live a good live. But the marriage vows are increasingly becoming impossible to keep. I have the greatest admiration and respect for those that are able to love and cherish, keeping to thee only, till death do us part, just like my parents. But more and more people today change and are able to change. We all only have one life and sometimes life moves on. I think it is so regrettable that successful happy marriages or partnerships break up just because one of the pair has a "little bit of sex on the side". Where is forgiveness? We should stop using the word unfaithful, jealousy and possessiveness. These two things I can honestly say I have never experienced even though five of my seven lovers have left me. They say 50% of married men have committed adultery.

Love is something that can die and the one simple single cause most likely to bring this about is sex. Sex with someone you love is the most wonderful thing in the world. But after a few years, the "seven year itch", (it's more like just two or three for so many now-a-days) Egg and bacon for breakfast every day can become a bit boring. You think you know everything there is to know about each other in that department.

Complete trust and openness in a relationship is paramount, a loving relationship where both are completely compatible. Someone you just love to have around and come home to. Someone you miss when parted, someone with whom you have built up a comfortable home, where there may be children. Is just about the most wonderful thing in the world not easily found or come by with out a lot of give and take on all sides.

Many times one reads or hears that all this is thrown away just because one of them is "unfaithful". I can well understand if "an affair" is going on, but why is it that a single act of sex is so important that it can destroy a relationship. Quick sex with a stranger for the first time is exciting. It has nothing to do with loving the person. The problem is more to do with deceit, lies, secrecy, humiliation and loss of face. But if there is an open relationship with a few rules like, only once with same person and never sleep all night. With complete and immediate openness and honesty. I can tell you that it strengthens a relationship and invigorates the sex life.

In some of us the sex drive is extremely powerful and unlike some popular belief, in some of us it remains so well into old age. An 80 years old man was asked. "What age were you when you found you could no longer have sex?" He replied. You had better come back in ten years and ask me again.

I was a devout believer in Christianity and every thing in it, up until about the age of sixty by which time I had lost both my parents, and a Brother. I wanted to believe I should see them again putting the words "see you later", a "family saying" over the family grave. Always rushing away from a gay pub to get to midnight mass on Christmas Eve. But then I stopped being brain washed and started to think seriously about it all. I decided, if the church cannot accept me as I am, then no longer could I accept the church. But I still listen to "Songs of praise".

BETTER DEAD THAN GAY.

I very rarely videotape any thing that I watch on television. Being a Patternmaker I have never liked making the same thing twice and I can't think of any film that I have wanted to see twice, not even the life story of Oscar Wild, although I have seen the film three times by different leading actors. But I do have a video, one with the above tile. I read about it before it was screened. It's about an "all American" boy hansom, clever, kind, polite, very much loved by his family who are very religious, he takes his religion very seriously. It seems to others he has every thing going for him. But he doesn't have a girl friend, when most of his contemporaries do, there is something missing in his life. Then he meets someone and realises he is gay. The feelings he gets when he is with his lover is so wonderful he feels complete and he experiences complete release and relief, he has never been so happy, he falls completely in love.

Then the guilt sets in, especially when he is in church and asking his god to forgive him his "sins". So he tries to stay away from his lover. His lover is patient and understanding telling him to seek advice. This he does from his priest, who tells him to be strong, to resist temptation and above all to pray for help from God. He goes to see his old head master, for whom he had the utmost respect, he is more or less told to "pull him self together" and not to risk the terrible hurt it would bring to his family. He goes to see his doctor who tells him he is going through a phase. His father is the last one he would think of going to for help, he had made it clear that if he had his way all homosexuals would be put on a desert island.

From time to time he goes and falls into the arms of his lover and forgets it all for a few hours, then the guilt starts all over again stronger than ever. He then commits suicide.

This is a true story and I have no doubt there have been many suicides just like this one, where the true cause was never found out. But in this case someone made it their job to see everyone he ever met including his lover, to find out just why. When his father discovered the reason, the words he used were, "Better dead than gay". The last words on the tape are spoken by the lover, who said.

"Religion has a lot to answer for".

I have thought a lot about that film and the comment from the lover. When you think of all the conflicts that are going on in the world as I write. Most of them are about one religion or cult against another.

When I heard a senior Roman Chatholic official on the radio I could hardly believe my ears I know many religions will not allow the use of condoms, but he said not even if the husband was HIV positive. So as well as being responsible for there being too many unwanted children in the world, they condone manslaughter.

The most terrible thing that any of us have ever seen live on the television was the Sept. 11th suicide bombing of the World Trade Centre. Then there have been the Tamil Tigers and the Palestinians. None of these would have done what they did, if they did not believe what their religion has taught them, that there us a paradise where all will be perfect.

SMOKING

People who smoke especially in a restaurant annoy me. Some of them will have two or three cigarettes during the course of their meal. They can go twelve hours or so without one on a flight, why can't they abstain for an hour until they are out side? Any one who smokes goes down a lot in my estimation. Smokers are drug addicts. Air polluters. Litter Bugs and Arsonists. Smokers and cigarette manufacturers are directly responsible for the early death of non-smokers and so maybe guilty of manslaughter. Cigarette smoke produces microscopic particles of carcinogenic substances that land on clothing skin and hair. These particles are stirred up with every movement and drift off the air and can be inhaled by those around them long after the cigarette is out. People who are subject to second hand smoke have four times greater chance of getting lung cancer than those not exposed.

I read an article by a respiratory therapist who works in paediatric intensive care, who says he is always outraged when he has a paediatric patient who is struggling to breath and Mum or Dad or a relative comes into the room reeking of tobacco. He explains that even if they go out of the room to smoke, when they return they bringing particles into the room that have clung to their clothing.

Smokers should take a paper towel and wipe down the windows of their cars. That yellow stain of the paper is not a gas but an accumulation of microscopic particles, that also lodge in people's lungs. Smokers who are near or who want to hold a baby should shower and change their clothes since their last cigarette.

They have banned smoking on busses, the underground on all aircraft and many other public places. Why on earth don't they ban it in all restaurants? I can see that it will be a long time before they are able to ban it in pubs, but they could start by having no smoking areas in them. Note - (There is now a ban on smoking in all restaurants and public buildings in Thailand) How about that England?

Non - smokers need to protest more and make it plain to smokers just how anti social they are. I look forward to the day (and it will come) when it is forbidden in any pubic place, that would include all public transport, the beach, the parks, the street, so that the only place they could slowly smoke themselves to death would be in their own house, so long as all living there were smokers and no children, or in special smoking rooms.

The media should make more of famous people who die before their time from smoking. Three were from the most famous family in the world. King George the VI, Princess Margaret, The Duke Of Windsor, George Harrison, Kojack and then there is Kirk Douglas an actor who has had to learn to speak again after an operation for throat cancer, plus many thousands more, including at least six close friends of mine.

<u>People and things that annoy me.</u>

Those that drive at forty miles an hour in the centre lane of a motorway.

Litterlouts who drop their litter even when they are near a bin.

Those who blow their car horn unnecessarily.

Those who take away the kitchen scissors and fail to put them back.

Those who will not say who called on the answer phone.

Those who don't say thank you to a shop assistant.

Americans, who cut up all their meal, then eat it with just their fork.

Americans who say "They must go to the bathroom" in a forest or pub.

The Tate modern Is a waste of a fine building, full of con tricks.

Classic FM, CNN and Hallmark, who advertise them selves constantly,

People who slam doors at any time, particularly late at night.

Neighbours who play mindless "so called music" with too much bass.

Raising the school leaving age to 16 for 20 to 25 %. Probably the cause of the greatest amount of delinquency

Homophobes who condemn all homosexuals "out of hand".

People who always combine the words smoking and drinking, Alcohol in moderation is good for you.

Those who use the term "chosen way of life" when referring to gays.

Those who class all homosexuals as paedophiles.

Persistent Paedophiles, who should be "put away" just as those who are viollent with severe mental problems are and not released until they are deemed to be no further danger to children (that means for life, for they connot be cured)

I saw an article in the newspaper about a fourteen-year-old male prostitute; I think his name was Jason, who was murdered by paedophiles in what the Daily Mail called a homosexual orgy". I wrote to the Mail and asked them. "If the victim had been a girl, would they have substituted the word heterosexual for homosexual?" This is a typical example of the way the press generate homophobia. There is no paper more homophobic than the Daily Mail. Fortunately most of the general public have now come to realise that there are even more very young female victims than there are male. And that there is no more connection between Homosexuality and Paedophilia than there is between Heterosexuality and Paedophilia.

SECTION 28

Forbids anyone in the teaching profession from promoting Homosexuality. I don't believe it is possible to promote it. Approximately two or three percent of boys are born gay, That means there are half a dozen or so in every average size school, some of whom go though a most difficult time, have no one they can turn to for help and advice. We all know and the kids know that parents are the last one's to go to over something like this. The teachers, or at least one in each school should be a sympathetic and fully informed person, to whom a boy or girl can go or be referred.

From the age of eleven all pupils should be made aware that such a person exists and to whom they should go if they think they have problems over sexuality. They should be told that they are not the only ones by a long way, that it is nothing to be ashamed of. But the law, brought in by the conservatives under Maggie Thatcher forbids this. At the moment there is total confusion and doubt over where teachers stand with regard to the law, so that the end result is nothing is done and no advice is given. I wonder how many young suicides are due to this? We shall never know.

As I go to print it now seems that this hateful law will be changed in spite of all the old "fogies" in the House of Lords.

SOMCHAI MY PRESENT LOVER & PARTNER

About the time I finalized the sale of "Woodside", but before I had held my Auction, or sold my Koi Carp I went to the Quebec with out any intention of "picking up" anyone but just for a drink with many of my gay friends that I always saw there. I was standing about twelve feet from the door talking to one of my young Oriental friends. I was facing the door and glancing at those that came in (as one does) while chatting to a friend named Chris, when suddenly there in the doorway, walking towards me was, in my opinion one of the most good looking young men that I have ever seen in there. He was looking straight at me with such a beautiful smile that can only come from a Thai. He walked towards me still smiling without taking his eyes off me; he kept on walking but looking back at me. Chris said. "I think you have 'scored' I had better leave you he will think I am your boy friend"

Somchai, I discovered later is one of those that take some time to make up their mind about most things. Chris moved away and left me standing on my own. Somchai had bought a drink by this time and came up to me and said. "Hello" we exchanged names, he told me he was in England for two more weeks, I told him I lived in the country twenty five miles away, he said straight away. "Can we go back to your place?" With-in five minutes he has finished his drink and we were on the road back to Farnham Common.

We spent the weekend together during which time I fell in love with him. I'm sure that is the quickest I've done that, well at my age there is not time to waste. He told me he had to be at Oxford on the Sunday evening to register for a course that would last for a week. I said. "I would take him in the car". Then it was decided that if he was there before nine o/clock Monday morning that would be OK. So that meant we could have another night together. I got him to the hotel where the course was to be held by eight o/clock. We exchanged phone numbers saying "We would ring each other sometime during the week" we rang every night.

The following weekend we were again at Woodside when we suddenly realised that it was Gay Pride week. There was to be a very large gay gathering at Clapham Common that Saturday afternoon. We set off in the car but found we could not park anywhere near one of the entrance gates. We could see thousands on the pavements walking from an underground station towards the common, so we managed to park the car and joined the walkers. I shall never forget how happy and proud I was to walk with Somchai, arm in arm, in public, as most of the others were doing, male with male, female with female.

Somchai and I stayed together for the rest of the next week getting to know each other and then he had to go back to Thailand. During the next six weeks we phoned each other at least four times a week and wrote express letters to each other, those we still have. Then as arranged I flew out to meet him, stayed there for three weeks during which time he resigned from his job, gave up his flat, obtained a students visa, then we both came back to England.

We were extremely fortunate that just about this time the newly elected labour government brought in a bill that allowed us to apply for a "same sex partnership". This was the first bit of legislation as part of an equalization policy getting rid of discriminatory differences between homosexuals and heterosexuals. At that time it was possible for heterosexuals to gain entry or to stay together in the U.K. if they could prove that they had been living together for one year. For homosexuals there was no such concession no matter how long they had been together. Now they made it possible for both to stay after proving cohabitation for two years. The Hets. Did not like the increase to two years from one year brought about on behalf of the homos.

Somchai started a folder, keeping all letters, Birthday and Christmas cards with the envelopes. He took photographs that proved we were together like standing in front of a poster with the date on it. We were down looking at the millennium dome when it was half built, he took a photo with the dome in the back ground, then when it was finished we did the same thing again. We changed all suppliers" accounts into our joint names and our bank accounts, all statement and receipts went into the folder. We went to the theatre and concerts at the Albert hall at least once a month; we kept all ticket stubs and programmes, plus all boarding cards and tickets when we flew anywhere. Then when the two years was almost up we wrote to about twenty friends who had known us both for some time asking them to write a letter confirming that we had been living together as a "loving couple" for two years. The file was now by this time about three inches thick.

Then we put in our application and waited, and waited. Then when it was getting near the time for us to go to Thailand for six months; we went down to the home office at Croydon. A female who, for a home office official was quite pleasant saw us just before lunch. She told us that there was no chance of our application being considered before the spring, it was towards the end of September. We asked her about the possibilities of applying in Bangkok; she said she thought there might be a chance of getting it while we were in Thailand. This would mean withdrawing our application and if we did so Somchai would have to leave the UK with-in three weeks. So this is what we did. As soon as we arrived in Bangkok we submitted the application at the British Embassy. I think it must have been the first one they had come across they were not too sure what to do with it. However after a bit of pressure we received an interview date, the 7th Jan 2000.

On the due date at eight in the morning we were at the British Embassy and quite soon shown into a cubicle, I was told that they only interviewed the applicant. Somchai in fear and trepidation stayed to answer the questions, again by a female. The only question that he faltered on was, why was he in a partnership with a man so much older than he? Like the great majority of people she would not have heard of the term. "Gerontophile".

She seemed quite knowledgeable about us, and told Somchai that she had taken our file home the evening before and spent most of the evening reading it. After twenty minutes she told him we had been successful, he collected his passport that now has, "same sex partnership with Mr. G.S.Montague" written in it. As we left they said please take away your file we do not have room to keep it. This now meant that Somchai could come and go in and out of the UK as often as he pleased and could work legally. In June 2002, as I write we will have been together for five years, he will be thirty three, and I shall be seventy nine.

LETTER TO OUR FAMILY's & FRIENDS
8th December 1998

Soon after we arrived at the ten years old Bungalow we have bought, Somchai's brother was engaged to renovate and paint everything. He turned up from about 150 miles away with seven workmen they took over for two weeks to complete the renovation. We had to move out into a nearby condominium. They then proceeded to sleep "on the job" literally, working from first light in the morning until late in the evening, then each night they just slept on the floor.

Every inch was refurbished both inside and out including the surrounding parameter wall, there were carpets in all the bedrooms, which were removed and parquet flooring was laid, you've never seen such dust as they were sanded down. More men came to put up the guttering, more came to modernize the electrics and still more to service and repair the air conditioning. The front patio was made waterproof with translucent and extended to form a carport. The cost was about a quarter of what I would have expected.

None spoke any English; I supervised the work with Somchai as interpreter. Very little was done the same way that we would do it at home, we found ourselves under some considerable stress. While Somchai's general knowledge of English is very good, it fell down when it became too technical. I have come to the conclusion that if a relationship can survive two weeks of that then it can survive anything.

The existing patio was supported by two nicely decorated columns. The extension needed another. I said to Somchai. "I don't suppose they will be able to find another to match". A plain concrete post arrived and I thought, "Well we can't have every thing" and was prepared to put up with it. Some time later when it had been erected I noticed one of the older members of the gang working on it, he had built up each of the four sides leaving an attractive recess, which he then proceeded to sculpture to exactly match the other two.

At long last they were finished, we had a little party, gave the gang a large beer each, took some photos and waved goodbye as they set off for home all piled into a "pick up truck". Despite my mid way doubts, they had done a really excellent job. But what a mess they made, all the floors including the patios with the exception of the bedrooms are marble or tiles, despite us constantly handing out old newspapers and under felt they just did not cover up, saying they would clean it up at the end. But that would have meant another day and we had had enough. In keeping with all the other houses in the "Village" every where was done in white, We were still cleaning off spots of white paint or emulsion including the plants weeks later.

Having sold my Rover car before leaving Blighty we bought a Toyota. There are no taxi's here, only what are called "Baht busses". A pick-up-truck with a canvas roof, which can seat 10 on two hard benches down each side, not one of them would pass an MOT, the exhaust system, "usually blown" belching out fumes which are drawn back at you by the slip stream. When you ring the bell to get off, they set you down in the middle of a very wide road with motorcyclists (which make up half the traffic here) and cars hurtling past on either side, you take your life in your hands each time.

Somchai does all the driving, I've long since lost the joy of it and I never drive at night now. Apparently Farang's, (that's mainly white westerners) are easy meat for the police who will stop you often for no good reason at all and demand a fine, which goes straight into their own pocket. This is understandable I suppose for they are paid practically nothing. I also sold my boat "Woody" shortly before leaving the UK and I do miss sailing so we Chartered one for the Christmas period. Edward Davis, a great friend and sailing companion of many years, together with his partner Daniel came and stayed with us for a few days. Then we all flew down to a Marina at Phuket

The house is situated just a few hundred yards from a beautiful sandy beach several miles long, a part of which nearest to our house is where all our local friends go. The sea water is body temperature. The 'Village' consists of about 40 house's, also two very large high rise condominiums which funnel the light but constant sea breeze's straight to our patio and through the house where the temperature is rarely above 80 f. There is a large swimming pool, tennis courts and never less than six security guards on duty, all for a service charge of about £100 a year. We have a maid who comes in five days a week, she does all the house work the washing and ironing, even cutting the grass and looking after the garden.

Having finished the house we looked at the garden. The few plants that we had were paint splattered and damaged. So we went along to the local garden center. The owner came around, we told him he had a free hand to do what he thought best. Two men for a whole day, dozens of beautiful mature plants, some 10 ft. high to give more privacy, all for a fraction of what the plants alone would cost in the UK.

Tucked away in the corner of the garden was what had once been a very attractive fountain that had probably been put there because it didn't work any more. We renovated it, put in a new submersible pump, got it working, added some fish, now we had the pleasant sound of running water.

The smallest of the four bedrooms we have turned into a study. Somchai now spends a lot of his time there, working as the "self employed breadwinner" of the partnership doing a research assignment for the international press similar to the work that he was doing and gave up when we met and came to live with me in England. Where although he was already a Graduate he was not allowed to work and the only way he could stay for longer than six months was to take another degree.

We let the London flat to a company based in Bangkok, one of whose young employees is a long time friend of Somchai's. Ton is his name and he's working on contract in London as a computer programmer. We were paid in Bahts into our Bangkok joint account. How about that for a bit of luck?

What do I do? I tap away on this computer when I can get on it continuing my memoirs. I do a little watercolour painting and I swim nearly every day and spend some time on the beach. BBC World keeps us in touch and the satellite TV shows constant films in the evenings in English with no adverts. We shall be here until the end of March'00, when I'm told it gets a lot hotter. Then all being well we shall return to our first home in England "when April is there". In my 77th year I have at long last learnt to relax and take it easy.

Our big day of course will be Jan 6th, 2000, when we are interviewed for our "same Sex partnership, approval at the British Embassy in Bangkok We shall take 'the file' all 4" of it, (A complete record and Proof of our 2 two years together) along several days before. When we tried to leave it with them they said. "Oh take it away and bring it with you we have nowhere to store it". If by some remote bad luck we are refused, then we shall have to appeal and Lord knows how long that would take. Somchai will be unable to return to England, in which case I shall stay here with him. But we are quietly confident of the out come.

To both our families and all our many very good friends in many parts of the world we are sending this edition of G&S news with Love and our Christmas and very special New Year good wishes in plenty of time hoping that they will be returned. So that even if we don't have a Christmas tree and all the trimmings we shall have some Cards to put around and our new post box on the outside gate will be used. E-mails are very convenient but very impersonal, they will never be so welcome as a hand written envelope with a stamp.

Love, George & Somchai.

<u>Note we received over 50 cards.</u>

With Somchai

Sailing in Phuket, Thailand, over Christmas (22-28 December 1999)

During a telephone conversation with my great friend and many time sailing companion Edward Davies discussing Somchai and my forthcoming six months stay in Thailand. Edward mentioned that he and Daniel had not yet decided what to do or where to go for their end of year holiday. I told him we had thought of sailing from Phuket. Straight away it was decided we would make up a foursome.

Between us we obtained information from the Internet of what was available and where. Then Edward took over. He chartered the boat (an Oceanis 320), paid the deposit, booked the flights and invested in a Chart of the area and pilot, he also did a great deal of preparation on the Chart that proved to be indispensable. We all met up in Bangkok a few days early and spent a couple of evenings showing them the gay nightspots, which included the aptly named "Screwboy Bar". In Bangkok these days each cabaret turn starts with "the full Monty". Edward was intrigued by the act I call the "Catherine Wheel". In another bar the coupled performers move about the audience and, in an eye-popping variation of lap dancing, performing a "pas de deux" in your lap!

By a happy accident Edward and Daniel found their visit to Bangkok coincided with the "Carnival", set to become an annual event. One of the main streets is closed off. Stalls, open air bars, restaurants and pop group stages are set out and there is a procession of floats in the late afternoon. One float stood out by far as being the most dazzling, with gorgeous costumes and the most vivacious and prettiest performers. Need I say more.

Next day we drove our visitors out to our Thailand home just outside Pattaya, which is only a short walk to the gay beach. They were very impressed with our 3-4 bed roomed house which, following a lot of work is now looking great. After showing them the most interesting bits of Pattaya for a couple of nights and a terrifying ride by rickety cable car to lunch on the top of the local Post Office tower, we set off back to Bangkok Airport.

The flight down to Phuket is only just over an hour; there the Sunsail mini bus met us. Vinai, a long time Thai friend of ours arrived on a later flight, we had invited him to join us as a Thai-speaking companion for Somchai and as 'Ships cook'. He is a delightful, bright young environmental Consultant and computer expert, a non-swimmer on his very first sail. We had decided that we would all eat Thai food for the entire cruise. Somchai and Vinai then set off for the nearest supermarket to stock up with provisions. This was a formidable task for there would be only one stop on the planned route that we would be unable to replenish stocks or go to a restaurant.

After all was stowed aboard "Loreto", including the bottles of Moet and Thai whiskey, courtesy of Sunsail, we had dinner on the marina, and then turned in for the first night on board. Unlike the rest of Thailand that was having its coolest December for 40 years, it was quite warm, much too warm to have the hatch or the windows shut. This marina has been built on a swamp. Mosquitoes plagued us, so we got very little sleep that night Even if my eyes and fitness were as they were, I would have insisted that Edward be Skipper. He reluctantly agreed, and said I would then be the Commodore.

The channel to the open sea was very long and winding, we were piloted out. We left at high water, but with the echo sounder set at 3 meters it was constantly bleeping. As we got nearer to the fairway buoy the wind was increasing all the time. It reached Force 6 gusting to seven at times and yes wouldn't just know it, exactly from the direction of our first destination. We managed to claw our way half way, passed Ko (that means island) WA YAI (that means big.) and anchored with as much shelter as we could find at Ko YAO YAI. (That means long and big!). It was a very rough night. The wind every now and then would die away completely. We would breathe a sigh of relief. Then back it would blow just as hard again. If you look at the map you will see that there is very little landmass between the Gulf of Thailand and the Indian Ocean.

The next day was just the same. To cover the route Edward had planned, which was to see the best of the beautiful islands, we just had to get ourselves north. By lunchtime we were at AO LABU (we didn't get an interpretation for that one). Skipper was a little concerned about the anchorage, so the three young ones and I went ashore. It's good not being skipper! There was no sign of life, but the long stretch of beautiful sand was the softest and finest I've ever seen. Before getting into the dinghy we had a skinny dip and a sea soap wash, then when getting back to the boat there was a fresh water shower on the stern to rinse the salt off each other. The water was body temperature, so we did this several time a day.

That afternoon's sail was the best until then: two reefs in the main with no "in-mast reefing" - 8 to 10 knots. We thought the log was a little generous. Later that afternoon the wind did die down for a few hours so much so that Somchai was towed at 4 knot. In the noddy of course, a very pretty sight, at least we two older ones thought so. Anchored that night at AO LO PALAL, so remote our Thai crew did not know the meaning. Eating our Thai meal so tastefully prepared by Somchai and Vinai as always, the skipper said "Hey! It's Christmas eve". We had completely forgotten. That was for me, one of the highlights.

Up at 7 o/c on Christmas morning, we set sail for Phi Phi Don. Two reefs in the main again. But this time on a course that gave us a Broad Reach, after a while we were able to shake out the reefs one at a time. This time when the log read 8 to 10 knots, it felt like it. We were really moving maybe the log is ok after all. Phi Phi Don is about the most beautiful island of them all. We came up to the East face then sailed close in right round to the West. The cliffs are spectacular so many varied colours. A 100 ft. or more, sheer from the top to the sea, then down another 30 meters according to the chart, which agreed with the echo sounder. With the sun shining on the rock face no film could begin to do justice to the scene. On turning a corner, suddenly there was the most amazing sight that I have ever seen in all my 25 years sailing. One large sheltered bay with similar cliffs down one side. At the base of these cliffs the water was a bright emerald green, caused by the coral. We had snorkels and flippers for all on board, so just as soon as we had anchored we were in the water. I have seen some very impressive samples of coral in aquariums. But when you see it in it's natural setting, it is breath taking. The fish fascinated me, camouflaged to exactly match the coral. They seemed to be very inquisitive, and would swim right up to your goggles.

There were several restaurants ashore, so the cooks had a night (Christmas) off. We wished we could have spent another whole day at Phi Phi Don Island. But we were now furthest away from base and more than half way though the cruise. So in the morning, reluctantly we up-anchored yet again and set off for BAN NIT that is on the main island of Phuket south of the main town. An excellent sail got us there in record time. Again a very attractive sheltered bay, but unlike our last port of call, no small boats on the beach, only another three large ocean going yachts, at the anchorage. We knew from the chart that there was coral all around for some distance from the shore, but with a marked channel. The (spring) tide was very low and we found the marked channel in the dark by looking at the reflection of the lights ashore in the water. Unfortunately, as the tide was on the turn, we could only leave the very heavy RIB, (inflatable) complete with outboard, above the high water mark. It was decided it was not a good idea to drag it over the shorn coral and so, in a grand gesture, we bribed some locals, all wearing boots, who were collecting shellfish by torchlight to carry it up to the beach for us.

We had not been able to stock up with any thing at Phi Phi Don. So eventually we managed to get a taxi into Phuket, where again the cooks got a rest. Then the same taxi took us to a super market. On returning to the dinghy the tide had come in and there was plenty of water to motor back blithely over the coral to Loreto.

Every-where we stayed we had to anchor. And (would you believe it?) getting the anchor up, took all five of us. A large electric windlass needed the engine to be run at $1/_2$ revs. The one controlling the windlass could not at the same time feed the chain into the locker. With the wind being very strong most of the time, we needed to motor up to anchor. I was on the tiller and the throttle changing the gear from drive to neutral as required. But as I could not operate the red clutch button, which was stiff, Vinai had to do that. Skipper stood amidships playing conductor.

Now to our last anchorage at Ko Rang Yai, yet another beautiful island, all coconut palms and perfect white beaches, with a pearl factory where we watched them 'seeding' the oysters. Edward bought some pearls. He tells us they're not to go with his twin set, but for dress shirt studs.

On the whole we were satisfied with Sunsail. The boat was in reasonably good nick and they let us off the end of charter cleaning. The only slight problem we encountered on the voyage was a blocked sink. On Woody the outlet was at the water line. On the Oceanis, it was a foot below. Nevertheless Somchai got his head down and did a blowjob with the dinghy pump!

We knew we had to be careful with water because there are very few places on the route we had chosen where we could have topped up. Stinginess was the order of the day and in the end we did not switch on to the reserve tank until the last day. How about that for economy?

It was altogether a very memorable and thoroughly enjoyable charter, and one that we highly recommend. The cost for the boat worked out at £250 per head for five, not including the flight. Foodstuffs (including the meals ashore), booze and all other costs amounted to approximately £10 pounds per head per day! We all thought two weeks would be better than one, if possible. Then one could linger longer at the best spots and 'do' some of the best islands we did not have time for.

On the end of charter report sheet, it asked all sorts of questions. The last one was "How many times did you go aground?" Our skipper was very well qualified to write proudly "NONE".

Me ✳ Vinai ✳ Somchai ✳ Daniel ✳ Edward On Chirstmas Day 1999

Letter from George & Somchai from Thailand
16th January 2001

We must apologize for not being in touch for so long to some of you, but for all but three months of the year 2000, has been "the most difficult time of both our lives". I became ill the last few days of our last trip here, spent a while in two hospitals one in Patttaya and then at the best hospital in Bangkok. Then we went back to England, me in a wheel chair through both airports. I spent some time in St, Mary's hospital Paddington, plus a great many visits there. Thankfully it's only a ten minute wheel chair ride, when pushed by Somchai.

At all three hospitals, many tests and scans were taken, the words then used by the many different doctors, following these tests and the examinations, will stick in my mind for ever, they all said, "something's going on". To cut a very painful story as short as I can, the final consensus of opinion is, that I had picked up a virus that made me extremely ill for the first time in my life. It has left me with Neuritis, (I hope that is the right spelling, it's not on my spell checker).

For those like me, who are not familiar with this, it is a complaint that affects the nerves furthest from the spine, i.e. the finger tips and the feet, making it extremely painful to walk without strong painkillers. In younger people it usually gets better, but takes a long time, with me, it might get completely better and it might not. It is certainly getting better very slowly all the time.

Somchai was not ill, but he had to put up with me, "I'm not a good patient!" He was a tower of strength and I am convinced that without him I would not have made it. For several months I was totally unable to do any thing for myself. He did every thing for me. He gave up his job, and spent most of his time, determined to MAKE me get well. He saw to it that I did everything I was told to do, go where ever and see who ever it was suggested I see, after listening to and questioning the doctors and others. I am ashamed to say that at times in my long life I did not have too much patience with some, "close to me", who said they were suffering from depression. I have learnt my lesson the hard way. Mine, (again thanks to Somchai) only lasted a few weeks, but I find it impossible to describe what it is like except to say that, a feeling of total panic wells up inside and try as you will not to take the pills you just have too (they are addictive).

I must say a sincere sorry to all those good friends who wanted to come to see me, whom Somchai as tactfully as he could "put off". I did not want to speak to any one except my caring partner, let alone see them. I was at my worst on my 77th birthday in June, "And I thought seven was my lucky number!" The sight of food made me feel sick. I lost thirty pounds of my body weight. My bones were sticking out so that I found it impossible to get comfortable in bed and I could not sleep more than a couple of hours at a time. I would get up at any time during the night, go down to my study and try and type some more of my Memoir. I just wanted to finish it, while as I thought at that time, while I still had some time. I really thought I was a gonner.

They say, "It's an ill wind that blows nobody any good". During my worst moments I felt trapped in the flat that I had, up to then been so happy with, I could not even get up the stairs to the street on my own. So we decided to sell. Somchai looked up the Internet and found a flat in Brighton, I was full of doubts. They say it's about the most stressful thing you can do to move house." The psychiatrist that I saw (yes me) said it was just what I needed. So we went ahead.

We had just caught a slightly falling market, which applied to both properties so we gave a reduction and we got one. But the fellow that wanted our flat had paid his surveyor and had retained a solicitor, was, fortunately as it turned out, "too clever by half" as the saying is, he kept trying to get us to reduce the price still further, on the pretext of possible future faults, blaming his bank. He said they wanted the surveyor to examine all the floorboards and the joists. I had covered everywhere with hardboard and then had under felt and new carpets fitted when I renovated the whole flat. At that time I had central heating put in and discovered that the whole flat had a new floor fitted following bomb damage during the war. I took photos at the time that showed the new timbers set up on "fletton" bricks, which did not exist when this Victorian building was put up 160 years ago. But he still persisted so we told him to forget the deal. He immediately said. I accept. It's OK now. But we had found that we could keep the London flat and buy the one in Brighton. He must have lost nearly a thousand pounds.

We went around to the Halifax building society, made some enquiries, did our sums, and have now got a joint mortgage on 166a, which together with funds I had, has now given me clear ownership of the Brighton flat. Somchai, now having gone back to work will need to stay in London during the week. We bought another car; I am now classed as disabled. I applied and got the blue (it is now) badge enabling me to park almost anywhere! I have no problem driving during the day.

My two sons Martin and Edward with two trips and a Ford Transit moved all our "very heavy" dining room furniture, other bits and pieces, on one trip, then "bargains" that we bought at the Xmas sales, on another, My very good friend Geoff came along and has been a great help throughout, so that "Brighton" is now almost fully furnished. We look forward to doing lots more refining in the summer. We also look forward to "entertaining" there.

I lost my "middle age" spread. I had been trying to do that for many years; I can now wear trousers that were too small for me that fortunately I had kept. My feet are getting less painful all the time, noticeably since arriving here, with the warm weather. In Brighton and in London I can put the wheel chair in the car, by my self, the smaller shops I can walk around, the bigger super markets and stores. I wheel myself around. I am now independent again.

At the moment we are at the condo in Bangkok, we go everywhere by taxi. Those who know Thailand will know it is extremely cheap, we hope to go to Jomtien later this week. The house is too far from the beach for me to walk (normally ten minutes), but as those who have visited us there, will remember, there is a "sky train type" pedestrian walkway, that goes to with-in a hundred yards of the beach. I shall trundle my way along as far as the steps. Leave the wheel chair In the care of the security guard, and walk the rest of the way to the beach, where we both look forward to renewing many old acquaints.

All best wishes for 2001. (We have written off the year 2000!).

LOVE GEORGE & SOMCHAI

<u>Letter to all friends and family</u>
8th December 2001 Thailand.

We escape the English winter for the fifth time, on the 17th Nov. this time via New Delhi India we are met at the airport by a long time friend of Somchai's, the most senior minister at the Thai Embassy with the chauffer driven CD Mercedes. We receive VIP through immigration and customs. Then we are off to our four-day stay at the Thai Embassy. Leaving behind our London flat, the Brighton flat and our car, (sitting on it's own personal parking spot), in the care of our very good friends Geoff & Jimmy.

We saw a great deal of New Delhi, but the star trip was to see the Taj Mahal. It took 4 hours each way in the CD car. The roads are very bad and everybody drives, walks or rides in the middle of the road. There are very few vehicles with any driver's mirror, if there is one it is folded in, so everyone drives on the horn. The lorries even have a notice on the back telling you to "horn please". There are Tricycles. - Bicycles, - Cars, - Cows, - Chickens, - Camels, - Donkeys, - Dogs, - Motor Cycles, - Mopeds, - Rickshaws, - Roadblocks, - Horse & Carts, - Handcarts, ' Vans, - Lorries, - Pedestrians and Tucucs.

At road junctions nobody is given the "right of way" and nobody gives way, not even for the CD Merc unless they are made to. The noise confusion pollution and congestion is quite frightening. Then suddenly we turn into a large beautiful forecourt of a luxury hotel all fountains and flowers. We are obviously expected, for we are greeted by name by several very tall commissionaires all dressed in Rarsatan Costume. We are now at Amarvilas Agra.

The transformation in just one minute is quite astounding; there are no vehicles or anything with wheels on in sight, except just one, a large "six seater golf course" style electric buggy. Nothing that makes any pollution is allowed. There are very many people all well dressed, all walking towards the monument that can be seen quite some distance away. After we are given refreshments in the hotel lobby we are taken in the buggy and then left to walk the last few hundred yards. The solid marble architecture was everything that we expected, but we were surprised and a little disappointed with the inside.

We were taken to two receptions. At the Oman and Monaco Embassy's. We expected the Oman one to be very grand, but they were both very large and like palace's. One could not help thinking about the abject poverty, as bad as any where in the world only a mile or so away. We were introduced to many Ambassadors. The British one was not there, so, being the only Englishman; and the fact that so many made a point of shaking my hand, I think some may have thought that I was he. I could not help but note the several hundred at each event were all speaking English.

On the evening of our departure the minister was at a function in the embassy. Two hours prior to the time of our flight with a half hour drive to the airport we were still waiting for his return almost an hour later we were still waiting convinced we would miss our flight to Bangkok. Then we were off we arrived with 30 mins to spare. There at the entrance was a wheel chair for me. I was taken to the security check where there was a long queue that I was taken straight to the head of and then to the door of the aircraft, I waited five mins. Then along came Somchai with the boarding tickets ten minutes before the aircraft door was closed. On arrival at Bangkok I was the first one off and there was another wheel chair. We were straight through immigration marked Corps Diplomatic and disabled only. My Thai pusher was walking very quick, poor Somchai had a job to keep up and I thought there's no hurry the bags will not be there yet. But there they were! Just ours, with a red priority labels on. We were in the taxi and as it was 5. 30 in the morning we were at the hotel 30 mins from leaving the aircraft. Somchai told me that the Ministers guest that evening had been the manager of Thai Airways.

Love George & Somchai.

Letter from Thailand
Christmas/Newyear 2002/3

About this time of the year we always write to all our family and friends with an update of what we have been doing and what we have planned then we send it out to everyone by "E-mail to those who have it, and by post to those who don't. Then the letters have been put on to my Memoirs, this time is it going to be slighty different For the last few days Somchai and I have been visiting printers, getting quotations, placing an order for printing. So instead of receiving it by E-mail or post all close friends and relations will be getting a copy of the book.

Each year we come to Thailand we include a trip to somewhere else. A few years ago I eventually plucked up the courage to send an update to all my relations in Australia which made it very clear that I was gay and living a gay life style with Somchai. By return we received an "e- mail, which only those who have agonized over "coming out to those they love will understand the joy I felt when I read- "thank God I'm not the only one in the family"- My cousin Joan, to whom I always addressed the mail usually sent it around to all the family, this time she only gave it to her daughter Anne. I've always had a problem reading mail on the screen, unlike what I am doing now the letters are always small and to my eyes rather faint, so I tell Somchai to print them out for me. This time as soon as he read out thiose words I pushed him away squinted and read with delight.

Anne told us that she was in a relationship and living with Julie, that they were completely accepted by all the other members of the large family, that they slept together at my cousins (her mothers) house and that for the first time in her life she was completely happy. So, much sooner than we otherwise would have done, (in fact I might never have got around to it), we decided. This year it must be Austrailia.

The last time I went was 16 years ago, to Perth to see my aunt Violet (my fathers sister) I was so glad I did for she died the following year at the age of 92. Also to see the Americas Cup Yacht race. I had intended to go down to Sydney, but when told it was another four hours flying time, I "chickened out" on that one. So this time we said we would include Sydney. Somchai is an expert at planning and finding the best deals.He said we can book a return ticket to Sydney from London, stopping off at Bangkok, then back to Bangkok stopping off at Perth much cheaper than booking separate flights.

First was a conducted tour of the Opera House, it really is, still to this day about the most unusual building in the world. We were told of the history of it. Estimated cost 14$ million it turned out to cost 110$ the designer had a row pulling out half way though. He never has seen it completed. How sad we thought. The last part we came to was the opera house itself. We were stoped at the door and there was some doubt that we would be allowed in for they were rehearsing the Messiah. Then all was well, so long as we were very quite. Now Handel is my favourite composer The Messiah is, well all I can say is The Messiah IS. Then what should the Bass soloist be rehersing? but the aria I have sung a hundered times. "Why Do The Nations So Furiously Rage Together". I had great difficulty keeping silent while I mouthed the words coming in and pausing "on que" all the time. As you get older it is a source of great regret that your memory fails you. But I can tell you it does not for some thing you have known and loved so well so many years ago. The thought went though my mind. If my life had taken a different course, that could have been me down there on that stage.

There is a great deal of walking to do. I am glad to report that my feet have improved a great deal, I could not have done it a year ago. The long promenade leading back to the city is called Writers Walk. Every few yards there is a three foot diameter bronze plaque that is highly polished by all the walkers. On them is inscribed the names of all the most famous writers and one of their quotations, with one date or two according to whether they were still alive or not at the time the disc was laid. Then I had the thought. "I'm a Writer!" and I'm about to be published. We stopped for a rest and refreshments half way, when I made sketches of the Opera House and the Bridge. I did not bring my paints this time to make more room to bring back the most number of books. As I was sketching I noticed tiny match sticks in groups of ten moving along on the top of the arch of the bridge. Somchai looked though the telephoto lense of the video camera and could plainly see the groups walking up. Apparently it takes three and a half hours dressed up in overalls and harness and roped together. He said no to that one.

We stayed in Oxford street (info from the internet) where for about a mile every cafe, shop, bar, hotel and restaurant is gay or gay friendly. and oh yes! there is also three saunas. I've been around a bit as you know and this must be the gayest street in the world. Half of all those you see are same sex partners many walking hand in hand. We "did" the city as the saying is, at a very good time of the year for they really "go to town" on the Christmas decorations We walked in Hyde Park and went around the circle of the monorail. Sydney Harbour is, I would say just about the finest in the world, we saw most of if from a pleasure boat.

One of Somchais older man friends told him if ever he was "down under" he must go and see him. We rang him and he was delighted. Being a gay man who had lived most of his working life in London we found he was often lonely now that he had retired to a place called Woy Woy about an hours train journey from Sydney. He picked us up from the station, then later that evening took us on a tour of his housing estate where there was a competition for the best decorated house, most had taken part and they were an amazing sight with some of them having lights all over the whole house including the roof. Arthur you could see did so much enjoy our visit and showing us all of his most beautiful house, when he told us we could not believe how little it had cost him. He was just such a lovely man, I thought what a waste that he had never had a lover. I think he was a.little envious of our relation-ship. He very reluctatanly took us back to the station then waited by his car to wave to us as we went by. On the way back we could see the result of some of the bush fire's.

We arrived about midnight Perth time which was three hours earlier than Sydney time so it was about three in the morming to us. Anne met us at the airport and on the way to her home apologised about the small size of the house. But an Aussie's idea of small is a bit different from our's, We met Julie whom we both took to right away, she and Anne look so right for each other. In spite of the time we talked for hours. I'm sure you don't need me to tell you what about. They told us they had made plans for us to meet all the rest of the family and for Somchai to be shown Perth. Then I told them about my last visit and how I had tried to get away from them all for an afternoon 16 years before to visit the local sauna that I had read about. I had told them I wanted to go shopping on my own in the city and how they had all said "You can't the whole city is closed on a Saturday afternoon". So Anne said. You shall both go this time, I'll tell the family you have frirends to meet "Which is only a little white fib really" So Anne ran us to a resturant nearest to the sauna leaving the house open and telling us it did not matter what time we got back. Oh I forgot to mention when we arrived they said you must sleep in our bed, it's the best one, how about that for hospitality. They have both promised to visit us at Jomtiem hopefully next year. They all thought Somchai was wonderful they liked him.

We are now back in our bungalow near Pattya, and what do you know? The 20th world Scout Jamboree has just started only a few miles away from here. Talk was of 30 thousand. But they now say there are 20 thousand I shall not be going, first because of security only organized approved groups can go as visitors and second I understand there will be as many girls there as boys. Now I am gay, but I am not a misogynist, I disapprove of girls in a boys choir, the voices are different. Boy don't join the Girl Guides. "Why should girls be in the Boy Scouts"? I hear it's all in the national press in England that Condoms are being supplied and the press here have a cartoon about it

Somchai has bought a new car. He has always been reluctant to pay to hire one, and it seems that over here for several strange reasons it's not much cheaper to buy second hand. It's a Honda and a brand new model. It reminds me of the pleasure I got from my first one. The pleasure that is very plain to see on his face, much more than any of the properties we've bought, make it all very worth while. While we are in England It will be looked after by his family who have strict orders to use it to run his mother around

By the time you all read this it will be a little late to wish you all the compliments of the season. But better late than never as they say. We will get back to "normal" in 2003/4.I wonder how many have sent a letter by book before.

Love
George & Somchai

EPILOGUE

Now we come to the difficult part, so far every thing I have written has been easy to do, I have just tried to tell it as it was and to put down the way I feel about things. Fortunately my long-term memory is very good. Then I still have drawers full of diaries, minute's of meetings, newspaper cuttings, old programmes, letters, dozens of photograph albums, boxes full of transparencies and thousands of feet of cine film, much of which has now been made into a video. I am a very nostalgic person having enjoyed immensely going through it all. And hopefully I shall continue to do so for the rest of my days.

So far I have had a wonderful life, I have had a great deal of luck.
For most of my adult life I have been "in love" and I have been very much loved in return and it is still just like that right now.

I am just as happy as it is possible to be and I don't feel my age at all.

Regrets — Frank Sinartra sang. "There are a few". Edith Piaf "sang" No regrets. I think I have to go along with Edith, I really can't remember anything that I have done that I regret, except perhaps one.

I would like to be able to say that I never ever intentionally hurt anyone physically. But I did just once.

During the time that Asif was still living with me, but we were no longer lovers. I had a very short relationship with a chap named John who turned out to be an alcoholic and drug addict. I tried my best to help him, but he was dishonest and was often violent. Some time after the last time I saw him I was with Asif in a pub at Nottinghill Gate. John was in there and saw us together. Asif had met him and quite understandably didn't like him. We left the pub and I walked ahead to the car, when I heard a scuffle behind me. I turned around and saw that John had attacked Asif from behind. Asif was on the ground John had kicked him. I confronted John and after a few blows knocked him to the ground. Then it was that I lost control, I kicked John very hard in the ribs while he was on the ground. We always say you should "never kick a man when he is down" I have remembered and regretted that ever since.

I would plead extenuating and mitigating circumstances, for he attacked the man I was still in love with.

You may think that I might regret my conviction for "Gross Indecency." But whilst I was many times guilty of this most unfair and discriminatory piece of victimless legistration. Ironically on this occasion I claim I was innocent.

Acquiring this criminal record drastically changed my life. It set me free from my addiction to Scouting, so that I spent much more time with my family. I bought and fitted out Woody, and then took up sailing, which we all enjoyed together. It also gave me a campaign to fight.

In all my many activities. Dealing with so many people usually as the leader, the boss or in charge, I have always tried to be fair. I look forward to the day (and I hope I will live long enough}, to see that we have full equality and that life is fair for people like me living a gay life style. at my age those who are interviewed, usually famous people are asked. What would you like others to say about you? I would wish them to say. He rarely wasted his time. He always tried to be fair. He did his best to keep the Scout promise, as far as the first and third lines are concerned.

On my honour I promise to do my best.
To do my duty to God and the King/Queen.

To help other people at all times.
And to obey the Scout law.

I have well exceeded my "three score years and ten" people find it hard to belive me when I tell them I am just a few months short of eighty they ask me what is my recipe. I would not presume to tell people how to live their lives, I can only tell what seems to have worked for me and the letter S seems good

The first is something none of us can do anything about .... Seed.
I'm not thinking of aristocrats, they often "inbreed", but heathly .... Stock
I have always kept myself fit and tried not to put on weight .... Slim
To do that as I got older I had to exercise more. I played .... Squash
The very best all round exercise I still do 2 or 3imes a week .... Swimming
Like a car the heart needs to go fast. I find jogging boring I go to........ Sauna
When I was young almost every adult male did I have NEVER............ Smoked
Lungs are important I keep them exercised by deep breathing & ....Singing
There are few better way of getting fresh air and exercise than .... Sailing
Money is not every thing but to help others you need to be .... Successful
I know that what gave me the best start and most out of life was ..... Scouting
The "feelgood" factor I had for many years was got by giving .... Service
I've never had a wet one I always use an electric one to .... Shave
Keeping busy when retired can be a problem I paint & .... Sketch
Drinking in moderation is good for you, I like a drink but I stay .... Sober
Not everyone is cutout for it, but my zest for life has been as ... Self Employed
Being a work-a-hollic, inherited from mother has given me ...... Staying power
Everyone looks their best, I've found you meet people if you .... Smile
Since I was 25 I've always had a wife or partner & not been................ Single
I've had every possible inch of a naked body touching me when........ Sleeping
Many 1/3 my age find me good looking and sexy. It pays to .... Socialize
No prizes guessing what I've had more than my fair share of .... Sex.

If asked what I would wish for if I had only one wish I would wish that I may live long enough to see my Grandchildren grow up

....

The End
....

With Grandsons Daniel & Simon

My dining room furniture

My Crest